The European Union:
Annual Review 1998/1999

Edited by

Geoffrey Edwards
and
Georg Wiessala

General Editors: Iain Begg and John Peterson

Copyright © Blackwell Publishers Ltd

ISBN 0-631-21598-0

First published 1999

Blackwell Publishers Ltd
108 Cowley Road, Oxford OX4 1JF, UK

Blackwell Publishers Inc.
350 Main Street,
Malden, MA 02148, USA

British Library Cataloguing in Publication Data
A catalogue record for this book is available from the British Library

Library of Congress
Cataloging in Publication Data applied for

This journal is printed on acid free paper
Printed in Great Britain by Whitstable Litho, Kent

CONTENTS

List of Abbreviations

ACP	African, Caribbean, and Pacific Countries
APEC	Asia–Pacific Economic Co-operation
ASEAN	Association of South East Asian Nations
ASEM	Asia–Europe Meeting
BSE	Bovine Spongiform Encephalopathy
CAP	Common Agricultural Policy
CBSS	Council of Baltic Sea States
CCEE	Countries of Central and Eastern Europe
CCP	Common Commercial Policy
CFI	Court of First Instance
CFP	Common Fisheries Policy
CFSP	Common Foreign and Security Policy
CJTF	Combined Joint Task Force
COM/COM DOC	Commission Document
COREPER	Committee of Permanent Representatives
DG	Directorate General
EAGGF	European Agricultural Guidance and Guarantee Fund
EBRD	European Bank for Reconstruction and Development
EBU	European Broadcasting Union
ECJ	European Court of Justice
ECHO	European Community Humanitarian Office
ECSC	European Coal and Steel Community
ECOFIN	Council of Economic and Finance Ministers
ECU	European Currency Unit
EDF	European Development Fund
EDU	Europol Drugs Unit
EEA	European Economic Area, also European Environmental Agency
EEC	European Economic Community
EFTA	European Free Trade Association
EIB	European Investment Bank
EMS	European Monetary System
EMU	Economic and Monetary Union
EP	European Parliament
ERDF	European Regional Development Fund
ERM	Exchange Rate Mechanism
ESF	European Social Fund
EURATOM	European Atomic Energy Community

EUROPOL	European Police Office
FYROM	Former Yugoslav Republic of Macedonia
GAC	General Affairs Council
GATT	General Agreement on Tariffs and Trade
GDP	Gross Domestic Product
GNP	Gross National Product
GSP	Generalized System of Preferences
HOSG	Heads of State or Government
IIA	Interinstitutional Agreement
IFOR	Implementation Force (of NATO)
IGC	Intergovernmental Conference
JHA	Justice and Home Affairs
KEDO	Korean Peninsula Energy Development Organization
KIE	Committee for European Integration (Poland)
MAGPs	Multiannual Guidance Programmes
MEP	Member of the European Parliament
NAFTA	North Atlantic Free Trade Area
NATO	North Atlantic Treaty Organization
NGO	Non-Governmental Organization
NPT	Non-Proliferation Treaty
OCTs	Overseas Countries and Territories
OECD	Organization for Economic Co-operation and Development
OJ	Official Journal of the European Communities
OSCE	Organization on Security and Co-operation in Europe
PCA	Partnership and Co-operation Agreement
PDS	Party of the Democratic Left (Italy)
PE DOC	Committee Report of the European Parliament
QMV	Qualified Majority Voting
SACU	South African Customs Union
SADC	South African Development Community
SEA	Single European Act
SEC	Internal Commission General Secretariat Document
SEM	Single European Market
SFOR	Stabilization Force (of NATO)
SIS	Schengen Information System
SMEs	Small and Medium-Sized Enterprises
SPA	Special Protection Area
SVC	Standing Veterinary Committee
TACs	Total Allowable Catches
TAFN	Task Force for the Accession Negotiations
TEN	Trans-European Network
TEU	Treaty on European Union
UCLAF	Anti-Fraud Co-ordination Unit
UFE	Union for Europe
WEU	Western European Union
WHO	World Health Organization
WTO	World Trade Organization

Journal of Common Market Studies

Volume 37, Annual Review
September 1999

Editorial: 'Plus ça change ...?'

GEOFFREY EDWARDS
University of Cambridge
and
GEORG WIESSALA
University of Central Lancashire

I. Introduction

Transition seems to be a dominant theme in several of the contributions to the *Review* this year. To begin with, the European Central Bank (ECB) emerged, together with the euro. Both were accompanied by sighs of relief on the part of many of the 11 Member States who are participating in it, whether because the whole venture had avoided being derailed or because they were actually a part of it. Possibly one of the most surprising things about the emergence of the Euro-zone – Euroland, or even *Eurolande,* being condemned as yet another instance of attempted linguistic hegemony by the Académie Française, which declared itself in favour of consistency, along with the franc-zone (or even the DM-zone?) – was that it was so smooth. This was despite the volatility of financial markets, a sharp deterioration in economic activity in many parts of the EU, and notwithstanding the very public row between France and Germany over the ECB's first President. At the same time, the Amsterdam Treaty progressed in stately and largely unchallenged fashion towards ratification, and preparations began for its implementation. There was, too, growing excitement as the European Parliament (EP) first called into question, then almost called into question and, finally, even by somewhat unorthodox means, eventually brought about the resignation of the Commission in March 1999. The Committee of

Experts which had been appointed to enquire into allegations of – at the very least – mismanagement, found against it.

The year also saw the start of undoubtedly a rather longer period of transition with the opening of negotiations on the accession of the countries of central and eastern Europe (and Cyprus). Closely tied to the accession negotiations are, of course, the politically sensitive issues of agricultural reform, structural funds and budgetary contributions, all of which are tied up in *Agenda 2000*. The Commission's proposals inevitably elicited all the usual signs of moral outrage and political fury that often presage relief that things are not quite as bad as they might have been – as Brigid Laffan suggests in her article. The full story is analysed by David Galloway in this year's keynote article.

If 1998 saw enough preparatory work on *Agenda 2000* to allow the German Presidency to reach agreement in March 1999, elsewhere in Europe – in the Balkans – there was so very much less to celebrate. The crisis in Kosovo deepened. What Lionel Barber in the *Financial Times* described as 'pin-prick diplomacy' (1 July 1998), left much of the initiative to the United States on behalf of the Contact Group and NATO. The arms embargo, visa ban, freezing of assets and, in June, the ban on investment in Serbia and the near farce of the ban on flights failed to contain the crisis, prevent ethnic cleansing or bring about the hoped for peace. The year ended with the Holbrooke/Hill ceasefire widely ignored and new peace efforts undertaken – with the use of force to halt the conflict envisaged even by the UN Secretary-General Kofi Annan on his visit to NATO in January 1999 (Weller, 1999, p. 221).

In almost grotesque counterpoint, the US and the EU were engaged in a dispute over bananas. The pros and cons of the spat tended to be lost, especially in the British press, in the welter of rumour about dubious pay-offs to political parties in Congress and the White House. Certainly, the significance of the dispute to both the West Indian economies heavily dependent on maintaining their banana exports, and the proper functioning of the World Trade Organization (WTO) and its disputes procedures, were frequently played down. But as Dave Allen and Mike Smith point out in their review of external policy, there seems to be an infinite capacity for compartmentalization in the EU–US relationship, such perhaps is the density of the relationship.

There were, too, some fairly radical changes in several Member States during 1998, not least, of course, in Germany with the defeat of Chancellor Helmut Kohl. After some 16 years in office, the CDU-led coalition was ousted in favour of a new Red–Green coalition under Gerhard Schröder as Chancellor, Oskar Lafontaine as Finance Minister and Joschka Fischer as Foreign Minister. In Italy, too, while a change in government is rarely path-breaking, the appointment of Massimo D'Alema as Prime Minister – the first former Communist Party member to form a government – meant that the EU began 1999 with 13 of the

Member States having centre-left governments. With such an emphasis on 'the third way', *'Neue Mitte'* etc., it is not surprising that, at least as reported in December, a new draft manifesto for the socialist group of finance ministers, was being drawn up at the Pörtschach summit, called 'The New European Way' (*Independent on Sunday*, 6 December 1998). However, even the centre-left appears to be a broad church, and not all finance ministers were quite so committed to measures for tax harmonization as perhaps the new, though temporary, German Finance Minister, or were as convinced that the 'obsession' with inflation could be overturned as the (equally temporary) Italian Finance Minister in Prodi's government, Vincenzo Visco (*European Voice*, 1998). Indeed, agreement on co-operation on tax matters was put off from the Cologne summit to that in Helsinki in December 1999. Lafontaine's enthusiasm for progress on tax matters won a perhaps predictable British reaction. Nonetheless, the Schröder–Jospin initiative for a comprehensive employment pact was agreed at the Vienna Council.

II. The Franco–German Axis Revived?

As Desmond Dinan points out in his article on Governance and Institutions (pp. 37–61 this issue), the Brussels European Council of May 1998 was memorable for the dramatic dispute between President Chirac and Chancellor Kohl over the appointment of Wim Duisenberg as the first President of the European Central Bank. The subsequent Chirac–Kohl letter on institutional reform appeared to do little to paper over the cracks in the Franco–German relationship, always regarded as the most potent of relationships for deepening the integration process. Shortcomings in the management of the relationship had inevitably occurred in the past but the dispute over the ECB seemed to focus, as rarely before, on the pragmatic nature of Franco–German co-operation. Given the thinness of the proposals in the initiative put forward at the Cardiff European Council, the effort of trying to reconcile more fundamental differences between Kohl and Chirac appeared to be simply too much. As *European Voice* suggested, 'the love had gone out of the marriage, and the stage was set for Schröder to end it' (17 December 1998). But as Andrea Szukala and Wolfgang Wessels suggested when analysing the Franco–German relationship in the run-up to the 1996–97 Intergovernmental Conference, it was somewhat premature to argue that the 'swan-song' thesis had won the day. There may have been few 'easy' policy areas left and the move towards EMU may have been full of pitfalls, but there remained a lowest common denominator of a 'shared lack of alternatives': neither partner can act alone, and the new relationship has obviously to be based on the recognition of this, whatever the divergences on particular issues (Szukala and Wessels, 1997, p. 78).

The prematurity of writing off the Franco–German relationship was shown only too clearly in both the difficulty the UK had in establishing a close working partnership with either during 1998 (see below) and the rapidity with which the new German government revitalized its relationship with France. Both Chirac and Jospin immediately welcomed Schröder on his election and the latter's first visit on taking office was to Paris. In addition, the French Finance Minister, Dominique Strauss-Kahn, seemed to be able to work with Oskar Lafontaine in a way that completely eluded Gordon Brown at the British Treasury. By the time of the Potsdam Franco–German bilateral summit at the beginning of December, a working consensus had been established on a whole raft of issues, not least on the need for majority voting on tax harmonization measures and on resolving the difficulties over future financing within the framework of *Agenda 2000* so that a satisfactory conclusion could be reached under the German Presidency. It was as if the very determined Keynesianism of Lafontaine struck a sympathetic chord with the French. The latter, having been thwarted in their attempt at 'Keynesianism in one country' in the early 1980s, were now able to experience it vicariously under the German Finance Minister and perhaps even to work on the possibilities of a Europeanized version of it. This was, of course, notwithstanding the *Neue Mitte* of the new German Chancellor and his seeming identification with the ideas and approach of the British Prime Minister, which did not seem to survive long after the election – though perhaps all was again in a state of flux with Lafontaine's resignation in March 1999.

III. A Near Triumvirate?

1998 was a year of tremendous potential for the UK though full, too, of many pitfalls: to take on the Presidency after barely six months in government is no easy task for any government least of all one that came after governments that had become ever more marginalized. The EU and its procedures and processes had been an extremely steep learning curve for incoming ministers – almost vertical according to one who reported that his extended briefing for his first European meeting continued in the lift to the negotiating chamber. But lack of governmental experience, as well as a continuing ambivalence within its highest counsels about quite what was wanted in Europe, inevitably had its impact. That unfamiliarity was also compounded by the pull of alternative poles, especially in foreign policy and particularly from the US – Britain's strong, isolated support for the bombing of Iraq being a case in point. The media hype surrounding the hosting of the Commonwealth Heads of Government meeting added other, further conflicting signals to Britain's partners in Europe as to where Britain's priorities lay.

But certainly the UK began their term at the helm with a clear change of tone:[1] the strutting lion of the past Conservative Presidency giving way to the cheerful daubs of children; New Labour's slogan, 'Europe Working for the People', was one difficult to imagine Mrs Thatcher agreeing to. 'New Labour, New Logo' – it was difficult perhaps not to be cynical.[2] It inevitably engendered wariness and suspicion as much, perhaps, as admiration and even some emulation. The EU had, after all, heard British claims – or demands – to be at heart of decision-making many times before. Moreover, the foci of the Presidency seemed still to be those of the Conservatives: the single market, deregulation, preventing fraud, reforming the CAP and enlargement. And, despite noises about a pro-European, even a pro-euro government – and a huge majority in the House of Commons – there was clearly concern about the possibility of alienating a still overwhelmingly Eurosceptical British press, especially that of Messrs Murdoch and Black.

It took some time for British ministers to realize that their expectation – that any sensible British leadership would always be followed by the rest of the EU – was over-optimistic. There was not always any great awareness of the extent to which they had to overcome the political negligence of Britain's European partners in the past. Nor did change or the prospect of change in Europe bring hoped-for support. The possibility of a more pragmatic leadership in Germany in place of the federalist Chancellor Kohl was exciting, but not without its uncertainties. After all, the problem with pragmatists is that they are pragmatic, and are not always predictable on any particular issue. This had certainly been the case with the French socialists under Lionel Jospin. Clearly they were not hard-line socialists, they were after all the heirs of François Mitterrand. Yet, equally clearly, they were not a 'modern' party in the New Labour sense. The German SPD under Gerhard Schröder seemed much more modern (Oskar Lafontaine notwithstanding) and, insofar as it had flattered New Labour through emulation, it engendered much greater hopes of new relationship at the centre of decision-making.

And yet, it proved to be no easy task – as others had found before – to break into the Franco–German duumvirate even at a time when it was going through a period of strain. New Labour was no longer Keynesian in its approach. With Lafontaine in such a key position, problems were perhaps inevitable, though they were exacerbated by the emphasis the German Finance Minister placed on the importance of tax harmonization, withholding taxes, etc. and which added to German demands for an end to the British rebate. The knee-jerk reaction of the British Chancellor of the Exchequer in vetoing any harmonization and the Prime

---

[1] This section is based on Edwards (1998).
[2] It should, however, be added that this was part of a deliberately created new image of the UK, another element of which was the establishment of a 'Panel 2000', which was recruited to fight the myth of a 'tired UK' and to promote the transformation of 'Little England' into 'Cool Britannia'.

Minister's flat rejection that the rebate was negotiable echoed earlier adminis-trations, suggesting that perhaps little in the British approach to things European had, indeed, changed in substance. Increasingly desperate attempts by ministers to persuade a Eurosceptic press rushing to demonize the German Finance Minister, that harmonization did not mean uniformity of taxation were not particularly successful; any subtlety in the distinction was somewhat lost in the tabloid translation.

But nonetheless a learning process was underway. Mr Blair may have sought to play a Presidency role in May over the ECB but it came ever clearer that the UK's position was fundamentally weakened by its absence from the Euro-11 councils. As Philip Stephens, neatly summed up in the *Financial Times*, 'Outside the eurozone, the British Prime Minister will have to shout to be heard' (5 June 1998).

Significantly, when the shouting came, it was about defence and in the company of the French. There was a fascinating development in British thinking within the space of only a few months in 1998. In July, the Ministry of Defence published its long-awaited Strategic Defence Review. It focused, perhaps naturally with such documents, on the British defence effort. There were few, very few, references specifically to European defence and security, though as the Defence Secretary had pointed out, the review was 'firmly grounded in foreign policy' as well as 'sound military experience'. A few months later, however, at St Malo, the British discovered a European vocation and sought with the French to move towards a stronger European defence and security identity. It was, as far as the Prime Minister's spokesman was concerned, a logical development:

> It is widely accepted that we pack most of the EU's conventional military punch. We and the French have been looking at achieving a stronger and more coherent voice in international affairs and combining this with an ability to back it up with military force if necessary. (*Financial Times*, 3 December 1998)

As the Prime Minister himself put it, he had begun 'opening up the British position' at Pörtschach with his fellow Heads of State or Governments (Press Conference, 4 December 1998). The St Malo declaration nonetheless came as a considerable surprise.

The imminent introduction of the euro by 11 of the 15 Member States may have been purely coincidental; it may, on the other hand, have been just too clear a signal of continued UK marginalization. The Franco–British summit also followed rapidly on a successful Franco–German bilateral meeting in Potsdam. But however rapidly engineered for whatever reason, the British shift of emphasis on defence and security seems to have been one that has stuck, and work was immediately started to give substance to the extremely brief declara-tion at St Malo.

Less extensively reported at least in the British press perhaps, were the remarks of both the French President and Prime Minister on other issues. Both were at pains to point out the work that remained to be done on the future financing of the EU. This, President Chirac held, was 'doomed to failure' unless all Member States participated in a spirit of give and take – a reference less to France giving than the need for the British to cease taking its rebate. The firmness of such French remarks was in marked contrast to the consensus reached at Potsdam. France and Germany may not be condemned to agree, but British self-exclusion from the deepening of the EU through EMU faces them with few alternatives except perhaps via the uncertainties of either closer co-operation under the Amsterdam Treaty or greater flexibility outside the EU framework. The British, themselves, firm advocates but not always enthusiastic supporters of flexibility in the past, appear to be moving slowly towards a more inclusive EU, a deepening process of 'Brusselsization' even if not of communitarization.

But if the British were being obliged to rethink their European strategy, they were at the same time entering a new era of uncertainty about the country's national identity. In 1998, the UK began to face up to the prospect of unprecedented constitutional change with devolution in both Scotland and Wales. With the constitutional niceties out of the way, preparations for both the Scottish Parliament and the Welsh Assembly then proceeded apace. As Brigid Laffan points out, the devolution process is transforming the last centralized state in western Europe into a multi-levelled system of governance. The consequences of this for the traditional dominance of Whitehall and Westminster, not least in European politics, will doubtless be the source of many new research projects. But what it is also creating, apart from an even fuzzier concept of sovereignty, is a growing interest in English nationalism. Hitherto, there has been no need for the English to think in terms of their 'Englishness': there was an implicit assumption that to be English and British were one and the same – except, of course, on the sports field. Whether a new sense of English identity will become subsumed within a new English nationalism and with what consequences, remains to be seen.

IV. Changes in the Annual Review

There is change, if not transition, too, even in respect of the *Review:* not only is there a new cover but we welcome several new contributors: Desmond Dinan and Nigel Grimwade – with our thanks to Richard Corbett and Drew Scott for having seen in the transitional phase of the new editorship – and three innovations – a regular update on the accession negotiations by Chris Preston and brief reflections on the two EU Presidencies of the year, in this case the British (Peter Anderson) and the Austrian (Richard Luther). In other ways, we have been only too delighted and relieved to follow the path laid down by Neill Nugent and his team.

Finally, the editors would like to extend our sincerest thanks to David Galloway for so generously stepping into the breach at less than short notice to provide such a valuable keynote article on *Agenda 2000*.

References

Edwards, G. (1998) 'The British Presidency and the Complexities of European Governance'. In *Britain's Role in Europe,* Report of the Conference, The Hague 16 January (Clingendael: Netherlands Institute of International Relations).

Szukala, A. and Wessels, W. (1997) 'The Franco–German Tandem'. In Edwards, G. and Pijpers, A. (eds) *The Politics of European Treaty Reform* (London: Cassell).

Weller, M. (1999) 'The Rambouillet Conference on Kosovo'. *International Affairs,* Vol. 75, No. 2, pp. 211–51.

Journal of Common Market Studies

Volume 37, Annual Review
September 1999

Keynote Article:
Agenda 2000 – Packaging the Deal*

DAVID GALLOWAY
Council of the European Union

I. Introduction

The political backdrop to *Agenda 2000*, the shorthand label describing reform of the EU's major spending policies and of the financial means to fund them, did not augur well for a smooth or straightforward negotiation. Member States were struggling to meet the Maastricht convergence criteria ahead of the final decisions in May 1998 on the introduction of the euro, while confronting the implications of a number of external factors in drawing up a new seven-year financial framework for the Union. Reform of the Common Agricultural Policy (CAP) would be undertaken on the threshold of a new millennium round of World Trade Organization (WTO) multilateral trade negotiations in which agriculture would feature prominently. With the EU embarking on its biggest ever enlargement, the financial implications of admitting a large number of less wealthy applicants were likely to be hotly disputed among existing Member States. Amid the general squeeze on public finances across Europe, the issue of payments to the EU budget by the large net contributors (Germany, the Netherlands, the UK, Sweden and Austria) was being propelled to the forefront of

* David Galloway is an adviser in the private office of the Secretary-General of the Council of the European Union. Any views expressed in this article are entirely personal, and are not the official view of either the Council or its General Secretariat. The author would like to express his appreciation to Jacques Keller-Noëllet, John Peterson, Geoffrey Edwards and Georg Wiessala for helpful comments and suggestions.

domestic political agendas;[1] in Germany in particular, the perceived 'excessive' net contribution to the EU budget was developing into a major electoral issue in the run-up to the September 1998 general elections. The UK government, faced with calls from other Member States either to abolish the 1984 budget abatement mechanism or to make significant concessions in relation to the cost of enlargement, argued that the UK's continued status as a major net contributor meant that the abatement was non-negotiable.

Given that drawing up a financial framework and reframing spending policies is essentially a zero-sum exercise in dividing up a given budgetary cake, Member States began their tactical positioning based on calculations of net gains and losses which might result from the Commission's *Agenda 2000* proposals, the external pressures outlined above and demands likely to be pressed by other Member States. The prospect of a rough ride ahead on one of the most complex packages ever processed by the Union loomed large at the start of 1998.

1998 began with something of a phoney war following the initial frenetic activity on the Commission's *Agenda 2000* communication in the run-up to the Luxembourg European Council in December 1997. Based on the Union's first cardinal principle that it can conduct only one major internal negotiation at any one time, the Commission had presented its communication in July 1997 in the wake of the Amsterdam Intergovernmental Conference (IGC), in order to test the water before submitting its formal proposals. In political terms, the main question facing the December 1997 Luxembourg European Council was the extent to which markers on the future financial framework would have to be laid down at this early stage as a prerequisite for the European Council to launch the enlargement process. While the Commission harboured ambitions of the European Council providing guidelines in support of the broad principles underlying its proposals, Member State governments saw no need to hold any part of *Agenda 2000* hostage as a condition for giving the green light to the start of the enlargement process.[2] Hence the minimalist and general blessing of the Commission's ideas as 'an appropriate working basis for further negotiations for an

---

[1] It is worth noting that none of these countries objected to being a net contributor as such, nor sought a 'juste retour'. Their complaint was that they deemed they were contributing excessively in relation to their relative prosperity, with no safety net (except for the UK) to prevent further deterioration in their negative budgetary positions in future.

[2] The Commission's opinions on enlargement advocated opening negotiations initially with six applicant states: Poland, Hungary, Czech Republic, Slovenia, Estonia and Cyprus. Member States were divided between those which advocated the Commission's 'staggered start' approach and those which advocated the 'regatta' approach (i.e. opening negotiations with all applicants at the same time without determining when each would arrive at the finishing line). The European Council in Luxembourg in December 1997 endeavoured to bridge this division and agree a non-discriminatory approach by launching an 'accession process' under Article O of the TEU in which *all* applicants are involved on an equal footing and are destined to become Members of the Union on the basis of the same criteria. Within this process, formal negotiations would be opened with six countries and five others would undertake 'preparations for negotiations' with the prospect of moving to formal negotiations as soon as they were ready and able to do so.

agreement on the Union's policies and the financial framework'. The major substantial element to emerge from the Luxembourg European Council conclusions was the requirement to ringfence expenditure for EU-15 in the next financial framework from that reserved for future acceding countries.

Nothing had therefore been pre-empted when the Commission duly presented its raft of proposals on 18 March 1998. The range and complexity of the *Agenda 2000* reforms underlined the magnitude of what was at stake: a new financial framework fixing, in an Interinstitutional Agreement (IIA) between the European Parliament, the Council and the Commission, the medium-term financial limits within which the annual budgets for the Union should be drawn up for the period 2000–06; six draft regulations reforming the Union's structural and cohesion funds; eight draft regulations reforming the arable crops, beef, veal and milk production sectors, including modifications to CAP financing, direct support schemes and rural development regulations; amendments to the financing of trans-European networks (TENs) and loan guarantee fund regulations; and three regulations on co-ordinating the pre-accession strategy and establishing two new pre-accession instruments respectively on agriculture and structural policies. The package lacked one vital element, which would only arrive in October (i.e. after the German general election): the Commission's report on the operation of the 'own resources' system (the system for raising revenue for the EU budget).

Such a far-reaching and potentially explosive reform package, covering the two major spending items in the Union's budget (CAP and structural policies) would clearly impose a considerable strain on the Union's legislative process. This article looks in turn at the method of handling and managing the negotiating process in the Council and the European Parliament (EP), at some of the main substantive political issues which emerged during the negotiation and, as a postscript, offers a tentative initial assessment of the final outcome achieved at the Berlin European Council on 24–25 March 1999.

II. Managing the Negotiating Process

Although precedents for this type of package negotiation existed in the shape of the Delors I and II financial packages following, respectively, the Single Act and the Treaty on European Union, the *Agenda 2000* negotiations were compounded by two further complicating factors. Firstly, because of the tight timetable if formal adoption were to be achieved before the June 1999 European Parliament elections, work would have to be pursued simultaneously on the overall political package to be agreed by the European Council, and on the actual texts translating the political deal into legislative form. Many of these texts required Parliament's approval in one form or other. In the case of Delors II, the legislative proposals were presented only after the Edinburgh European Council had struck an overall political deal. Secondly, the Union would have to ensure that the content of its reforms and its financial framework would enable it to cope with the accession of new and less wealthy Member States during the period of the new financial perspective. While the EU has not committed itself to any date for the completion of accession negotiations, the working assumption used by the Commission in its proposals and in drawing up the new financial perspective was the accession of six new Member States in 2002.

Furthermore, the economic and financial context within which the negotiations took place was very different from the one that prevailed at the time of the Delors II reforms. At that time, the Community was undertaking a rapid expansion of its structural expenditure, to enable poorer regions and countries to derive maximum benefit from the internal market. The Cohesion Fund was created expressly in order to assist less wealthy countries in meeting the demands of preparing for the single currency. In 1998, however, the watchwords of budgetary rigour and efficient expenditure were writ larger than ever, with many Member States, particularly the net contributors to the EU budget, seeking to impose on the Union's expenditure similar budgetary discipline to that being exercised at home in the context of preparing for the introduction of the euro. The big question mark was whether the European Parliament would be as willing to subscribe to a financial perspective which would probably give it substantially less leeway for increasing non-compulsory expenditure in the annual budgets than the Treaty provisions on the so-called maximum rate of increase (Art. 272(9) of the EC Treaty).

Work in the Council

Council Presidencies were confronted with two main management problems. First, *Agenda 2000* extended across the preserve of the General Affairs, Agriculture and Ecofin Councils. Processing such a complex and wide-ranging programme through the Council's vertical structures ran the real risk of fragmentation of the various components of the package, with civil servants in different national ministries naturally taking negotiating positions defending their own turf rather than in the interests of the overall balance of the package. It was therefore vital for the Presidency to obviate this risk by putting in place mechanisms to ensure consistency of approach on the dossier as a whole. Secondly, the UK and Austrian Presidencies each had to consider carefully what their overall objective should be in terms of the outcome of their respective European Councils as important staging posts along the road to Berlin. This required striking the right balance between sustaining an adequate degree of momentum throughout the negotiations, while avoiding over-ambition at too early a stage, with the attendant risk of incurring a major setback in a Council or European Council meeting.

Careful planning was required in order to deal with both of these potential pitfalls, while following the twin track of paving the way for an overall political agreement and undertaking a detailed examination of the legislative texts. The Council agreed early in the UK Presidency on a procedure for ensuring unity of work. The General Affairs Council, given its role in preparing the European Council, would have overall responsibility for *Agenda 2000*, and for preparing the reports to be submitted to the European Council. The Ecofin and Agriculture Councils would provide their input on the aspects of the package that concerned them. The Committee of Permanent Representatives (Coreper) was to have its usual responsibility for preparing the General Affairs Council, assisted by a 'Friends of the Presidency' Group.[3] In practice, however, while Coreper and the General Affairs Council had overall responsibility for the financial amounts to be fixed for agriculture, actual work on the detailed content of the CAP reform was carried out by the Agriculture Council and its preparatory bodies, given the highly specialized and technical nature of these negotiations. Provided the agriculture ministers and their civil servants respected the financial parameters to be laid down as part of the overall negotiation, they would be left largely to their own devices on the content of the reform. The question was whether an acceptable reform package could be achieved in the context of a desire to impose strict curbs on agriculture spending.

Much of the initial work by the UK Presidency on the Commission's proposals involved clarifying their content and what they actually meant, as well as assessing the assumptions underlying them. Discussions in the 'Friends' Group and Coreper were structured by Presidency questionnaires in order to highlight relevant issues, and ensure that all delegations were talking about the same thing at the same time (something that is not always necessarily self-evident nor easy to achieve!). It became clear early on that three broad types of issue would have to be tackled:

- First of all certain issues which were *fundamentally political in character*, such as the overall financial amounts in each heading, the agricultural guideline, or eligibility criteria for the structural funds. It was generally recognized that, on these matters, agreement could be reached only in an

---

[3] The Friends of the Presidency Group was a group 'close' to Coreper composed of a mixture of ambassadors' assistants (*'Anticis'*) and financial or political counsellors, under a single chair, although the composition of delegations varied depending on matters under discussion. Its main task was to carry out a detailed examination of various issues for Coreper and to remit more specific technical work on certain parts of the legislation to either the Structural Actions Working Group or the Financial Counsellors Group. The group was particularly active during the UK and Austrian Presidencies, when much of the work involved clarifying the content of the Commission's proposals by requesting and examining supplementary explanatory documents and background information from the Commission.

overall context in the end-game, and that the focus of work would be to clarify the Commission's underlying assumptions and calculations.

- *Substantive issues* on which the broad contours of agreement could be reached, such as the structure and breakdown of the financial perspective, the content of the IIA other than on the end-game issues, the financial management provisions of the structural funds, or the pre-accession instruments. On these issues progress, even on fairly political aspects, could be expected at the level of Coreper or the Council.
- Finally, *more technical issues*, such as the organization and programming of structural funds and the pre-accession instruments, where experts could get into the nitty-gritty detail of the legislative texts from the outset.

The report drawn up for the Cardiff European Council in June 1998 provided a useful overview and description of the key issues which would have to be addressed in the subsequent negotiation, as well as an indication in general terms of the main tendencies emerging among Member States. It became clear that Cardiff could not be expected to make much headway on the substance of the negotiations only three months after the proposals had been submitted, and given the fact that the Commission's own resources report would not be presented until the autumn. However, Cardiff was able to reach two tangible conclusions. First of all, it fixed a deadline of March 1999 for wrapping up the political package in the European Council, with the aim of completing the legislative work before the European Parliamentary elections in June 1999. Second, it again underlined the ringfencing requirement by stating that 'a clear distinction must be made in the presentation and implementation in the financial framework between expenditure relating to the Union as currently constituted and that reserved for the future acceding countries, including after enlargement'.

Armed with an annotated 'bible' in the shape of the Cardiff report, and knowing that work on the package could not be completed by the Vienna European Council in December, the Austrian Presidency was faced with a daunting challenge: how to keep work focused and achieve 'substantial progress on the key elements of the package' in the knowledge that final agreement could only come later. Careful management was required to avoid investing too much political capital in trying to move substantially towards an agreement at Vienna, without the constraint of a hard deadline and an end-game scenario to concentrate ministerial minds. The Presidency nevertheless had to ensure that real progress was achieved at Vienna, while dispelling early on any misconceptions that Vienna would somehow have failed if no final agreement was struck.

Work was pursued actively at the technical level and by the Friends of the Presidency examining the detail of the Commission's proposals, particularly on middle-order issues relating to the structural funds, as well as on the pre-accession instruments where tangible progress was achieved. The first stage of the Presidency's work involved looking at issues which had only been given a cursory examination to date, or those requiring a more detailed examination as a precondition for advancing on substance. From September the Presidency, by tabling questionnaires and options papers, sought to flush delegations out by asking them to take a position on specific items. Work was brought forward rapidly on the pre-accession instruments, the TENs financing and the loan guarantee fund regulations, so that by the end of the Presidency political agreement on those issues had largely been achieved, subject to a number of reservations linked to the overall outcome on *Agenda 2000*. The third stage of work involved preparing a comprehensive report for the Vienna European Council which highlighted the main outstanding issues which would have to be resolved as part of the political deal. As regards the new financial perspective, the report managed to establish the upper and lower parameters within which further negotiation would take place (see below).

It was crucial for the Austrian Presidency to have an effective internal process for forging its Presidency (rather than national) position on both tactics and key issues of substance, particularly those to be addressed at each session of the General Affairs, Ecofin and Agriculture Councils.[4] Presidency positions were co-ordinated by a Strategic Co-ordinating Committee in Vienna consisting of senior civil servants from the Federal Chancellery and the foreign, finance and agriculture ministries, as well as from the Permanent Representation in Brussels. In hammering out a strategic line, often operating to tight deadlines required by the pace of work in Brussels, this Committee not only had to square the interests of different ministries within a Social Democrat–People's Party ruling coalition, but also to avoid taking an overtly partisan stance in Presidency papers on vital Austrian national issues (e.g. the negative budgetary position).

The German Presidency from 1 January 1999 marked the beginning of a new negotiating phase in which it would have to drive forward the process of narrowing the gap between delegations' positions on the key issues in order to meet the timeframe confirmed at the Vienna European Council. In early January, the Presidency tabled what was dubbed its 'negotiating box'. This document was an issue-based paper which did not set out delegations' positions; it constituted, in effect, a skeletal pre-draft of what would eventually become the Berlin European Council conclusions.[5] Developed language already existed in certain

---

[4] This also involved determining the nature and content of the report to be prepared for the Vienna European Council, in particular whether it should be a Presidency or a Council (i.e. agreed) report, whether it should be issue based or reflect delegations' views. On most of these points, the Council Secretariat provided counsel and suggested language to the Presidency at an early stage in their internal reflections as a basis on which the Presidency could construct the line it wished to take.

[5] While European Council conclusions are typically not negotiated in advance but tabled only on the second day of the summit meetings, *Agenda 2000* was an exception to this well-established rule. Given the complexity and political sensitivity of the subject matter, where the inclusion or omission of single sentences,

parts; other parts consisted of options, square-bracketed language or blanks! The content of the 'box' was fleshed out by means of a series of non-papers tabled in Coreper on the Presidency's responsibility.[6] In the light of successive discussions in Coreper, Council and by Heads of State or Government, the text would be gradually firmed up by a process of successive approximations. The Presidency had to steer work forward firmly, through successive revisions of the 'box' at the appropriate junctures, over the two-and-a-half months leading up to Berlin. Essentially, the Presidency had to organize and facilitate four types of activity:

• Holding preparatory meetings with the Commission and the Council Secretariat in order to prepare compromise ideas. Typically, an initial draft of conclusions' language or options ideas would be drawn up by the Council Secretariat and tested with the Commission before being sent to the Presidency as a basis for internal interdepartmental co-ordination. The texts would then be finalized in one of the weekly or fortnightly co-ordination meetings between the Presidency, Commission and Secretariat, with the Presidency, after hearing counsel from the Commission and the Council Secretariat, having the ultimate responsibility for the content of its papers.
• Conducting bilateral contacts throughout this period in both national capitals and Brussels in the margins of meetings in order to sound out informally some of the ideas being developed and to gauge what the market would bear in terms of possible compromises. The outcome of these discussions would assist the Presidency in selecting options most likely to constitute a basis for achieving political agreement.
• Organizing weekly discussions in Coreper on the 'negotiating box' or on supplementary non-papers fleshing out language and ideas for inclusion in the 'box'. At this stage in the proceedings, the Friends of the Presidency Group was less actively involved, since the work of preparing the European Council had moved on to a more political plane.
• Making best use of ministerial meetings of the Council as a forum for negotiating on the key political issues. Through the work carried out in Coreper, political issues would be identified by the Presidency for examination by the General Affairs and Ecofin Councils.

---

or even words, could cost individual Member States hundreds of millions of euros, 27 pages of densely drafted conclusions could not be sprung on the European Council without prior scrutiny and familiarity with the overall structure and the language to be used. This method mirrored that used in the run-up to the Edinburgh European Council in December 1992 which sealed the Delors II package.
[6] Presidency non-papers are texts prepared under the Presidency's responsibility but without formally committing it, which are tabled to test the temperature by sounding out ideas, language and options so that the Presidency can subsequently come forward with a more formal position based on its feeling for what the market will bear.

Deft handling was required to keep all the negotiating strands moving forward in unison. The Presidency, as is the case in most package negotiations of this nature, had to keep several moves ahead of the game in dealing with the rapid succession of Councils and an informal Heads of Government meeting in Petersberg one month before Berlin. While most experts intimately involved in the negotiation could roughly sketch out the contours of a final deal as early as January, the skill lies in charting a path that ensures the negotiation remains on track over the various political hurdles before the finishing line is reached. Although the broad contours of a fair and balanced overall outcome may have been discernible ahead of a final deal, the specific details of the many aspects of a negotiation such as this could have a significant financial impact on any individual Member State, which meant that the Presidency had to remain vigilant right up until the last moment.

Legislative Handling in the European Parliament

At the same time as the Council was pursuing its *Agenda 2000* work, the European Parliament had also begun putting in place its internal arrangements for examining the legislative texts. A Steering Committee was established within the Parliament under the Chairmanship of its President, José Maria Gil-Robles, in order to co-ordinate work between the various Parliamentary Committees, and to prepare the overall position which the Parliament would take towards the Council and the Commission. The *Agenda 2000* proposals covered practically the whole gamut of legislative procedures, including consultation, co-operation (which would become co-decision after the entry into force of the Treaty of Amsterdam) and assent. From the outset, the European Parliament's view was that the proposals should be considered as a single political package, that it would need to be fully associated with discussions in the Council and that it would be seeking arrangements for handling the proposals involving two readings by the Parliament on all of them. Initially, it sought to formalize these arrangements in an Interinstitutional Agreement with the Council.

The Council recognized the need for and the importance of collaborating effectively with the Parliament, given that a constructive attitude would be required from both institutions if the legislative work was to be completed on time. It also acknowledged the need for regular contacts between the two institutions to ensure co-ordination and an exchange of information on discussions. However, the Council was more circumspect on the question of agreeing an IIA on how to handle the package. Its view was that the Treaties provided for a specific legislative procedure for each proposal, and that while these legislative proposals had to be considered in an overall context, the pace of work on each should take account of objective timing constraints, which were not necessarily the same for each one. Moreover, the Parliament's goal of achieving a *de facto* co-decision procedure on the whole *Agenda 2000* package went beyond the letter and the spirit of the Treaties, and what the Council felt able to accept.

The European Parliament's tactical response was to follow a two-stage approach for all of the *Agenda 2000* texts. It first of all delivered proposed amendments on the Commission's proposals by late 1998 or early 1999, but at the same time withheld its formal legislative opinion on the texts until after Berlin (except for those subject to the co-operation procedure, where formal opinions were produced before the end of 1998). This enabled it to assess the direction the Council was taking, and the extent to which its proposed amendments had been taken on board before delivering its definitive view.

However the Council, building on the precedent followed during the Delors II negotiations, agreed that, over and above the formal procedures of assent and co-operation, an approach would be followed allowing the Parliament to undertake a second reading on all the structural and cohesion fund regulations. There was a certain logic to this approach. Given that co-decision would apply to both the regulations on the European Regional Development Fund and the European Social Fund, it would be difficult not to give serious consideration to the Parliament's view on the general regulation containing the provisions on issues such as eligibility criteria for the various structural fund objectives, transitional support and financial management issues, for which the assent procedure would apply. Indeed, a number of amendments were negotiated on the general regulation before the final text was formalized by the Council with Parliamentary assent. This serves to demonstrate the general unsuitability of the assent procedure for legislative texts, given that, formally, it only allows the Parliament to give a general thumbs up or thumbs down on a text finalized by the Council, without any scope for negotiation.

Throughout the *Agenda 2000* negotiations, therefore, the Presidency had an important second front to deal with in keeping the European Parliament informed about work in the Council in order to pave the way for the intense period of negotiation with the Parliament which would follow any political agreement in Berlin. The Parliament had set up three working groups dealing respectively with agriculture, structural funds and the pre-accession instruments designed to act as fora for dialogue and exchange of information among members of Parliament, as well as with the Council and the Commission. The Presidency, over and above the regular series of trialogue meetings with the Parliament and the Commission, participated informally in each of these working groups on behalf of the Council in order to ensure co-ordination of work between the Council and the Parliament and to exchange information on the progress of work in the various policy areas. This allowed the Council, through the Presidency, to be informed about the mood of the Parliament. The Parliament, particularly on pre-accession instruments and on structural funds, expected even before Berlin to enter into a detailed dialogue on its proposed amendments. However, it was difficult for the Council to respond to these in detail as long as no formal common positions existed. Some minor concessions were made to the Parliament on the pre-accession instruments in February in order to demonstrate the Council's goodwill, and it was only following the Berlin European Council that a meaningful dialogue could take place between the Parliament and the Council on the Parliament's specific amendments to the structural fund regulations.

III. Survey of the Main Political Issues

While half a dozen or so points could be singled out as first-order political issues which could only be agreed as part of a final package, three in particular merit attention: the requirement to ringfence expenditure for EU-15 and that for countries joining the Union in the course of the new financial perspective; the approach for determining the overall expenditure ceilings in the new financial perspective in general, and the main spending categories in particular (agriculture and structural operations); and issues relating to the Union's own resources, in particular the efforts by four of the largest net contributor Member States to achieve a reduction in their negative budgetary imbalance.

Ringfencing of Expenditure for EU-15 and New Member States

It became apparent as early as the Luxembourg European Council that provision would have to be made in the financial perspective to ensure watertight separation between expenditure for EU-15, and that for the new Member States, including pre-accession expenditure. This conveniently killed two birds with one stone: it provided reassurance for Member States who were net recipients of EU funds that enlargement during the new financial perspective period would not place in jeopardy their portion of the cake, and it sent a clear political signal to applicant states that monies set aside for them, both immediately in the form of pre-accession assistance, and later following their accession to the Union, would not be eroded due to any unforeseen spending contingencies confronting EU-15. The Commission's approach involved setting aside resources in the financial perspective from 2002 until 2006 as maximum amounts in payment appropriations to cover expenditure resulting from new accessions over the period.[7] These figures would represent the Union's common negotiating position for the accession negotiations. Under the Commission's original proposal, there was insufficient scope to cover the full cost of enlargement in terms of payment appropriations under the financial perspective EU-15; the remaining

---

[7] The Commission's initial approach involved reserving part of the margin (as a percentage of EU GNP) to cover part of the cost of enlargement. There was, however, a firm desire from all Member States to include this cost in the financial perspective table in absolute amounts.

cost would be met by having recourse to part of the additional resources available as a result of the new accessions. It is indicative of the extent to which the overall financial perspective levels agreed at Berlin fell short of the Commission's original figures that the full cost of enlargement in terms of payment appropriations could be accommodated in the financial perspective for EU-15, as well as enormous margins for unforeseen expenditure (0.14 per cent of EU GNP by the end of the period;[8] by way of comparison, the margin for unforeseen expenditure in the 1999 financial perspective was 0.01 per cent of EU GNP).

The Spanish delegation considered at an early stage in the negotiation that this approach did not provide sufficient assurances that funds for EU-15 would be secure. Their preferred approach was to make the full cost of enlargement visible at this early stage by adopting a financial perspective for EU-21, including the full cost of enlargement in a separate financial perspective heading. The amounts in this enlargement heading would cover the requirements following enlargement for all expenditure categories, and would remain in this heading after enlargement without being reallocated to the other Headings 1–6. This implied that no adjustment of the financial perspective would be made upon enlargement. This approach appeared, however, at the very least to be complex and impracticable to apply in drawing up the annual budget and was criticized by other Member States for being contrary to budget orthodoxy as well as discriminatory against what would become fully-fledged Member States.

The underlying political problem in this case was a desire to highlight clearly the maximum cost of enlargement over the period in the various financial perspective headings, and to ensure the safety of expenditure for EU-15, particularly for structural operations, a concern widely shared by all the cohesion countries. The solution was to draw up alongside the financial perspective an indicative financial framework for EU-21, including additional own resources resulting from the accession of six new Member States, and set out in an additional Heading 8 in that framework the cost of enlargement as maximum amounts in commitment appropriations (see Tables 1 and 2). Since Table 2 is purely indicative in character, upon enlargement, the financial perspective for EU-15 will still have to be amended, taking account of the actual number of acceding Member States. In order to underline the fact that enlargement posed no risk for current spending in EU-15, the Berlin European Council conclusions expressly provided that in the event of any development of actual expenditure as a consequence of enlargement proving likely to exceed the ceiling on payment appropriations, the financial commitments for EU-15 agreed in the financial perspective will have to be respected.

[8] The margin for unforeseen expenditure in the indicative financial framework for EU-21 (i.e. taking account of the own resources available from six new Member States) is 0.18 per cent in 2006 (see Table 2).

Table 1: Financial Perspective EU-15 (m euros – 1999 prices)

Commitment Appropriations	2000	2001	2002	2003	2004	2005	2006
1. Agriculture	40920	42800	43900	43770	42760	41930	41660
CAP (not including rural development)	*36620*	*38480*	*39570*	*39430*	*38410*	*37570*	*37290*
Rural development and accompanying measures	*4300*	*4320*	*4330*	*4340*	*4350*	*4360*	*4370*
2. Structural operations	32045	31455	30865	30285	29595	29595	29170
Structural funds	*29430*	*28840*	*28250*	*27670*	*27080*	*27080*	*26660*
Cohesion fund	*2615*	*2615*	*2615*	*2615*	*2515*	*2515*	*2510*
3. Internal policies[a]	5930	6040	6150	6260	6370	6480	6600
4. External action	4550	4560	4570	4580	4590	4600	4610
5. Administration[b]	4560	4600	4700	4800	4900	5000	5100
6. Reserves	900	900	650	400	400	400	400
Monetary reserve	*500*	*500*	*250*	*0*	*0*	*0*	*0*
Emergency aid reserve	*200*	*200*	*200*	*200*	*200*	*200*	*200*
Loan guarantee reserve	*200*	*200*	*200*	*200*	*200*	*200*	*200*
7. Pre-accession aid	3120	3120	3120	3120	3120	3120	3120
Agriculture	*520*	*520*	*520*	*520*	*520*	*520*	*520*
Pre-accession structural instruments	*1040*	*1040*	*1040*	*1040*	*1040*	*1040*	*1040*
PHARE (applicant countries)	*1560*	*1560*	*1560*	*1560*	*1560*	*1560*	*1560*
Total commitment appropriations	92025	93475	93955	93215	91735	91125	90660
Total payment appropriations	89600	91110	94220	94880	91910	90160	89620
Payment appropriations as % of GNP	1.13	1.12	1.13	1.11	1.05	1.00	0.97
Available for accession (payment appropriations)			4140	6710	8890	11440	14220
Agriculture			*1600*	*2030*	*2450*	*2930*	*3400*
Other expenditure			*2540*	*4680*	*6440*	*8510*	*10820*
Ceiling on payment appropriations	89600	91110	98360	101590	100800	101600	103840
Ceiling on payment appropriations as % of GNP	1.13	1.12	1.18	1.19	1.15	1.13	1.13
Margin for unforeseen expenditure (%)	0.14	0.15	0.09	0.08	0.12	0.14	0.14
Own resources ceiling (%)	1.27	1.27	1.27	1.27	1.27	1.27	1.27

Notes: [a] In accordance with Art. 2 of Decision No 182/1999/EC of the European Parliament and the Council and Council Decision 1999/64/Euratom (*OJ* L 26, 1.2.1999, pp. 1, 34), the amount of expenditure available during the period 2000–02 for research amounts to 11510m euros at current prices.
[b] The expenditure on pensions included under the ceilings for this heading is calculated net of staff contributions to the relevant scheme, within the limit of 1100m euros at 1999 prices for the period 2000–06.

Table 2: Financial Framework EU-21 (m euros – 1999 prices)

Commitment Appropriations	2000	2001	2002	2003	2004	2005	2006
1. Agriculture	40920	42800	43900	43770	42760	41930	41660
CAP (*not including rural development*)	36620	38480	39570	39430	38410	37570	37290
Rural development and accompanying measures	4300	4320	4330	4340	4350	4360	4370
2. Structural operations	32045	31455	30865	30285	29595	29595	29170
Structural funds	29430	28840	28250	27670	27080	27080	26660
Cohesion fund	2615	2615	2615	2615	2515	2515	2510
3. Internal policies[a]	5930	6040	6150	6260	6370	6480	6600
4. External action	4550	4560	4570	4580	4590	4600	4610
5. Administration[b]	4560	4600	4700	4800	4900	5000	5100
6. Reserves	900	900	650	400	400	400	400
Monetary reserve	500	500	250	0	0	0	0
Emergency aid reserve	200	200	200	200	200	200	200
Loan guarantee reserve	200	200	200	200	200	200	200
7. Pre-accession aid	3120	3120	3120	3120	3120	3120	3120
Agriculture	520	520	520	520	520	520	520
Pre-accession	1040	1040	1040	1040	1040	1040	1040
PHARE (applicant countries)	1560	1560	1560	1560	1560	1560	1560
8. Enlargement			6450	9030	11610	14200	16780
Agriculture			1600	2030	2450	2930	3400
Structural operations			3750	5830	7920	10000	12080
Internal policies			730	760	790	820	850
Administration			370	410	450	450	450
Total commitment appropriations	92025	93475	100405	102245	103345	105325	107440
Total payment appropriations	89600	91110	98360	101590	100800	101600	103840
Of which: enlargement			4140	6710	8890	11440	14220
Payment appropriations as % of GNP	1.13	1.12	1.14	1.15	1.11	1.09	1.09
Margin for unforeseen expenditure (%)	0.14	0.15	0.13	0.12	0.16	0.18	0.18
Own resources ceiling (%)	1.27	1.27	1.27	1.27	1.27	1.27	1.27

Notes: [a] In accordance with Art. 2 of Decision No 182/1999/EC of the European Parliament and the Council and Council Decision 1999/64/Euratom (*OJ* L 26, 1.2.1999, pp. 1, 34), the amount of expenditure available during the period 2000–02 for research amounts to 11510m euros at current prices.
[b] The expenditure on pensions included under the ceilings for this heading is calculated net of staff contributions to the relevant scheme, within the limit of 1100m euros at 1999 prices for the period 2000–06.

It should be noted that even though the Cardiff European Council called for ringfencing of expenditure 'including after enlargement', in actual fact once a new Member State is in the Union it will no longer be possible to earmark money solely for that Member State under the budget. Spending will be effected via the relevant budget lines in accordance with the applicable Community legislation. Theoretically at least, Member States could potentially receive amounts in excess of the allocation indicatively provided for in a Treaty of Accession, for example on agriculture, if applying the relevant legislation, say on price support, were to result in a higher figure.

Determining the Overall Levels of Spending in the New Financial Perspective

A clear split emerged from the outset between those Member States, particularly those with negative budgetary balances, which advocated a top-down approach based on determining the means available for spending before agreeing the content of policy reforms, and those (mainly the net beneficiaries) preferring a bottom-up approach in defining the Community's policy development needs before tailoring a financial framework to fit. In reality, both approaches were applied in parallel, with neither prevailing. However, a new watchword emerged to describe efforts by those advocating a Calvinistic budget disciplinarian approach for the Union's spending – 'real stabilization of expenditure'.

Stabilization is, of course, an elastic concept with potentially ambivalent meanings. However, the clear aim of the Member States which introduced the concept into the discussion was to maintain expenditure ceilings in terms of payment appropriations at an annual level of around 85 billion euros (i.e. close to the level of the 1999 budget rather than the 1999 financial perspective ceilings). The tactic behind this move was to pull the negotiating blanket downwards from the Commission's original proposals, which they deemed over-generous. Stabilization appealed of course to those countries that are large net contributors to the Community budget, given that every euro unspent by the Union represents a greater saving in terms of their contributions to the EU budget from the national public purse. Other Member States, particularly the net beneficiaries, felt that this approach did not take account of the objectives and scope of policy reforms, did not adequately meet the Treaty-based requirement for sufficient resources for the Union's policies, nor take account of the distinction between a financial perspective and the annual budget.

A key feature of negotiation on the overall level of the financial perspective is that it cut across the work of both the General Affairs and Ecofin Councils. Both endeavoured to stamp their mark by laying down principles for fixing the overall financial ceilings. However, while attempts were made to use the Ecofin Council to promote the concept of real stabilization of expenditure, no firm endorsement of this approach could be achieved by Ecofin. This clearly underlined the fact that a package negotiation like *Agenda 2000* is indivisible, and that even if finance ministers share the same 'religion', it was impossible to push through Ecofin a Calvinist approach on spending independently of other political considerations in the wider package which were of equal or greater importance for certain Member States. Playing one Council off against another cannot work where Member States have already carried out their internal arbitration. The Ecofin Council conclusions and press releases on *Agenda 2000* are striking in that they highlighted the disagreement at that stage in the process on many political issues, and therefore added little in terms of consensus-building. Nevertheless, the Ecofin Council made a significant contribution as a forum where advocates of real stabilization of expenditure could muster support for their idea and keep it alive on the political agenda. In doing so, they ensured that the Vienna report contained an alternative, 'stabilized' financial perspective table, thereby establishing the lower negotiating limit for further work. It was clear that the final compromise would have to be sought somewhere below the Commission's proposal, and above the figures in this alternative table. The implications of the stabilization approach would be felt most in financial perspective Headings 1 and 2 (agriculture and structural operations).

Agriculture (Heading 1). As far as agriculture is concerned, the Commission had proposed retaining the agricultural guideline as the ceiling for CAP expenditure. The agricultural guideline is a mechanism which has until now determined the level of Heading 1 by providing for an automatic annual increase of 0.74 per cent of the increase in EU GNP starting from a 1988 base. Its original purpose was to act as a brake on agricultural expenditure. However, in recent years, with CAP reform and implementation of strict budgetary discipline by the Agriculture Council, an increasingly large gap had opened up between the Heading 1 ceiling and the level of the annual budgets, which were substantially lower. The guideline therefore appeared somewhat anomalous since in practice it no longer served its original purpose as a means of containing CAP expenditure. While the Mediterranean Member States were concerned about the potential impact of enlargement on agricultural expenditure, there was growing pressure from the disciplinarian camp either to rebase the guideline or review its method of calculation, or to retain the guideline, and introduce a ceiling for Heading 1 at a lower level. The latter approach was preferred mainly for optical and psychological reasons.[9]

The difficulty lay in trying to establish what that ceiling should be, and whether it should be based on:

---

[9] While the guideline has remained unchanged, it now covers, in addition to the Heading 1 ceiling, the amounts in Heading 7 for the agricultural pre-accession instrument and the amounts set aside to cover the costs of agricultural expenditure after enlargement. In order to respond to concerns regarding the potential cost of enlargement in future, the European Council committed itself to review the guideline before enlargement, although without committing itself to any changes at this stage.

- maintaining a strict level of 40.5bn euros (i.e. the 1999 level of spending) for each of the years of the new financial perspective;
- taking 40.5bn euros as an annual average over the period, thereby allowing higher amounts at the start of the period, to be offset by lower amounts towards the end of the period;
- or taking 40.5bn euros as the spending target for 2006, and allowing a 'hump' in the intervening years, provided it permitted a substantial and far-reaching CAP reform.

While largely unsuccessful attempts had been made at a number of meetings of Ecofin and the General Affairs Council to fix a ceiling more in keeping with actual levels of spending, a strong (albeit not unanimous) preference emerged at the informal meeting of Heads of State or Government at Petersberg on 26 February for taking the 40.5bn euros figure as an average figure for the period (excluding rural development expenditure of around 2bn euros per annum transferred from Heading 2).

This was an important political signal to the farm ministers, engaged in the time-honoured ritual of a marathon Agriculture Council in order to hammer out an overall compromise on the agricultural reform package. The Council finally struck a deal on 11 March. The compromise reached, however, was open to criticism because it cost around 7bn euros more over the period than the figure which emerged with broad support from the Petersberg meeting. Moreover, some felt that the scope of reform did not go far enough, particularly by watering down the Commission's original proposals and by not providing for any 'degressivity' of direct aids over time. The risk was that negotiations on the rest of the financial package might stall, making it practically impossible to reach agreement in Berlin. Politically, the Agriculture Council could not revisit the deal without the risk of it unravelling, given the finely balanced content of such compromise packages. Introducing some measure of degressivity in direct income support provided to compensate farmers for price reductions also appeared to be a politically untenable option, given the firm opposition expressed by a number of Member States in the Council. Even more politically unsellable for reasons of principle (creeping 'renationalization' of the CAP), particularly for France and others, was the idea, originally floated by the Commission, of part co-financing direct income support, in order to share the burden between the Community budget (75 per cent) and national exchequers (25 per cent), thereby reducing the overall level of agriculture spending financed through the Community budget. A further idea was to provide a mechanism for reducing each year a certain amount earmarked for direct income support under Heading 1 and increasing the Heading 1 sub-ceiling on rural development (where co-financing is the usual practice) by some portion of that reduction. This would in effect maintain total agricultural financial flows unchanged, while reducing significantly the amount channelled through the Community budget. While this idea offered a number of attractions, it also encountered resistance from certain Member States, and it would have required the Commission to come forward with proposals to ensure that certain rural development measures were applied in such ways as to support farmers' incomes.

At the Berlin European Council, it was clear that bringing the CAP back into line would probably involve some substantive reopening of the compromise. This was indeed what happened, with President Chirac leading requests for a number of changes to be introduced in order to achieve the objective of stabilizing agricultural expenditure in real terms at an annual average over the period of 40.5bn euros (excluding rural development). The financial target for expenditure was achieved mainly by postponing implementation of the dairy reform until 2005–06, along with a less ambitious reduction in the intervention price for cereals. Attempts to pre-empt the Union's mandate for the forthcoming WTO negotiating round in the Berlin conclusions were, however, watered down in the face of objections from Member States seeking to ensure that the Union's hands were not immutably tied at this stage. The decisions adopted regarding the reform of the CAP within the framework of *Agenda 2000* will constitute 'essential elements in defining the Commission's negotiating mandate for the future multilateral trade negotiations at the WTO'.

Structural operations (Heading 2). Heading 2, which contains the annual amounts for the structural and cohesion funds, proved to be another key battleground. The thrust of the structural fund reform proposals was to enhance the effectiveness of EU structural funding by concentrating assistance in areas of greatest need. This would be achieved by substantially reducing the number of structural fund Objectives to three, and by strictly applying the 75 per cent of Community average GDP threshold for Objective 1 status, the most generous assistance level accounting for nearly 70 per cent of structural fund allocations. This would be coupled with reasonably generous transitional assistance arrangements for regions and areas no longer eligible for Objective 1 or 2 funding in the next financial perspective.

Regarding the overall levels for Heading 2, the initial negotiating position of the cohesion countries was that the Commission's proposal represented a step back compared to the Union's 1999 level of structural spending. For these delegations, if stabilization of expenditure were to be used as a concept to guide further negotiations, the point of departure had to be the 1999 target level agreed at Edinburgh (0.46 per cent of EU GNP for EU-15). Under this approach, any reduction in that figure had to correspond exactly to reductions in eligible regions in the 15 Member States during the period. The Commission's proposal, representing some 240bn euros over the period, was based on maintaining the political commitment of 0.46 per cent of EU GNP for structural operations, but applied to the enlarged Union. The advocates of a rigorous approach, however, considered that stabilization had to be based on the annual average of amounts over the period 1993–99, rather than solely the 1999 level. This discussion was compounded by the fact that the advocates of the rigorist approach, which felt that the Commission had been far too generous in its proposals given the economic and financial climate, questioned whether Member States receiving assistance under the Cohesion Fund should continue to be eligible for such assistance if participating in the single currency. Despite the logical inconsistency of defending stabilization in terms of an annual average over the period rather than the 1999 spending level, while for all other headings, the 1999 budget levels were the yardstick, these delegations advocated an overall figure for Heading 2 in the vicinity of 190m euros, or lower, for the new period. Clearly, a wide gulf would have to be bridged if positions were to be reconciled into an acceptable outcome.

Reconciling the seemingly irreconcilable is the essence of the work of the Council and the European Council. The concept of stabilization was one which advocates of both approaches could accept, albeit with different meanings. The key was to build on the concept in such a way as to find a politically acceptable outcome somewhere in the middle between the two extreme positions.

The concept developed for determining the overall level of expenditure for the structural funds was that of maintaining average per capita aid intensity levels in the new period for Objectives 1, 2 and 3 at the 1999 level.[10] This could be accomplished by fixing the overall level of allocations for the new period at around 195bn euros. The Cohesion Fund was maintained for all of the current beneficiaries, although the final total of 18bn euros over the period (62 per cent of which will go to Spain) was down on the Commission's original proposal of 21bn euros. Final agreement on Heading 2 was therefore reached on an overall figure of 213bn euros, which as it happened was neatly placed near the mid-point between the upper and lower limits set for the negotiation. While haggling over numbers could be (and sometimes is) done on a purely arbitrary basis, it is always preferable to seek an underlying rationale which can be used by politicians in order to sell a negotiating outcome.

[10] While the Commission had proposed an increase in Objective 3 spending (development of human resources) which would apply in all parts of the Union outside Objective 1 regions, some of the net budget contributors, who stood to 'benefit' from increased Objective 3 funding, still preferred an across-the-board approach which contained structural expenditure, including Objective 3, within acceptable financial limits, relying on side-payments as part of the overall deal to improve their individual situation (see para. 44 of the Berlin summit conclusions). It is important to note that the concept of stabilization by maintaining average per capita aid intensity levels under these three Objectives was one used for determining the overall financial envelope for Heading 2, and did *not* mean that each eligible area would receive the same amount as during the previous period. The actual allocation among eligible regions would depend on the programming process based on applying the relevant criteria laid down in the general regulation.

Own Resources and Budgetary Imbalances

Nothing excited the media, the politicians and the civil servants more than the question of the Union's own resources, and the issue of negative budgetary imbalances which, in a number of Member States, especially Germany, had become a highly politically charged topic.

As far as the own resources system itself was concerned, there was general acceptance that the Union's financial system should be equitable, cost-effective, transparent and simple, and that pursuit of other goals, such as financial autonomy, should not undermine these four generally accepted principles. It was politically impossible to contemplate the introduction of new autonomous own resources at this stage, because providing an autonomous source of funding (i.e. one that does not rely on 'contributions' from Member States' exchequers, even if they are as of right due to the Union) would probably not result in a predictable and acceptable distribution of payments from Member States' into the Union's coffers.[11]

The European Council agreed on a number of specific changes to the own resources system (see below). Given the room available beneath the own resources ceiling, there was no need to increase this ceiling above its current level of 1.27 per cent of EU GNP, although net recipients were reluctant to endorse this figure until the end of the negotiation given concerns about the financial ramifications of enlargement. On this question, those who favoured maintaining the ceiling unchanged were in a comfortable position, since the present own resources decision which entered into force in 1994 would remain in force indefinitely.

From the outset of the discussion, improving the net budgetary situation as soon as possible was a domestic political imperative for the major net contributors. Their solution was a straightforward one: introduce a correction mechanism to act as a safety net if any Member State's budgetary imbalance exceeded a certain proportion of national GDP, drawing inspiration from the 1984 Fontainebleau European Council at which the UK's budget abatement mechanism was agreed, which stated that:

> Expenditure policy is ultimately the essential means of resolving the question of budgetary imbalances. However, it has been decided that any Member State sustaining a budgetary burden which is excessive in relation to its relative prosperity may benefit from a correction at the appropriate time.

A measure of the sensitivity of this question can be gleaned from the Cardiff European Council conclusions, where para. 54 reads as follows:

---

[11] For a detailed examination of these issues, see the Commission's report on the operation of the Union's own resources system.

In this context, the European Council notes that some Member States have expressed their view that burden sharing should be more equitable and have called for the creation of a mechanism for correcting budgetary imbalances, but that some other Member States have opposed this. In the same context, it also notes that some Member States have made proposals for changing the own resources, e.g. by creating a progressive own resource, but that others have opposed this.

Divisive language such as this is highly unusual in European Council conclusions. Staking out the ground and putting down political markers in this way, highlighting the fact that no common view yet exists among Member States purely as a hook for politicians to demonstrate their firmness of stance to domestic political and public opinion on matters of important national interest, serves no useful purpose in terms of building consensus within the Council. In the absence of the Commission's own resources report at this stage, more general or procedural language would have been more appropriate.

The request for a correction mechanism faced strong objections from other Member States. They deemed such mechanisms to be contrary to the basic principles of the Community, and queried the validity of the Fontainebleau conclusions given the changes in the level and scope of Union finances since 1984. They also considered that the concept of net balances was a poor measure of the benefits of EU membership. While a number of Member States voiced sympathy for the net contributors' plight, there was a feeling that a proper assessment of the magnitude of the problem could only be made after evaluating the impact of expenditure stabilization efforts and of policy reforms, given the emphasis in the Fontainebleau conclusions that, 'expenditure policy is ultimately the essential means of resolving the question of budgetary imbalances'.

Once the Commission's report on the operation of the own resources system was submitted in the late autumn, notwithstanding the continued efforts of the net contributors in pressing for a generalized correction mechanism, it was clear that an approach had to be found combining various measures to meet the political objective sought by these Member States. They recognized that, despite arguing a robust case, they would not be able to garner sufficient support in the Council to establish a safety-net correction mechanism to limit their net contributions to a certain proportion of their national GDP. Ways had therefore to be found of achieving a sellable political outcome for these countries by addressing their concerns through other means. Their concerns were largely met in the following general and specific ways:

- by following a restrictive approach in the growth of the Union's finances, endeavouring to stabilize or at least limit the overall increase in resources channelled through the Community budget;

- by continuing the shift from the VAT to the GNP resource by reducing the maximum rate of call of the VAT resource from 1 per cent to 0.75 per cent in 2002 and to 0.50 per cent in 2004, thereby continuing the process of making allowance for each Member State's ability to pay and of correcting the regressive aspects of the current system for the least prosperous Member States. Given its regressive effects, phasing out the VAT resource is likely to be a long-term objective; however, since doing so at this juncture would have placed a significant burden on Italy, it was not possible to complete the phase-out during the period of the new financial perspective. It should be noted, however, that the actual impact on the net budgetary situation of the main contributing countries of this measure was marginal;
- by taking a number of specific measures on the resources and expenditure side targeted at individual net contributors. For example, the charges retained by Member States for collecting so-called 'traditional own resources' (i.e. mainly customs duties on goods entering the Union) will be increased from 10 per cent to 25 per cent from 2001, a measure designed principally to help the Netherlands. Moreover, a number of specific additional payments were made on the expenditure side for the Netherlands and Sweden under the structural funds (see footnote 13);
- finally, and perhaps most importantly, by altering the financing key for the UK budget abatement in order to reduce the cost of the abatement borne by Germany, Sweden, the Netherlands and Austria. The UK budget abatement is financed by all Member States except the UK under the method set out in the current own resources decisions. Under that decision, Germany already benefited from a reduction in its normal contribution to the abatement to 66 per cent of what it would otherwise be. This idea has been taken a step further by reducing the contribution of Germany, the Netherlands, Sweden and Austria to financing the UK abatement to 25 per cent of their normal share!

The question of the UK budget abatement was a focus of discussion right up to the wire at the Berlin European Council. The UK's basic negotiating position was that the abatement was non-negotiable. However, it was apparent that any satisfactory outcome on *Agenda 2000* would require some inroads being made on the abatement. The UK government made a robust case for retaining it unchanged since, according to the Commission's analysis, the UK remained a larger net contributor to the EU budget than Member States with a higher capacity to pay, and that its ranking would not be likely to change following enlargement. Other Member States, in particular France, while recognizing that its abolition was not a realistic prospect, at least expected the UK to shoulder its full, unabated contribution to the cost of enlargement. It was politically inconceivable for the Prime Minister to return to the House of Commons having made major concessions on this question, although it was recognized that some quarter would probably need to be given. However, the margin for negotiation was limited, given the media attention to this issue (although UK media reporting on the abatement at the Berlin European Council was largely crowded out by the situation in Kosovo).

The UK government accepted the principle (already accepted in 1988 and 1992) of continuing to neutralize 'windfall' gains resulting from the reduction in the VAT resource, as well as those resulting from increasing the percentage of 'traditional own resources' retained by Member States to cover their collection costs (this latter element being a new concession). The more substantial concession was to agree to remove part of the accession-related expenditure from the calculation of the abatement. Like so many successful outcomes, this concession had to follow a defendable rationale, for reasons of political presentation. The UK abatement is calculated on the basis of so-called allocated expenditure, which does not include expenditure made outside the Union. Pre-accession expenditure would not therefore be included, and would consequently remain unabated. Given the particular characteristics of pre-accession expenditure, which is similar to expenditure that would be received by the new Member States when joining the Union,[12] its nature would not in essence change after enlargement. The UK was therefore able to accept a reduction in total allocated expenditure by an amount equivalent to the amount being received by the new Member States in the form of pre-accession expenditure, thereby ensuring that this expenditure continues to be unabated after enlargement. The overall combined impact of the concessions accepted by the UK was estimated at 220m euros by 2006.

Given the challenges mounted in the earlier stages of the negotiation, it was somewhat surprising that more pressure was not applied on the UK government for concessions at Berlin. There are two explanations for this. First, a great deal of the negotiating effort in the European Council was deployed on the content of the CAP reform, leaving little time or inclination for Heads of Government to cross swords in the early hours of the morning to enter into what would be in any case the near impossible task of wresting further concessions from the UK. Second, and perhaps more telling, in altering the financing key for the UK abatement, the four Member States which benefited from this measure now had a clear vested interest in retaining the abatement as it stands as a means of securing a significant reduction in their own net contributions to the Union budget! This can only be described as a resounding victory for the UK, which

---

[12] One of the stated objectives of pre-accession expenditure is to familiarize applicant countries with the procedures and methods used for implementing programmes within the Union.

also managed to obtain in the Berlin conclusions the unequivocal statement that 'the UK abatement will remain'.

IV. Postscript: Berlin and Beyond – a Good Agreement for Europe?

March 1999 was the self-imposed deadline set by the Cardiff European Council for wrapping up the political package. Timing was of the essence in the end-game scenario. Completion by this date was desirable for a number of reasons: it would be the only chance for the Council and the European Parliament to complete the legislative work within the lifetime of the Parliament before the June 1999 elections. It would ensure that the Commission could begin structural fund programming and prepare the implementation of the new pre-accession instruments. It would also clear the way for the Union to take up work on its institutional reform agenda. Other than these political imperatives, there were no absolute legal deadlines compelling agreement by that date. The current own resources decision would remain valid beyond 1999, and in the event of denunciation of the IIA and the absence of agreement on a new financial perspective, the Treaty provisions on the maximum rate of growth of non-compulsory expenditure would apply.

In general terms, it can be said that interinstitutional co-operation on *Agenda 2000* worked well. Following the political agreement reached at Berlin, the process of finalizing negotiations on the new interinstitutional agreement was a relatively smooth one, and the Parliament and Council managed to reach agreement on a number of modifications to the structural fund regulations to enable formal approval to be achieved by June 1999. Good co-operation also took place in the agriculture sector. The interesting feature of the process of co-operation between the Council and the Parliament on *Agenda 2000* is that it threw up a twin paradox. Firstly, unlike previous negotiations on the IIA and the financial perspective, where the Council had taken the view that the financial perspective amounts agreed by the European Council were untouchable, the Council was willing this time round to accept the Parliament's requests for an increase in the figures for Heading 3 (internal policies), and a *de facto* increase in Heading 5 expenditure (administration) by fixing the amounts net of staff contributions to pensions. This constitutes an interesting precedent for a Parliament ever on the lookout for extending its informal as well as formal powers. The Council was willing to contemplate these concessions in circumstances where, unlike at Edinburgh in 1992, the financial perspective represented an overall volume of expenditure significantly well below what could be achieved by the Parliament by applying the provisions of the Treaty. Secondly, the European Parliament, while receiving some minor concessions on its role in the conciliation procedure and on the establishment of a new flexibility provision totalling

200m euros per annum, was willing to sign up to an IIA in which it in effect renounced some of its budgetary powers under Art. 272 of the Treaty (amounting to tens of billions of euros over the period). Clearly, the Parliament was responding to the prevailing political climate by tacitly recognizing that even if the Treaty gave it extensive powers and the theoretical right to increase non-compulsory expenditure up to the 'maximum rate of increase', a mature and responsible Parliament could not have wielded these Treaty powers to their full extent in current economic circumstances.

Regarding the content of the policy reforms effected under *Agenda 2000*, a detailed assessment – in particular the precise impact of the agreement on the net budgetary positions of Member States – will have to await implementation of the policy reforms which have been agreed. However, some lessons can be learnt from this experience and preliminary conclusions can already be drawn.

On the positive side, three broad political objectives evident from the start of the negotiations were largely achieved. For the cohesion countries, their prime concern was to ensure that future enlargement of the Union did not occur at the expense of the Union's structural and cohesion policies. The overall amounts agreed in the financial perspective for Heading 2, which retain their status as spending targets rather than financial ceilings, have enabled the Union to consolidate its structural assistance at a level corresponding to 1999 average per capita aid intensity levels, thereby meeting their concern. The relatively small price to be paid in the form of a shopping list of side-payments to various Member States was an acceptable part of the final political deal.[13] Secondly, an important political signal has been sent to the applicant countries queuing at the Union's door that, in the context of a single currency in which the applicants are all aspiring participants, enlargement of the Union will have to take place within tight budgetary constraints. The financial perspective has been drawn up to accommodate the full cost of enlargement until 2006, along with a significant increase in the pre-accession strategy, while also substantially increasing the margins for unforeseen expenditure under the own resources ceiling fixed at 1.27 per cent of EU GNP. There will clearly be pressure to maintain that ceiling beyond 2006. Finally, politically unacceptable anomalies which had emerged in burden-sharing among the Member States in the cost of financing the Union's budget have been corrected to a sufficient extent to make the overall *Agenda 2000* package politically acceptable without having recourse to new budgetary correction mechanisms.

[13] Some of these additional payments included 500m euros to Lisbon for Objective 1 phasing out, 500m euros for Northern Ireland, 550m euros to Ireland under Objective 1, 350m euros for certain regions in Sweden, 100m euros for East Berlin in Objective 1 phasing-out, 300m euros for the Highlands and Islands of Scotland for Objective 1 phasing-out (i.e. a similar allocation to what this region would have received if it had retained Objective 1 status), payments to Greece, Ireland, Spain and Portugal to maintain the average level of per capita assistance reached in 1999, etc. For the complete list, refer to para. 44 of the Berlin European Council conclusions.

Costs are, however, involved. One of the *leitmotifs* of the reform of the Union's structural operations was concentration of assistance. The question can be legitimately put as to whether the Union has gone sufficiently far down this road in preparing for enlargement. As far as Heading 2 is concerned, to what extent can concentration of assistance be tightened further in the future? While both Ireland and Spain will probably have dropped out of the Cohesion Fund by 2006, and the 75 per cent average EU GDP threshold for determining Objective 1 eligibility will fall as new and less wealthy Member States join the Union, it is easy to foresee the tough political bargaining ahead as current Member States seek to preserve as far as possible financial flows they are currently receiving within the Union. Similar questions can also be raised about the scope of the CAP reform. Although reform has been achieved while maintaining an annual average ceiling on expenditure over the period of 40.5bn euros (excluding rural development), the price for doing so was to undertake a less ambitious reform than that initially proposed. One of the peculiar features of agriculture spending is that reforms always cost more during the transitional stage to a new regime. Hence, the more ambitious the reform, the more expensive the cost. At the end of the day, cost prevailed over ambition. However, it is a fair guess that the Union will come under further pressure for reform in the not too distant future, through pressures created by new accessions and the next round of WTO negotiations.

The outcome of the *Agenda 2000* negotiation on these items seems to bear out the Union's second cardinal principle that any agreement reached will always be no more than the bare minimum necessary to secure consensus.

Over and above the political content of the reforms, there are fundamental lessons to be drawn about the conduct of future negotiations of this type within the Union. The fact that agreement was reached at all is in itself an achievement, given the prevailing political circumstances surrounding the negotiation. This was one of the most complex packages ever processed through the institutional system. It says much about the driving skills of the UK, Austrian and German Presidencies that the vehicle was held firmly on the negotiating road without skidding off at the first bump. *Agenda 2000* would still be under negotiation if a firm hand had not been used in managing the negotiating process by the Presidency, the Commission and the Council Secretariat. While there was never any guarantee that the method of the 'negotiating box' would work, what is certain is that it at least provided a reasonable opportunity for the Berlin European Council to reach agreement. As the Union enlarges to 26 or more Member States, the methods of work used by the Council will have to undergo a radical rethink in order to ensure that the Council can continue to be an effective decision-making body in the Union. This rethink has already begun.[14]

---

[14] See the report by the Secretary-General of the Council on the functioning of the Council with an enlarged Union in prospect, which sets out 143 suggestions for improving the workings of the Council.

With the successful completion of *Agenda 2000*, the way is now clear for the final piece of the Union's pre-enlargement jigsaw to be put in place – institutional reform. This will be the focus of the Union's work over the coming 18 months, with the decision taken by the Cologne European Council on 3–4 June 1999 to convene an Intergovernmental Conference for March 2000 to examine the institutional changes in connection with enlargement, and to press ahead with reform of the working methods and operation of the institutions, in particular the Council.

Journal of Common Market Studies

Volume 37, Annual Review
September 1999

Governance and Institutions:
A Transitional Year

DESMOND DINAN

Netherlands Institute of International Relations

I. Introduction

1998 was a transitional year for the EU. Most obviously, it was a year of transition from negotiation to implementation of the Amsterdam Treaty (a transition that stretched into 1999 because of ratification delays in several Member States) and from the preparatory stages to the final stage of Economic and Monetary Union (EMU) (a transition that saw the birth of the European Central Bank and other important institutional innovations). In the key policy areas of enlargement and the budget, 1998 also saw accession negotiations started with six candidate countries and, of more immediate concern, Member States began to tackle the challenge of *Agenda 2000*.

The political situation in Germany greatly influenced EU governance and institutional developments during the long run-up to the September 1998 general election and the lengthy formation after it of a new ruling coalition. German domestic concerns, for example – as well as a Franco-German desire to patch up differences following the selection of the European Central Bank's first President – drove the debate on more far-reaching institutional reform of the kind mooted during the 1996–97 Intergovernmental Conference (IGC) but conspicuously absent from the Amsterdam Treaty. However, the debate generated few new ideas and fizzled out as soon as Chancellor Helmut Kohl lost the election.

Although not due to take place until mid-1999, elections for the European Parliament (EP) also cast a long shadow over institutional developments in 1998. Eager to raise the profiles of their institution and their political groups before launching electoral campaigns, Euro-parliamentarians grew increasingly assertive and partisan. This was evident not only in the conduct of such routine (albeit important) interinstitutional business as the negotiation of the 1999 budget and a new multi-annual Framework Programme for Research and Technological Development, but especially in the growing conflict between Parliament and the Commission over discharge of the 1996 budget. Despite having dragged on for much of the year, it was only when the discharge dispute escalated in December 1998 that the Commission's vulnerability became fully apparent.

The budget discharge dispute galvanized calls in the EP and elsewhere for major reform of the Commission. Paradoxically, the Commission was then in the throes of a reform effort initiated by President Jacques Santer as early as 1995. By contrast, the Council embarked in 1998 on a far less radical reform effort that focused on the need to reduce the workload and improve the co-ordinating role of the General Affairs Council. Other Council reforms, of a purely procedural nature, were linked to the impending implementation of the Amsterdam Treaty. Similarly, the Amsterdam Treaty occasioned two significant reform efforts in the EP, one dealing with direct elections and the other with parliamentarians' pay and conditions of service.

II. Towards Implementing the Amsterdam Treaty

Preparations to implement the Amsterdam Treaty continued throughout the year, although their intensity diminished when it became obvious that the Treaty would not be ratified in all Member States until 1999. Preparatory work focused on the most important areas and issues covered by the Treaty: the Common Foreign and Security Policy (CFSP), Justice and Home Affairs (JHA), legislative decision-making and flexibility.

Member States looked forward to the availability of a new instrument – the Common Strategy – to help improve the effectiveness of the Common Foreign and Security Policy (CFSP). So much so, indeed, that in December 1998, the General Affairs Council endorsed a preliminary list, drawn up by the Political Committee, of possible common strategies for the EU's 'near-abroad': Russia, Ukraine, the southern Mediterranean and the Balkans, that covered a range of issues for each subject, such as human rights and democracy. The test of the new instrument's effectiveness will, of course, have to await the Treaty's implementation. Preparations to establish the post-Amsterdam Policy Planning and Early Warning Unit (PPEWU) began in late 1997 and continued throughout 1998. Member States debated the unit's precise role, responsibilities and structure, as well as the flow of information between the PPEWU and national foreign ministries. A key question concerned the relationship between the PPEWU and the High Representative for the CFSP, a position established by the Amsterdam Treaty. The High Representative was to have been named at the Vienna summit in December 1998, but treaty ratification delays gave Member States an excuse to defer a difficult decision. Nevertheless a consensus had emerged that the High Representative should be a well-known politician (ideally a former foreign minister) rather than an anonymous diplomat (with possible candidates mentioned at the Vienna summit such as Dick Spring, a former Irish Foreign Minister, and Carlos Westerndorp, the international community's High Commissioner in Bosnia).

Throughout the year, Member States considered issues relating to the implementation of the Amsterdam Treaty's provisions on JHA. Procedurally, the impending move of six areas of common interest from the third to the first pillar of the EU would affect the functioning of JHA working parties, as would the incorporation into the EU of the Schengen Agreement and its working groups. Art. 36 of the post-Amsterdam TEU calls for a new steering committee of high-ranking officials for the truncated third pillar; but the extent to which this committee should or could also co-ordinate JHA activities in the post-Amsterdam first pillar remained unclear. What should have been a relatively simple issue – the incorporation of the Schengen Secretariat into the Council Secretariat – proved contentious, not for substantive reasons, but because of the politics of national representation in EU institutions. It took several months of often bitter debate in the Committee of Permanent Representatives (Coreper) before agreement was reached to hold a special competition that would ostensibly meet the requirements of the Council staff regulations, while effectively guaranteeing the success of the current incumbents of the Schengen Secretariat. France took the moral high ground, with President Chirac reportedly warning at the Cardiff summit that underhand recruitment procedure would diminish French confidence in the communitarization of a substantial part of the JHA dossier (*European Report*, 20 June 1998, p. I-1). Behind Chirac's rhetoric lay the reality that not a single A-grade official in the Schengen Secretariat was French. Belgium fought hardest to smooth the integration of the Schengen Secretariat, as currently constituted, into the Council Secretariat. Not surprisingly, most of the Schengen Secretariat's A-grade officials were Belgian.

The Amsterdam Treaty's simplification and extension of the co-decision procedure greatly strengthens the EP's legislative power. As a result, MEPs were eager, in 1998, to explore co-decision's new potential in order to maximize the EP's authority once the Treaty came into effect. Hence their adoption on 17 July of the Manzella Report on the future operation of co-decision. The report emphasized the possibility of reaching agreement with the Council on draft

legislation at the first reading stage. To be able to do so, the EP needs to improve
the legal quality of its own first reading texts and lengthen the time between the
tabling of amendments and the taking of a final vote in a plenary session, thereby
providing ample opportunity for linguistic and legal improvement of texts and
for informal discussions with the Council. The report advocated closer contacts
between EP committees and Council working groups and recommended procedural improvements in the second and third reading stages, especially for the
operation of the conciliation procedure.

MEPs' interest in the legislative provisions of the Amsterdam Treaty demonstrated the EP's determination to exploit co-decision to the full. However, as
Commissioner Oreja observed during the debate on the Manzella Report, the
main problem with co-decision so far was not procedural but political: more
often than not the Council and the Parliament could not agree on which
implementing procedure (comitology committee) to specify for a particular
legislative act. Co-decision had therefore become the principal battleground for
the comitology wars that raged between the Council and the Parliament. As it
happened, the Commission submitted a proposal in 1998 for a new Council
decision and interinstitutional agreement on comitology (see below).

Whereas MEPs were eager to see many of the Amsterdam Treaty's provisions put into effect as soon as possible, they were decidedly unenthusiastic
about implementation of the Treaty's flexibility clause (Art. 11). After all,
flexibility was one of the few areas of the Amsterdam Treaty in which the EP's
power had not been strengthened. In an own-initiative report (the Frischen-
schlager Report) adopted in July 1998, the EP's Committee on Institutional
Affairs urged Member States to use flexibility only in exceptional cases, if at all.
Predictably, the report suggested that flexibility be subject to the EP's democratic control and stressed the importance of budgetary unity in the event of recourse
to it (thereby giving the EP some leverage over the procedure).

III. Towards Stage 3 of EMU

Preparations for the launch of the euro saw a number of important institutional
and decision-making innovations. Institutionally, the most significant developments were the wrapping-up of the European Monetary Institute (EMI) and the
launch of the European Central Bank (ECB), and the metamorphosis of the
Monetary Committee (a special committee of the Council of Economic and
Finance Ministers) into the potentially powerful Economic and Financial Committee. On the decision-making front, the Commission, the Council, and the EP
took a series of decisions during a hectic two-day period in early May, all in
accordance with the terms of the TEU, that made it possible to move to Stage 3
of EMU by 1 January 1999.

The final decision-making process began with the publication by the EMI and the Commission, on 25 March 1998, of separate 'convergence reports'. As both institutions asserted that 11 Member States were qualified to begin Stage 3, it was inevitable that there should be a consensus in Ecofin, meeting in Brussels on 1 May, to recommend the same 11 members for participation in Stage 3 and that the EP, meeting in plenary session next morning, would in turn endorse Ecofin's recommendation (which it did by a vote of 468 to 64, with 24 abstentions). Later on 2 May the Council – meeting in the form of the Heads of State or Government (HOSG) – took the advice of Ecofin and the EP and formally selected the charter members of the Euro-zone. Only 12 months earlier, the Brussels summit had been expected to be contentious because of the possibility that the HOSG would have to decide by qualified majority vote which countries would participate in Stage 3. By early 1998, however, consensus on the composition of the Euro-zone threatened to rob the summit of all drama. In the event, the Brussels summit was highly memorable because of drama of a different kind: a bitter row between President Chirac and Chancellor Kohl over the Presidency of the ECB.

The row originated in a decision by central bank governors, in May 1996, to nominate Wim Duisenberg to succeed Alexandre Lamfalussy as head of the EMI, on the understanding that Duisenberg would then become President of the ECB. Although the ECB was to be independent of national influence, the choice of ECB President was, nonetheless, a political decision. The TEU acknowledged this fact by giving the Council of Ministers – in the form of the HOSG – responsibility for selecting the ECB President. Realizing that this would occur several months before the launch of Stage 3, the Central Bank's governors had won in May 1996 what they thought was their national leaders' approval of Duisenberg's eventual succession to the ECB Presidency. In fact, Chirac was unhappy about Duisenberg's selection both because Duisenberg was clearly the German government's candidate (having won the battle to locate the ECB in Frankfurt, Germany could not also have pushed one of its own nationals to head the new bank; Duisenberg was the next best thing), and because the selection procedure smacked of unelected central bankers usurping the prerogative of elected government leaders. However, Chirac objected publicly to Duisenberg's otherwise uncontested nomination only in November 1997, when he nominated Jean-Claude Trichet, governor of the Bank of France, for the job.

Thereafter, the issue was Chirac's insistence on a Franco–German trade-off: a German location for the ECB (already decided) and a French President for the ECB (not yet decided). To everyone's surprise, Chirac pursued this nakedly nationalistic position to the end, compromising only to the extent that Duisenberg could begin the ECB Presidency's first eight-year term but would have to step down for Trichet half way through. Chirac held out for a written commitment by Duisenberg to resign on 1 January 2002. Following prolonged negotiations, which Kohl described as among the most difficult in his lengthy EU experience, Chirac accepted a decision by Duisenberg, supposedly reached 'of my own free will ... and not under pressure from anyone', to step down sometime after mid-2002 (Duisenberg's statement was attached to the conclusions of the meeting). As part of the compromise, the HOSG agreed that another Frenchman would become Duisenberg's vice-president and that Trichet would succeed Duisenberg for a full eight-year term (a decision recorded in the minutes of the meeting).

The Duisenberg row obscured from public view a considerable amount of crowing by the Prime Ministers of Spain and Italy that citizens of their countries had been appointed to the ECB's Executive Board, and considerable carping by the prime ministers of many of the smaller Euro-zone participants that their countries were not represented on the Executive Board. At Portugal's behest, the HOSG issued a statement endorsing 'a balanced principle of rotation' in the selection of future Executive Board members.

The conduct and outcome of the Brussels summit suggested that the ECB's independence was compromised even before the Bank came into being, and that the French government in particular would attempt to interfere in European monetary policy-making. Such concerns were largely assuaged by Duisenberg's robust performance before the EP the following week, when he effectively repudiated his earlier statement, and by the composition of the ECB's governing board (all are experienced, independent-minded central bankers). The significance of Chirac's behaviour was not what it portended for EMU, but for Chirac's relations with his EU partners, and especially for Franco–German leadership in the EU.

The conduct of the summit also led to considerable criticism of the British Prime Minister's chairmanship of the meeting. One of the Presidency's jobs is to anticipate and defuse high-level rows. Beginning in November 1997, the row over the ECB Presidency was easily anticipated, but could hardly have been defused. Given Chirac's dogged support for Trichet, it is difficult to imagine that the outcome would have been different had Tony Blair acted otherwise or had another country been in the chair.

The May summit also reinforced an obvious point about the conduct of European Councils: despite the appearance of equality, some EU leaders are far more equal than others. In particular, the President of France and the Chancellor of Germany are in a league of their own. Beginning at lunchtime on 2 May, Chirac and Kohl, joined occasionally by Blair (because of Britain's Presidency) and Dutch Prime Minister Wim Kok (because of Duisenberg's candidacy) kept the other heads of government waiting for ten hours. As an exasperated Jean-Luc Dehaene remarked of the proceedings, this was 'the shortest European Council with the longest lunch' (*Agence Europe*, 4 May 1998).

The ECB was duly launched (and the EMI wound down) on 1 June 1998. During the next seven months, pending the launch of the euro, the ECB moved into its impressive headquarters (the Eurotower in Frankfurt), recruited personnel, assigned responsibilities among its Executive Board, and addressed a wide range of procedural and policy issues. Although language wars raged in other institutions, the ECB had only one working language: English. In accordance with the TEU, the Monetary Committee (a Council special committee) came to an end at midnight on 31 December 1998, and was replaced by the Economic and Financial Committee (EFC). With 34 members (two Commission officials, two ECB officials, and two treasury and/or central bank officials from each Member State), the new committee promised to become a powerful player in the formulation of economic and monetary policy in the EU. It has a much wider remit in terms of policy co-ordination than the old Monetary Committee. Accordingly, the Presidency of the committee became an important political prize on which France squarely set its sights. As a bargaining chip, France gave up what had come to be seen as its right to the Presidency of the European Bank for Reconstruction and Development and backed Romano Prodi's possible nomination for the Commission Presidency (thus buying off Italy, the only other country with a strong contender for the EFC presidency).

IV. Towards Institutional Reform

Member States had little enthusiasm for major institutional reform in 1998, a subject they had ducked during the 1996–97 IGC. Although all acknowledged the need for institutional reform before further enlargement (France, Belgium, and Italy had attached a declaration to the Amsterdam Treaty *demanding* institutional reform before enlargement), none seemed willing to begin what was bound to be a difficult and contentious debate. The non-imminence of enlargement and the delay in ratifying the Amsterdam Treaty let Member States off the hook. Only the EP urged immediate institutional reform, having adopted a resolution in November 1997 calling on the Commission to get the ball rolling by submitting a proposal on this subject to the Council and the EP. Already on the defensive politically, the Commission quietly let the matter drop.

It was surprising, therefore, that institutional reform suddenly came to the fore in May 1998, with the announcement by Chirac and Kohl that they planned a joint letter on the subject to the Council Presidency. High-level Franco–German initiatives resonate in the history of European integration (a letter from Mitterrand and Kohl in June 1990 had paved the way for the 1991 IGC on political union). The announcement of a Chirac–Kohl letter, the first since December 1995, inevitably fuelled speculation that the anticipated IGC on institutional reform might take place sooner than expected, perhaps as early as

1999. However, the context and content of the letter soon dashed any hopes and allayed any fears that Chirac and Kohl sought to launch a serious debate about far-reaching reform. In fact they wanted to dispel the gloom surrounding the recently-concluded Brussels summit, where they had fought so bitterly over the Presidency of the ECB. What better way to show that the much-vaunted Franco–German axis was back on track than to announce a major joint initiative? Moreover, Kohl was preoccupied with the forthcoming federal elections and felt increasingly harassed by assertive state governments. What better way to strike a domestic political chord than to advocate EU reform, defend the rights of sub-national governments, and bash the Commission, a notoriously easy target?

The letter itself was uninspiring. Despite calling for a debate on 'the future of Europe', it focused almost exclusively on subsidiarity, hardly a novel idea. Rather than elucidating its meaning, the two leaders urged that 'the principle of subsidiarity ... [be] applied even more strictly in the future, correcting certain debatable developments and taking into account national constitutional and administrative structures'. Next came a thinly-veiled attack on the Commission and a fillip for European summitry: 'Given the tendency of certain European institutions to remain distant from citizens and their daily problems, it is important to invite the ... European Council to hold a discussion on practical implementation of the subsidiarity principle in order to clarify the limits of the competences of the European Union and of the Member States and to examine the extent to which the current level of intervention is suitable'. The language was vintage Chirac and characteristic also of Kohl's increasingly populist approach to European integration. Kohl's eye was not so much on the future of the EU as on his own political future. As one MEP observed: 'Every time problems of internal politics arise in a large member state – in this case the German elections – the subject of subsidiarity is raised. More often than not it is just a thinly disguised attempt to renationalize elements of European policy and thus satisfy discontented voters' (*Agence Europe*, 20 June 1998).

Only at the end of their letter did Chirac and Kohl address the broader question of institutional reform, referring specifically to the need for an overhaul of the Commission and the Council. Calling on their colleagues to 'make a critical assessment of the EU's current situation' at the forthcoming Cardiff summit, Chirac and Kohl hoped that six months later, at the Vienna summit, the European Council would be able 'to deepen the debate on the topics broached today and, if possible, draw the initial conclusions'. Although Chirac had floated the idea of asking Jacques Delors to lead a high-level advisory group on institutional reform (like de Gaulle during the waning days of the Fourth Republic, Delors announced that he was waiting for the call), in their letter, Chirac and Kohl pointedly dismissed the idea, stating clearly that the European Council 'must not delegate [its] responsibility'. The idea of a group of 'wise men' to lay the groundwork for institutional reform never seriously resurfaced, nor did that of pressing Delors into service – after all, Delors' name was almost synonymous with the kinds of 'debatable developments' with respect to subsidiarity referred to in the letter.

Although miffed that he had been excluded from the Chirac–Kohl initiative, the British Prime Minister responded enthusiastically to it. Here was another opportunity for Blair to display Britain's enthusiastic involvement in the development of European integration. Accordingly, he arranged for a discussion of the letter to take place during lunch on the first day of the Cardiff summit. The Commission, alarmed by the Chirac–Kohl letter, prepared a self-exculpatory paper entitled, 'Legislate Less to Act Better: The Facts'. This purported to show that it had fulfilled its promise, made when Santer became President in 1995, to introduce fewer legislative proposals. Santer drove the point home in Cardiff, arguing forcibly that Member States were using subsidiarity to undermine Community policies and to upset the institutional balance – in other words, to demote the Commission in the EU system.

The Cardiff discussion hardly constituted a 'critical assessment of the EU's current situation', as Chirac–Kohl had advocated in their letter. Instead, the HOSG decided to explore the issue further at a special summit during the Austrian Presidency. However, by the time the summit took place, on 24–25 October, Kohl was out of office. Indeed, the summit's real significance may be that it was the first in 16 years that Kohl did not attend.

Free of the need to focus on institutional reform, the summiteers instead had a wide-ranging but inconclusive discussion on a variety of issues ranging from social policy to foreign policy. With the usual exuberance of a summit host, Chancellor Viktor Klima described the meeting as one of 'vision, study, ideas and impetus for the future'. But there had been little discussion of institutional reform, which Germany's Chancellor-designate, Gerhard Schröder, regarded as important but not urgent. Schröder later confirmed that he wanted to postpone a discussion of institutional reform until after Germany's Presidency in the first half of 1999.

V. Internal Institutional Affairs

The Council

Reform was uppermost in the minds of most foreign ministers in 1998: not reform of qualified majority voting – that would be part of a major institutional overhaul in 1999 or perhaps 2000 – but reform of the Council system and especially of the functioning of the General Affairs Council.

For some time, the co-ordinating role of the General Affairs Council (GAC) had been eroded from above (by the European Council) and from below (by

Ecofin). The increasing frequency of European Councils and the propensity of the HOSG to try to reach agreement on a wide range of sectoral issues undermined one of the GAC's most important functions. At the same time, Ecofin's primacy in the EMU process robbed the GAC of a role in one of the most dynamic areas of EU public policy-making. To make matters worse, Ecofin also rivalled the GAC for ascendancy in the negotiation of an *Agenda 2000* agreement. The British, who pride themselves on running a good meeting, had attempted during their Presidency to improve the GAC's efficiency. The French were also eager to recoup some of the GAC's lost ground. Chirac, with Kohl, asserted in their letter of June 1998 that 'the working of the Council must be substantially improved. In particular, there must be better co-ordination of the Council's decision-making processes and structures in order to ensure better coherence in the Union's decisions'.

Perhaps eager to deflect criticism from the Commission, Santer was one of the harshest critics of the GAC's decline. In a press conference before the Cardiff summit, he lamented that 'there is no one in charge of coordination any more between the too numerous formations of the Council, unless it is the European Council itself, which cannot do everything'. He then suggested that the foreign ministers in future deal only with external affairs (including trade policy, development policy and the CFSP) and that a new body, made up of deputy prime ministers or ministers of state, should 'be charged with co-ordinating European affairs at the national level and also in Brussels' (*Agence Europe*, 13 June 1998).

There was some discussion of GAC reform at the Cardiff summit, and the subject recurred throughout the Austrian Presidency. Foreign ministers themselves discussed the GAC's problems at length during their informal (Gymnich) meeting in Salzburg on 5–6 September, before which the Austrian Presidency had circulated a questionnaire on the functioning of the GAC. Based on the work of a few high-level officials (the so-called Trumpf group), the Council Secretariat prepared a discussion paper for the Salzburg meeting which painted a vivid picture of all that was wrong procedurally with the GAC (*European Report*, 2 September 1998):

- opening 'debates' consisted in fact of '16 successive monologues' (by the 15 foreign ministers plus the Commission President);
- each of the four Commissioners present tended to outline at length proposals on which the ministers had already been briefed by their permanent representatives;
- the GAC was the only council to have reneged on a pledge made in 1996 to reduce the number of officials present to six. As a result, 'attendance in the Council meeting room is sometimes such (too many people present – often standing – following the item under discussion or waiting for the next item) that the orderly conduct of business is severely hampered';

- ministers had a poor attendance record, sometimes turning up only for lunch (where key decisions were often made) and/or for a couple of agenda items of particular interest to them.

Clearly, the GAC was its own worst enemy. The solutions to many of its problems were obvious, as the Austrian Presidency and the Trumpf group pointed out: ministers should make a clear distinction between horizontal (co-ordination) issues and external relations issues; they should shorten their initial interventions; they should hold more frequent sessions; they should turn up to meetings and stay for the duration of them. They should, in short, go back to the future and implement guidelines for procedural improvements agreed upon by the GAC in 1988, 1992 and 1995. In all, a ten-point plan was suggested to improve the GAC's work. The possible use of video conferencing was a novel proposal, although interest in it waned following a number of feasibility studies that showed that it lacked political support and faced a major organizational problem – it was too difficult to get hold of ministers in their national capitals. When ministers were in Brussels, by contrast, they were generally at the Council's disposal. Foreign ministers did not endorse the more radical idea of establishing a separate co-ordinating council, which in any case was politically problematic because not all national governments handle EU affairs in the same way (some do not have European affairs ministers or deputy prime ministers).

Foreign ministers again called for a reduction in the number of Council formations (they had first done so in 1988). The Austrian Presidency was especially vociferous on that point, although that did not stop it from convening a new, unofficial council of defence ministers on 4 November. In the event, the defence ministers had little to say to each other (those from NATO and WEU member states have ample opportunity to meet in more appropriate forums) and were markedly unenthusiastic about meeting again under the auspices of the EU.

The Council's problems were far from resolved by the end of the year, and will undoubtedly be addressed in the IGC on institutional reform. In the meantime, the GAC has begun to regain some of its lost influence and make procedural improvements. During 1998, for instance, it sought to win control of the *Agenda 2000* dossier, although papers from Ecofin and the Agricultural Council did not always arrive on time for the GAC to work on them. Nevertheless discussions on *Agenda 2000* became a key feature of GAC meetings throughout the year. Ironically, this further increased the GAC's workload and highlighted the urgency of organizational reform.

Despite concerns about the proliferation of Council formations, a new one – albeit of a unique kind – came into existence when the Euro-11 Council was convened on 4 June, following the decision of the HOSG to select 11 countries for participation in Stage 3 of EMU. The UK, then in the EU Council Presidency and perhaps resentful of its exclusion from the Euro-11, turned up at the

Council's inaugural meeting. This obviated the need for the Euro-11 finance ministers to nominate one of their own as president but they agreed that, for the future, the next Euro-11 member in line for the Council Presidency will assume the Euro-11 Presidency when the Council Presidency is in a non-Euro-11 Member State.

As agreed by its members at their inaugural session, the Euro-11 meets for two hours in the morning before the opening of a regular Ecofin meeting. Over lunch, the Euro-11 president tells the non-Euro-11 finance ministers what transpired at the Euro-11 meeting. The Monetary Committee prepared meetings of the Euro-11 in 1998, thus establishing a procedural link between Euro-11 and Ecofin meetings (the Economic and Financial Committee took over this responsibility in 1999). Euro-11 finance ministers invited the other EU finance ministers to join their informal meeting before the Ecofin informal meeting on 25 September. This produced the slightly ludicrous spectacle of the 15 finance ministers meeting early in the morning as 'the enlarged Euro-11' and later in the day as Ecofin.

The Commission

While MEPs and others lambasted the Commission in 1998 for serious managerial lapses, the Commission itself was in the throes of a reform programme. This had begun in 1995, shortly after Santer became President. It was spearheaded by Santer himself, and by Commissioners Errki Liikanen and Anita Gradin, who were generally assumed because of their Nordic backgrounds to be ideally suited to put the Commission's house in order.

By 1998, the three-part Santer reform programme was at an advanced stage, although not sufficiently advanced or comprehensive to appease the European Parliament. The first part consisted of Sound and Efficient Management (SEM 2000). Launched in 1995, SEM 2000 sought to improve financial management in the Commission by separating operational and financial management structures within each of the directorates-general. The programme was still being implemented three years later and had already resulted in greater financial control over Community operations, although often at a cost of additional bureaucratization and delays in payments to contractors. A more telling criticism of SEM 2000 was that although financial control may have increased, it had not necessarily improved. Most Commission officials were unhappy about SEM 2000, objecting especially to the way in which the programme had been initiated – largely without consulting them. Ironically, Liikanen's own directorate-general – DG IX for personnel and administration – was one of the last DGs to be overhauled in accordance with SEM 2000 (beginning on 1 March 1998).

Liikanen had launched Modernizing the Administration and Personnel Policy (MAP 2000), the second part of the reform programme, in 1997. MAP 2000 consisted of a 25-point programme – ranging from managing vacation time and absences to ordering supplies and furniture – intended to improve administrative practices and personnel policy by means of decentralization, rationalization and simplification. A progress report approved by the Commission in December 1998 showed that MAP 2000 was being implemented reasonably successfully although unevenly throughout the Commission. At least MAP 2000 proved helpful to the environment: the report claimed that greater use of email had saved the Commission 76.6 million pages of printed text in 1998 (*European Report*, 2 December 1998). Inevitably, the most difficult aspects of MAP 2000 related to personnel issues such as training, mobility and equal opportunity. Suspicious Commission officials and their unions obstructed implementation of some personnel measures, resenting what they saw as yet another top-down managerial initiative, with little serious input from the staff itself.

The Commission of Tomorrow, the third part of the Santer reform programme, was a natural extension of MAP 2000 and formed the capstone of the entire reform effort. The pet project of Commission Secretary-General, Carlo Trojan, the Commission of Tomorrow dealt with such politically sensitive issues as consolidating and reducing the number of Commission portfolios (a subject that had come up in the 1996–97 IGC and would have to be resolved at the next IGC), strengthening the Commission Presidency (a subject mentioned in a number of provisions of the Amsterdam Treaty), and enhancing the role of the two Commission vice-presidencies, possibly by giving one responsibility for external relations and the other for economic and monetary affairs. The Commission of Tomorrow also addressed long-standing questions about the size and role of *Cabinets*, the number of directorates-general, and the promotion of officials into the Commission's senior ranks (A3 and above). On the basis of a report by Trojan, Commissioners discussed the Commission of Tomorrow at a seminar on 20 May. Despite making predictable noises about the need to improve the Commission's image and efficiency, they were reluctant to endorse specific recommendations until ratification of the Amsterdam Treaty. However, they agreed to establish an internal 'think tank' under Trojan and Jim Cloos, Santer's *Chef de Cabinet*, to flesh out some ideas for the Commission of Tomorrow. To provide data for their deliberations, Trojan and Cloos launched a 'screening exercise' in late 1998. This involved confidential reviews by teams of senior Commission officials of all the Commission's DGs and services – clustered into 12 functional groups or 'families'.

Based on the cynical internal response to SEM 2000 and MAP 2000, Santer, Trojan and Cloos did their utmost to allay staff suspicions and bring the entire 'house' along with them. Perhaps because the Commission of Tomorrow dealt with 'high political' rather than everyday personnel issues, most Commission officials seemed reasonably well disposed toward it. In any event, officials were more keenly interested in yet another internal report, this time by a group chaired by a former Secretary-General, Sir David Williamson, on reform of the 'European civil service'. The origin of the Williamson Report– a strike by Commission staff on 30 April 1998 – accounted in large part for Santer's solicitousness of staff opinion.

The one-day strike – the first in the Commission since 1991 – had brought lofty discussion of SEM 2000 and MAP 2000 crashing down to earth. It happened in response to a leak of the so-called Caston Report[1] on reform of the Statute of Service for Commission staff, which dealt with such sensitive issues as pay, pensions and promotion. The secretive way that Caston drew up his report, at a time when management was urging staff and trades unions to become fully involved in the SEM 2000 and MAP 2000 reforms, inflamed opinion inside the Commission. Some of his suggested changes then added fuel to the fire. The final straw came when Liikanen put the report on *Europe-plus*, the Commission's Intranet server, and refused to remove it. The strike was settled on terms that included the curious statement that the dissemination of information on the Intranet represents neither 'a means of communication nor a means of consultation' (*European Report*, 13 May 1998) and agreement on a report on civil servants' pay and conditions. The Williamson group delivered a surprisingly uninspired report on 6 November.

Neither side in the dispute was united, but the strike itself demonstrated deep staff resentment toward the senior levels of the Commission. A number of Commissioners repudiated Liikanen and sympathized with or even supported the strike, while similarly a number of Commission officials, especially those in the more reflective and less militant A-grade, were ambivalent about, if not outright opposed to it.[2] But staff morale, after years of bad management, had reached rock-bottom. Doubtless many Commission officials revelled in the difficulties experienced by Santer and some of the other Commissioners in the EP as various financial controversies gathered momentum throughout the year. However, Commission staff are not immune from the same underlying forces that eventually brought about the Commissioners' demise: public opinion is almost as critical of the pay and conditions of Commission officials as it is of the pay and conditions of the Commissioners themselves. Publicity surrounding the cancellation, due to mismanagement and possibly also corruption, of the Commission recruitment examination (*concours*) in September brought home the point. There seemed to be too obvious an answer as to why 31,000 people were competing for a few hundred positions in the Brussels bureaucracy. While Commission officials and unions tenaciously defend their interests in the statute

[1] Anthony Caston, an adviser in DG IX (personnel).
[2] Few officials actually turned up for work, possibly because the strike conveniently fell on the day before a long weekend, but regardless of why they stayed away, all lost a day's pay (stopping strikers' pay was an innovation in the Commission and a source of further staff resentment).

of service, they may well soon be subject to the same wave of public opprobrium that washed away the Commission in March 1999.

1998 was the last year before the HOSG were to select a new Commission President, a selection that ultimately took place earlier than expected and in highly unusual circumstances. Santer seemed interested in a second term, although his prospects looked slim even before the censure crisis gathered momentum toward the end of the year. The possible nomination of Oskar Lafontaine, Germany's new Finance Minister, was floated briefly in the German press, but the most plausible putative President was Romano Prodi, the former Italian Prime Minister, who staked a claim to the job in an interview in *La Republica* on 26 June. By the end of the year Prodi was the clear front runner, with NATO Secretary-General Javier Solana of Spain and Portuguese Prime Minister Antonio Guterres some distance behind him.

Anticipating greater influence in the selection of the next Commission President, the EP called for a strong, politically powerful President and demanded of the HOSG an input into the selection process. Delors, at a press conference in Brussels on 19 May, suggested that the next President be chosen by the HOSG from a list of candidates drawn up by the political groups in the EP – which might have the added benefit not only of enhancing the next President's political legitimacy, but also of invigorating direct elections to the EP. There was near consensus among Member States, current Commissioners and the EP, however, that Delors's proposal was premature and that a debate about a new presidential selection procedure should await the forthcoming IGC on institutional reform.

Apart from internal reorganization as a result of the rolling implementation of SEM 2000 and MAP 2000, the two most important organizational changes in the Commission's DGs and services in 1998 were related to the beginning of accession negotiations and the fight against fraud. The Commission's role in the enlargement process provides an opportunity for the institution to assert itself politically, but procedurally it requires considerable internal reorganization. This was the case in January 1998 when the Commission established a major new unit, the Task Force for the Accession Negotiations (TAFN), in anticipation of the formal opening of negotiations in March. The strengthening of the Commission's Anti-Fraud Co-ordination Unit (UCLAF) was another significant organizational development. This began in July 1998, when the Commission proposed granting UCLAF greater autonomy and authority, largely in anticipation of the implementation of Art. 280 of the Amsterdam Treaty on the protection of the EU's financial interests. Of course, the Commission was also responding to criticism by MEPs of its poor financial management, especially of tourism policy. As such attacks intensified and broadened later in the year, and following a report by the Court of Auditors that was highly critical of UCLAF itself, Santer proposed replacing UCLAF with an anti-fraud office completely independent of the Commission (*European Report*, 7 October 1998). On 1 December, the Commission formally adopted a proposal for a regulation to establish the Fraud Investigation Office. In the meantime, UCLAF had grown considerably in size and stature and had in effect became a task force attached to the Commission.

Partly linked to the issue of fraud, but also because of the obvious need to co-ordinate the management of its assistance to all third countries, the Commission established a new joint service for managing Community aid, drawn from the two external relations DGs (IA and IB) and the development DG (VIII). Under pressure from the EP, which has long been critical of the management and staffing of the Commission's numerous delegations in third countries (a total of 123 in 1998) and which wields the power of the purse, the Commission reorganized its external services further in 1998 and deployed more officials abroad. Although Commissioners and high-level Commission officials general-ly resent the EP's intrusion, many mid-level officials welcome and even encourage the EP's interest in the management of external services, seeing it as a way to bring about changes that the Commission itself would not otherwise countenance.

The European Parliament

The two most significant developments in the internal affairs of the EP in 1998 were directly related to the approaching implementation of the Amsterdam Treaty: the adoption by the EP of a proposal on common principles for direct elections; and a draft statute for MEPs covering issues such as remuneration and expenses.

Efforts to agree upon common electoral principles had eluded the EP since well before the introduction of direct elections in 1979. Britain's refusal to abandon its unique first-past-the-post system in individual constituencies (ex-cept in Northern Ireland, where a version of proportional representation (PR) was used) had always been the main stumbling block. That finally changed when the new Labour government introduced legislation in Britain to use a version of PR in 12 'Euro-constituencies' (including one in Northern Ireland), beginning with the elections of June 1999. Although this made it possible that common electoral principles might finally be adopted, the EP's Committee on Institution-al Affairs had decided well before most Member States had begun to ratify the Amsterdam Treaty that it would act on a provision in the Treaty (new first paragraph, Art. 190.4 TEC) that calls on the EP to 'draw up a proposal for elections for direct universal suffrage in accordance with a uniform procedure in all Member States or in accordance with principles common to all Member States'.

The Institutional Affairs Committee, founded by the veteran Euro-federalist Altiero Spinelli, has a reputation for flights of political fancy. Sensitive to this,

Georgios Anastassopoulos, a vice-president of the Parliament and rapporteur of the electoral principles report, took great care not to make excessive demands of Member States, not least because national governments would have to approve the EP's proposals by unanimity in the Council. With Britain finally on the side of the angels, France appeared to constitute the greatest obstacle to the adoption of uniform electoral principles. This was not because France opposed PR, but because it opposed the establishment of regional constituencies, a key EP demand. The government of Lionel Jospin promised to introduce regional Euro-constituencies, but backed down in July 1998 in the face of strong opposition from within its own ranks. Nevertheless Jospin's support for regional lists suggested that by mid-2004 – when the proposed electoral changes would come into effect – France will, indeed, have adopted regional constituencies.

Based on extensive consultation within the EP and with representatives of national governments, the Anastassopoulos Report – adopted by the Institutional Affairs Committee on 26 May and by the EP as a whole on 15 July – included the following recommendations:

- use of a list system of proportional representation (although Ireland's quaint system of proportional representation by the single transferable vote could be maintained);
- the introduction of regional constituencies for Member States with a population of more than 20 million;
- possible special arrangements for specific regions;
- a possible minimum threshold for representation in the EP, not to exceed at a national level 5 per cent of the vote (this point proved most controversial in the EP itself; after all, some current members might not have been elected had such a threshold existed in 1994);
- abolition of the dual mandate.

The EP adopted a draft statute for its members on 3 December 1998. This was the culmination of six months work by the Legal Affairs Committee under the direction of its rapporteur, Willi Rothley. Precisely because it dealt with MEPs' pay and allowances – a potential political minefield – progress of the Rothley Report was followed closely both inside and outside the house. MEPs have long wanted their own statute in order to enhance their political and institutional autonomy. An innovation in the Amsterdam Treaty – a new paragraph in Art. 138.4 TEC (now Art. 190.5) – made it possible for them finally to draft a statute: 'The European Parliament shall, after seeking an opinion from the Commission and with the approval of the Council acting by unanimity, lay down the regulations and general conditions governing the performance of the duties of its members'. As in the case of electoral principles, the EP decided to act on the TEC's new provision for a members' statute even before ratification of the

Amsterdam Treaty. The thrust of the Rothley Report was the urgency of standardizing MEP's salaries and, as a result, standardizing also their allowances. At present, MEPs' salaries are pegged to the salaries of parliamentarians in their national parliaments. Consequently, some MEPs (notably Italians) are paid four times as much as others (notably Portuguese). Unofficially, travelling and other expenses have been used to top up the salaries of less well paid MEPs. The abuse of allowances, however well intentioned, is a fertile source of criticism of the EP. Ironically, while seeking to end the practice, the Rothley Report drew further public attention to it at precisely the time when the EP set off on the moral high road in its budget discharge dispute with the Commission. A scathing Court of Auditors' report on MEPs' allowances, published in August 1998, further embarrassed the Parliament.

Much to the delight of most MEPs, the draft statute recommended that MEPs receive the same salary, based on that of a judge in the European Court of Justice (ECJ). In return, MEPs would be reimbursed only for expenses actually incurred in the course of their official duties – a novel idea for the EP. The EP sent its proposal to the Council before the end of the year. Given the controversial nature of the proposal in some Member States – national parliamentarians in Portugal, for instance, are unlikely to welcome a huge salary increase for Portuguese MEPs – the Council proceeded cautiously.

The big news concerning political groups in 1998, was the defection of 20 members of Silvio Berlusconi's Forza Italia from the Union for Europe (UFE) and their acceptance as individual members of the European People's Party (EPP). This was the latest development in the long-running saga of the reconfiguration of Italian delegations in the EP – a development directly linked to convulsions in domestic Italian politics since the end of the Cold War. The departure of the Forza Italia members dealt a crushing blow to the UFE, which had become the third largest group in the EP, eclipsing the Liberals; their membership in the EPP was a morale boost for the Christian Democrats, whose total membership by the end of the year topped 200 – only 13 behind the Socialists (PES). But the EPP's acceptance of the disaffected Forza Italia MEPs was not without irony or controversy: while supporting the centrist government of Romano Prodi in Italy, the EPP embraced the political party of Berlusconi, Prodi's sworn enemy.

The Economic and Social Committee and the Committee of the Regions

The Court of Auditors' report on the 1996 budget, which sparked the discharge dispute between the Commission and the Parliament, also included a stinging attack on the Economic and Social Committee (ESC), whose members' travel expenses were so extravagant that the Court called for an additional investigation. The Court's far greater criticism of the Commission deflected attention from the ESC's alleged misdeeds, which nevertheless cast a pall over the committee's 40th anniversary celebrations in May 1998. The ESC began a new four-year term in October, and for the first time elected a woman to serve at its head (for a two-year term). Perhaps because of the alleged financial irregularities there was a larger than usual turnover (over 33 per cent) in the composition of the committee (nominated by Member States). The Committee held its usual number of plenary sessions and produced a large number of reports, of variable quality. Most went unread by the Commission and the Council, their intended audience.

The Committee of the Regions (CoR) fared only slightly better in 1998. In its fourth year of existence, the CoR began a new four-year term in January. Members elected Manfred Dammeyer, a Social Democrat and Minister for Federal and European Affairs for North-Rhine Westphalia, the Committee's new president. By agreement with the EPP 'opposition' in the CoR, Dammeyer will hand over the presidency after two years to the current vice-president, a Christian Democrat (like the EP, the CoR operates a rotating PES–EPP presidency). Although disappointed with the outcome of the 1996–97 IGC, where it had fought for full institutional status and the right to bring alleged breaches of subsidiarity before the ECJ, the CoR nonetheless gained a higher profile and additional reporting authority in the Amsterdam Treaty. Yet like Edmund Stoiber, Prime Minister of Bavaria and a prominent member of the CoR, Dammeyer seemed more interested in using his position on the Committee to try to curb the power of the federal government in Bonn than to contribute to EU policy-making in Brussels. The CoR is a good platform for Dammeyer and other German federalists to assert states' rights – that is, the rights of the Länder – in the name of subsidiarity.

The early months of Dammeyer's presidency were overshadowed by a bitter staff dispute, a legacy of the separation of the staff and institutions of the ESC and the CoR. Indeed, the inaugural session of the Committee's new term, in February 1998, was marred by a staff strike. Dammeyer acted decisively by firing two officials, much to the consternation of those who expected a German-style consensual approach to internal dispute resolution. Dammeyer's action at least bought some breathing space while the aggrieved officials pursued their cases in the courts.

VI. Interinstitutional Relations

The Budget Discharge Dispute

Looking back on what happened in 1998 from the perspective of 1999, it is tempting to claim that the row brewing between the Parliament and Commission over 'discharge' of the 1996 budget, and over related allegations of fraud and mismanagement, would lead inevitably to the Commission's demise. Indeed, the issue of the Commission's resignation was raised at the outset, in March 1998, when the Budgetary Control Committee recommended that the EP delay granting a discharge to protest against the Commission's poor management of successive budgets, based on a highly critical report by the Court of Auditors. James Ellis, the Committee's *rapporteur*, claimed that failure to grant a discharge would be tantamount to a vote of censure and would therefore oblige the entire Commission to resign. Needless to say, the Commission disputed this interpretation.

Given the potential gravity of the situation, it is surprising that the Commission did not act with greater circumspection and deference to Parliament in the months ahead. Neither the Commission nor the Parliament expected or wanted a political crisis. Indeed, when the situation deteriorated later in the year, Ellis changed his mind on the consequences of failure to grant a discharge, claiming that it would not necessitate the Commission's resignation. By that time the situation had become highly charged and the political groups fully appreciated the gravity of the situation. The EPP was not inclined to embarrass the Commission Presidency of one of its own. The PES, the largest group in Parliament, also recommended granting a discharge, both to avoid a full-blown crisis and to protect the two most heavily criticized Commissioners, both socialists. Indeed, in early December the Budgetary Control Committee as a whole backed down and voted, albeit by the narrowest of margins, to grant a discharge.

The Commission seemed to have survived unscathed. And yet passions were running high in the EP as the discharge issue became entangled with other allegations of fraud, the most colourful of which concerned an alleged contract for a scientific report awarded by Commissioner Edith Cresson to a friend unqualified to carry out the work. The story broke in the newspaper *Libération*. Unlike other such allegations, it did not drop out of sight because public opinion – especially in France – would no longer indulge such practices. The situation was further exacerbated by Cresson's reaction of utter disdain toward her accusers in the media and her critics in Parliament and in the Commission itself.

To make matters worse, reports of the disappearance of huge sums of money from programmes administered by the European Community Humanitarian Office (ECHO) surfaced at the same time. The Commission went on the offensive, with no fewer than four Commissioners – Anita Gradin (Fraud), Emma Bonino (Humanitarian Aid), Manuel Marín (who had responsibility for ECHO when the money allegedly disappeared), and Erkki Liikanen (budget and personnel) agreeing to appear before the Budget Control Committee of the EP to explain the Commission's position. Despite their willingness to discuss the affair, the four Commissioners were clearly taken aback by the depth of public and parliamentary anger. Only Bonino, a former MEP, acquitted herself well before the budget committee (Marín was excused from making an appearance).

MEPs were incensed by the Commission's failure to make major reforms on the basis of previous criticism by the Court of Auditors and the EP itself. Moreover, MEPs sensed that they were riding a wave of popular indignation – a wave that they hoped would crest in June 1999 in the form of a large turnout in the direct elections. Even so, a political crisis could have been averted but for the extraordinary insensitivity and poor political judgement of Santer, who adopted a tone of indignation and self-righteousness. In effect, he challenged the EP to put up or shut up; to take a vote of censure or not. As the EPP had already decided to vote against granting a discharge – provided this would not result in the Commission's resignation – and the PES had decided to vote in favour of granting a discharge, Santer was sure that he had called the EP's bluff. In fact, he had left the main political groups, at the December plenary session, little choice but to table a vote of censure for the January plenary. Santer was confident that the Commission would survive the vote, which it did. Germany, about to assume the Council Presidency, made every effort to defuse the situation, fearing that its Presidency would be sullied and prospects for a conclusion of the *Agenda 2000* negotiations would be damaged.

The censure saga can be seen as further evidence of the EP's political assertiveness *vis-à-vis* the Commission or, more plausibly, as an example of political brinkmanship and bumbling. By the end of the year, it had set the Commission and Parliament on a collision course from which it seemed that the Commission would survive, but only with its reputation further weakened. By drawing attention to the Commission's slipshod ways and emphasizing the EP's powers of scrutiny and control, the episode at least portended a stronger EU system, one in which the Commission was better managed and more accountable.

Comitology

Preliminary work on a new Council decision and a new interinstitutional agreement on EU implementing procedures (comitology) began in 1998. Originally comitology had been a political battleground for the Council and Commission (the Commission often accused the Council of using comitology's complex committee system to curb the Commission's right to execute Community policy). Since the early 1990s, however, comitology was a battleground primarily for the Council and the Parliament (having acquired the power of legislative co-decision in the TEU, the EP resented its exclusion from a system dominated by the Council, the EP's co-legislator). National governments were to have reviewed comitology in the 1996–97 IGC. Instead, at the Amsterdam summit in June 1997, they called on the Commission to introduce a proposal before the end of 1998 for reform of the comitology regime. This the Commission did on 24 June.

As it unfolded in 1998, the comitology battle was fought not between the Council and the Commission or the Council and the Parliament, but between the Commission and the Parliament. The EP was disappointed with the Commission's proposal: although it included provisions for greater parliamentary involvement in comitology, especially through the provision of more and higher quality information to MEPs, the proposal did not envision a radical overhaul of the system. The EP expressed its dissatisfaction with the Commission's proposal in the Aglietta Report and in a resolution of 17 September. As well as a far-reaching overhaul of comitology, the EP wants a clearer distinction to be made between substantive legislation and implementing provisions so that important legislative acts cannot be introduced under the guise of implementing measures. As usual, the EP threatened to use its budgetary powers – in this case by putting funds for comitology meetings in a reserve – unless it got its way with the Council and Commission. The Council kept its powder dry in 1998 in anticipation of a bruising comitology battle in 1999.

The European Parliament and the European Central Bank

The European Central Bank (ECB) is one of the most powerful and independent central banks in the world. Given the nature of the EU, it is also unique. To whom should the Bank be accountable? How transparent should it be? Not surprisingly, MEPs believe that the EP should be the ECB's main institutional interlocutor both in order to build the Bank's legitimacy and make its decision-making procedures more open and transparent.

The EP–ECB dialogue began on 7 May 1998 (even before the Bank was established), when, under the terms of the TEU, the EP considered Wim Duisenberg's nomination for the Presidency. This was a congenial occasion for both parties: it allowed the EP to castigate Chirac and the other heads of government for their conduct of the Brussels summit earlier in the month, and it allowed Duisenberg to assert that he was not obliged to resign at any particular time before his eight-year term expired. Duisenberg appeared before the EP again on 15–16 September 1998, this time in his capacity of former president of the defunct EMI (the EP was debating the EMI's final report). The EP's regular, quarterly meetings with Duisenberg and the other members of the ECB's Executive Board (held under the terms of Art. 109(B)3 TEU), began on 22 September. In their appearances before the EP, ECB Executive Board members were sensitive to the issues of accountability and legitimacy and sympathetic to calls for openness and transparency. Duisenberg, a former politician, seemed especially to enjoy the give-and-take of meetings with the EP's monetary subcommittee. But Duisenberg and his colleagues set strict limits on public access to information on ECB decision-making, refusing especially to release the minutes of the Bank's policy-making committee. This insistence on confidentiality may eventually clash with the EP's preference for disclosure. If so, both institutions will look back on 1998 as the honeymoon of their relationship.

Transparency

Transparency is a key ingredient of good governance and a central element in efforts to improve the accountability and credibility of EU institutions. The Council's second report on transparency, published in April 1998 (covering the years 1996–97), was slightly self-congratulatory. Based on the Council's famous decision of December 1993 on openness in EU decision-making and access to Council documents (the so-called code of conduct), the report listed both an increasing number of requests for documents and an improvement in the ratio of document provision to demand. It also noted that those who request documents are often hampered by not knowing exactly what they are looking for (hence the need for a register of documents), while television broadcasts of Council 'debates' attracted a disappointingly low audience.

Any smugness on the part of the Council was shattered in June 1998, when the Court of First Instance issued a ruling highly critical of the Council's code of conduct. The Court came out in favour of the Swedish Journalists' Union, which had taken a case on behalf of some of its members who, in turn, had tested the Council's code of conduct by requesting 20 specific documents on JHA from both the Swedish government and the Council. The Swedish government had promptly produced 18 of them, the Council only two (and another two later), without explaining adequately why it withheld the rest. Based on the provisions of the code of conduct, the Court insisted that the Council give precise reasons for withholding documents, putting the onus, if necessary, on the Council rather than the individual requesting a document to justify the request.

The Council received another drubbing in July 1998, this time from Jacob Söderman, the EU Ombudsman. Citing the court ruling above, Söderman lent his prestige to a journalist whose request for documents on a US–EU working group the Council had rejected on the grounds that it was only a joint author of the documents in question. The journalist's ability to request the documents in Washington through the Freedom of Information Act highlights the distance that transparency in the EU still needs to travel. Continuing criticism of the Council seemed to be having an effect. Anticipating yet another negative report on transparency, this time by the Court of Auditors, at its meeting on 6–7 December the General Affairs Council adopted a set of conclusions aimed at improving the implementation of the code of conduct and generally enhancing its public information policy. The Council also welcomed the imminent publication on the Internet of a public register of Council documents.

At the end of the year, the Commission considered introducing a code of conduct for its staff covering everything from handling requests for information (officials should respond promptly and politely), to accepting gifts (officials should hand over gifts worth more than 250 euros to their supervisors), to teaching university courses (not to exceed 60 hours per academic year and not to be paid more than 3,500 euros). Those who telephone the Commission with any regularity will be pleased to hear that officials are now being urged to identify themselves 'immediately upon answering', and to return calls 'as quickly as possible'.

VII. Conclusion

With the notable exception of the launch of the ECB, the EU's institutional structure and system of governance underwent no profound changes in 1998. Even so, the ECB became fully operational only in January 1999. Similarly, although the Amsterdam Treaty had been concluded in June 1997, its impact on the EU's policies and policy-making process will not be felt before the middle of 1999. In the meantime, major institutional reform remained pressing in the EU, but little was done about it in 1998.

In the last full year of its tenure before the nomination of a new college, the Santer Commission carried out its statutory obligations in key areas such EMU, enlargement and *Agenda 2000,* but generally lacked vision and dynamism. Already on the defensive politically, the Commission was further weakened by serious allegations of fraud and mismanagement. The Commission's inept response to these allegations, ironically at a time when an internal reform programme was well underway, increased the EP's ire and set the stage for an interinstitutional conflict at the end of the year. Far from heralding the demise of the Commission, however, this and other developments in 1998 may have helped to strengthen the Commission in the long run by exposing some of its major deficiencies and forcing Member States to correct them.

The EP continued its seemingly inexorable struggle for mastery of the EU system. But MEPs are aware that their greatest strength – the fact that they are directly elected – is also potentially their greatest weakness. If the turnout in the June 1999 elections were to be lower or only slightly higher than it was in 1994 (which itself was lower than in 1989), the EP would be in a relatively weak position going into the next IGC. A closer look at the EP also reveals a tendency on its part to focus on big political events – IGCs, enlargement, censure and the like – possibly to the detriment of legislative decision-making. Arguably, the quality and efficiency of EU policy-making could be improved through reform of internal EP procedures and structures.

Regardless of the EP's ambition, the year 1998 showed yet again that the Member States remain masters of the EU system. The HOSG, meeting in the European Council or occasionally in the Council, are the EU's key actors. Although the Cardiff and Vienna summits were not especially memorable, the HOSG continue to play a greater role in everyday EU affairs. Often, they do so outside the EU's formal structure, notably through a dense network of bilateral and multilateral meetings. In 1998 as in previous years, some of the most important of these meetings were the pre-summit conferences of social democratic and Christian democratic leaders. Yet while dominating the policy-making process, both the Council and the European Council lacked strong leadership and direction during 1998. This was noticeable in their handling of two key policy areas: enlargement and *Agenda 2000*. The problem lay partly in Germany's preoccupation with domestic politics, but it also reflected growing introspection in most Member States. Similarly, strains in the Franco–German axis were exacerbated by the German election of September 1998, but reflected fundamental changes in priorities and perspectives on both sides of the Rhine.

Journal of Common Market Studies

Volume 37, Annual Review
September 1999

The British Presidency of 1998

PETER J. ANDERSON

University of Central Lancashire

For the declaredly forward-looking and modernizing New Labour leadership, the job of steering the EU through the final stages of a major policy initiative from which the British had excluded themselves clearly was an embarrassing one. However, the desires of some key Cabinet members for early entry into the EMU were blocked by a more important party goal, that of securing a second term of office. In this regard, given Blair's commitment to a referendum on the question of entry prior to any final government decision on monetary union, the virulent opposition of key UK newspapers – in particular the Murdoch mass-circulation, tabloid the *Sun* – to all things EMU, became a matter of serious concern and a reason for caution before committing to the euro. The government's response was to try to change the attitude of Murdoch and his editors by converting the electorate to a more favourable view of the EU, which in turn would force him to consider changing his stance on EMU if he wished to maintain his UK papers' circulation figures. One way in which this was to be achieved was by using the Presidency to secure a clear set of gains which could be held up as reasons for liking 'Europe'. Related to this was a declared intention to make the EU more responsive to some of the key concerns of ordinary voters on the street. This campaign appeared to have a second purpose also in providing a positive counterpoint to Britain's rather lonely position outside the euro-club from which the Major government originally had voluntarily excluded it.

In addition to the difficult job of steering through the final stages of the EMU project, the government was faced with the extremely complex question of EU enlargement.

All in all, Blair's performance in dealing with the above problems and aspirations was a proverbial mixed bag. He made a high-profile, 'back to the people' move in proceeding quickly on the implementation of the Working Time Directive. However, the 'good news' campaign descended into near farce when Blair released his half-term report in which 45 largely routine or minor 'achievements' were trumpeted as major successes. The government also unconsciously undermined the value of the EU in the electorate's eyes right at the beginning of its Presidency by making the Common Foreign and Security Policy appear worthless when the Iraq crisis arose over weapons' inspection.

The British attracted considerable flak from some Member States over their handling of the negotiations concerning the choice of the first President of the European Central Bank in May. However, there were also those who defended the government's performance, most notably the Austrians.

As far as enlargement was concerned, a largely symbolic EU meeting with prospective new members had been held during the early part of the Presidency. Given the various potential costs of admitting the relatively poor prospective eastern members, the British did not find themselves under great pressure from their partners to move with greater rapidity from symbolic to truly substantial progress.

What is clear is that, despite its failures in such ambitions as winning over Murdoch or taking Europe to the people, the British government did manage successfully the tricky task of helping efficiently to deliver a new common currency which it would not itself be issuing in the immediate future.

Journal of Common Market Studies

Volume 37, Annual Review
September 1999

Small and New, but Nonetheless Competent: Austria and the EU Presidency

KURT RICHARD LUTHER

Keele University

Austria, as the first of the newest EU members to assume the Presidency, was bound to be something of an unknown quantity. Not only had it limited EU experience but it also had a modest apparatus with which to discharge the significant burdens imposed by the office. Yet not least out of concern for its external image and in the light of domestic political considerations, including a general election in 1999, Austria was determined to ensure its tenure was a success, or could at least not be construed a failure.

Planning for the Presidency began even before Austria joined the Union. To enhance its EU expertise and address problems of potential administrative overload, Austria exchanged a number of its civil servants with other Member States. It proved a useful programme even if, in the event, Austria still had to draw extensively on the support of Commission and Council officials. Two further factors mitigated Austria's lack of EU experience. First, when the UK Presidency embarrassingly found itself unable to participate fully in the Euro-11 committee, the Austrians stepped in, which provided the latter with valuable hands-on experience, and their partners with insights into how the Austrian Presidency itself would operate. Second, Austria's traditionally consensual policy-making style arguably helped it engage in the kind of brokerage and package deals characteristic of a successful Presidency.

The bulk of EU business – and thus also of Austria's own declared priorities – was, of course, predetermined (an exception being Kosovo). EMU was a central item and though virtually all key decisions had already been made, Austria gained political capital from both its enhanced role in the Euro-11 and the fact that its 'watch' coincided with the eve of this major step in European integration. On the enlargement dossier, Austria carried forward the groundwork of the preceding presidencies in a workmanlike manner and prides itself in having pushed for the start of official entry negotiations on those chapters where *acquis* screening had been concluded, rather than waiting for the completion of the whole screening process. It was only to be expected that progress should have been limited to the less contentious chapters.

However, the enlargement dossier illustrates the mixed blessings which formal leadership of EU business can bring. Austria's elite is deeply committed to eastern enlargement for at least two strategic reasons: moving the EU eastwards relocates Austria 'from the west European periphery to the centre of Europe' (Luther and Ogilvie, 1998, pp. 3–22), while the only long-term solution to tensions caused by the economic gulf on its extensive border with east European states is seen to lie in enhancing the latter's economic position. As Foreign Minister Schüssel stated, 'the European Union will either export stability towards the applicant countries, or it will import instability. No country has a higher stake in this than Austria' (Luther and Ogilvie, 1998, p. 93).

Yet this strategic vision is politically problematic in a country which has such a long border with the aspiring states and whose public is concerned, above all, over what it sees as a threat to Austria's labour market. It is not only the threat from incoming migrant labour, but also from potential commuter labour traffic given the proximity of major eastern European conurbations to the industrial and commercial centres of eastern Austria. As the parties in government are faced with a strident and successful populist opposition, it is perhaps not surprising that Austria's political and administrative elite addressed eastern enlargement in a noticeably differentiated manner. In their Presidency role, the Austrians diligently promoted the accession process and were not without success, not least because of their historical ties with many applicant countries. In domestic discourse, however, more emphasis was placed on the need for long transition periods to safeguard the labour markets of existing EU members.

Significant progress on *Agenda 2000* proved elusive. The main substantive impediments were over post-1999 EU financing – including the CAP and reform of the structural and cohesion funds – while uncertainty about the outcome of the German General Election made agreement impossible. Future funding decisions were postponed until the Berlin summit – though many were sceptical about the prospects of a deal being reached there. It is thus unsurprising that a senior Austrian diplomat should claim that *Agenda 2000* had been 'by far the most difficult, work-intensive and at the same time most thankless of issues'.

The Presidency was keen to de-emphasize sterile 'in-house' EU disputes and to stress EU transparency and accountability, as well as 'citizen-oriented' issues such as promoting employment. The Austrians felt that the informal Pörtschach summit (October 1998) was a success on both counts. It provided an informal get-to-know-you session for Chancellor-elect Schröder, but also arrived at agreement on measures designed to enhance the public's perception of the relevance of EU affairs. Though substantive progress cannot yet be expected, the Austrians argue that the (rather pompously entitled) 'Vienna Strategy for Europe' of the subsequent Vienna summit (December 1998) marked a milestone in this process, by enshrining the significance of unemployment, as well as of the need to provide EU citizens with, for example, improved legal redress. It was agreed that by the Cologne summit, national reports on best practice in combating unemployment would be used to draft an EU-wide policy initiative.

In sum, Austria's Presidency was not marked by major agreements that are likely to be remembered in a decade's time, nor (with the exception of the euro) by other major events. Moreover, some dossiers were delayed by factors beyond Austria's control. Yet Austria provided a generally competent, albeit unremarkable, stewardship of EU affairs, confounding sceptics who doubted the capacity of a new, small state to conduct the Presidency. Accordingly, Schüssel's wish in June 1998 that 'a lot will be done, but nothing will happen' (Luther and Ogilvie, 1998, p. 100) was largely granted. Though for many a rather modest aspiration, it is one which one suspects the German Presidency would in retrospect have been quite content with, for there is nothing more worrying for politicians than the unexpected.

Reference

Luther, K.R. and Ogilvie, I. (eds) (1998) *Austria and the European Union Presidency: Background and Perspectives* (Keele: KERC).

Journal of Common Market Studies

Volume 37, Annual Review
September 1999

Internal Policy Developments

JOHN REDMOND

University of Birmingham

I. Introduction

The year was dominated by two policy developments due to reach fruition in 1999: the third and final stage of Economic and Monetary Union (EMU), and the agreement of the *Agenda 2000* reform package. Between them, these two issues set the agenda in the key internal EU policy areas. However, the EU did seek to develop other policies as well, particularly in the fields of employment, the environment, energy and transport. Moreover, long-standing problems relating to fraud and to the transposition and implementation of single market regulations continued, getting rather worse in the case of the former.

II. Economic and Related Policies

Internal Market Developments

The Commission's 1997 *Action Plan for the Single Market* provided the agenda and the framework within which efforts to complete the single market continued throughout 1998. A number of new initiatives were taken:

- An early intervention mechanism was introduced for cases where the free movement of goods is hindered.

- A 'test panel' of businessmen (the European Business Panel) was established to evaluate the costs and administrative effects of new single market legislative proposals (and thereby promote legislative simplification).
- The SLIM (Simpler Legislation for the Internal Market) programme was extended into a third and fourth phase.
- The liberalization of telecommunications services took effect on 1 January but problems continued, and by the end of the year over 80 infringement procedures had been opened.
- In February, the gradual liberalization cf the postal sector was begun (although, initially, only to a very limited degree, with no further measures until 2003).
- The Commission proposed (March) and the Council supported (May) measures to create a single market for commercial communications services (advertising, direct marketing, sponsoring, sales promotions, public relations and a packaging design).
- Also in March, the Commission published a communication setting out the broad guidelines for its policy on public procurement for the next five years, designed to simplify the existing framework and increase flexibility.
- In July, as a follow-up to the work of the Veil Group, the Commission announced a modest package of initiatives to facilitate free movement of people.
- In November a high-level group – the Financial Services Policy Group – was set up to define priorities and actions required to create a more integrated market for financial services; it is to report in mid-1999.

However, efforts to progress the European Company Statute continued to flounder on the issue on of worker participation. There were also persistent difficulties with standardization and mutual recognition, and the opening-up of public procurement; the latter remains one of the key areas to be addressed, with over half of the later directives in this field still not being applied in all Member States in mid-1998. Moreover, an earlier decision – to abolish duty-free sales in airports and on ferries on intra-EU routes in mid-1999 – began to unravel in 1998. In the face of growing pressure from various Member States to postpone this measure, the Vienna Council decided to ask the Commission to examine the employment problems that it may cause and raised the possibility of a limited extension for duty-free sales.

Furthermore, problems with transposition and implementation of the single market rules continued. The Commission sought to deal with the first of these by publishing its 'scorecard' three times during the year. The final version (November) indicated significant improvement, with the percentage of directives not yet applied by all Member States falling to 14.9 per cent from 26.7 per cent a year earlier, although certain Member States – Luxembourg, Ireland and Portugal – continued to perform poorly; the areas where most implementation difficulties occurred were telecommunications, public procurement and transport. In spite of this progress, the Action Plan's target – to complete the single market in line with the introduction of the euro on 1 January 1999 – was not achieved. The Commission responded to the implementation deficiencies by taking out a succession of infringement proceedings, with every Member State in the dock on numerous occasions. However, the worst offenders were France, Italy, Belgium and Greece, and over half of the infringements concerned free movement of goods and services or freedom of establishment. The speeding-up of infringement procedures has led to a significant increase in the number of cases, but the vast majority continue to be resolved without recourse to the European Court of Justice (ECJ).

Participation in the Schengen Accord continued to prove popular. In April, Sweden took the first steps towards membership while Switzerland expressed a desire to join in the medium term and, in September, a standing committee was created to facilitate the future accession of countries from central and eastern Europe. Meanwhile, the process of integrating the Schengen Agreement into the European Union, agreed at Amsterdam, was begun.

Economic and Monetary Union

Unsurprisingly, 1998 was dominated by the countdown to the introduction of the euro on 1 January 1999. The first key question – who would qualify for participation in the third and final stage of Economic and Monetary Union – was answered in early May, when a special European Council endorsed the recommendations of the Ecofin Council that the third stage should include 11 countries: Austria, Belgium, Finland, France, Germany, Ireland, Italy, Luxembourg, the Netherlands, Portugal and Spain. These countries were all judged to have met the Maastricht criteria, although the interpretation of the global debt yardstick – a maximum of 60 per cent (of GDP) total debt – was honoured more in the breach since only three Member States achieved this (and one of these was the UK), while Belgium and Italy actually had total debt of over twice the maximum permitted level. The EU was thus forced to draw rather heavily on the 'moving in the right direction' interpretation permitted by the TEU. (On 1 May, in the context of the excessive deficits procedure, nine of the ten countries previously judged to have excessive deficits were struck off the list, as was the tenth – Greece – in June.) Two countries were judged not to fulfil all the criteria – none of them in the case of Greece and just one (exchange rate stability) in the case of Sweden; this decision defused a potentially difficult situation caused by the unilateral resolution by the Swedish Parliament not to participate at least initially. Finally, Britain and Denmark chose to exercise their opt-outs.

The announcement of who would participate in the final stage of EMU was accompanied by the 'Waigel Declaration'. This, firstly, committed Member States to continue to pursue budgetary balance with the determination shown in the past; secondly, it anticipated and confirmed the application of certain aspects of the Stability and Growth Pact; thirdly, it reaffirmed the need to convert growth into more employment; and, finally, it emphasized the need for structural reforms – particularly relating to labour and capital markets – and also stressed the importance of more effective training and entrepreneurship and of increasing tax efficiency.

However, organizational matters also required attention. Specifically, three important new bodies were created:

- The European Central Bank, the ECB (and the European System of Central Banks, the ESCB) were established on 1 June, the former not without controversy over the choice of its head. Although Wim Duisenberg, head of the EMI, was confirmed in the post, it is expected that he will resign in the middle of his eight-year term to make way for a French successor (Jean-Claude Trichet, Governor of the Bank of France).
- The Euro Council (or Euro-11) designed to provide a political counterweight to the ECB, with (controversially) only those Member States participating in the launch of the euro allowed to be full members, held its first meeting in June. It was subsequently expanded to include all EU members and seems set to play a significant role.
- In December, the details of the Economic and Financial Committee, due to replace the Monetary Committee in 1999, were finalized.

There was also the contentious issue of the external representation for the euro, particularly at the G7. It was eventually agreed (in December) that G7 representation would consist of the President of the ECB and the President of Ecofin (or, if he/she came from a non-euro area Member State, the President of the Euro-11), assisted by the Commission.

Otherwise, normal business continued. On 16 March, the drachma entered the exchange rate mechanism (ERM) and the Irish punt was revalued by 3 per cent. At the end the year, ERM1 was replaced by ERM2, which was joined by Denmark and Greece but with different fluctuation bands (+/–2.25 per cent and +/–15 per cent respectively). In May, the Commission adopted its (annual) Broad Guidelines for Economic Policy which largely echoed the content of the 'Waigel Declaration'. The Commission stressed the importance of economic policy co-ordination in EMU and placed more emphasis on country-specific recommendations than in the past. In October, the Council examined the Greek convergence and the Finnish stability programmes and, in December, the Danish convergence and the Dutch stability programmes.

The Commission's efforts to address the problem of harmful tax competition continued in 1999. The code of conduct for business taxation was implemented in the shape of the Primarolo Committee which presented a preliminary report in December highlighting a range of potentially harmful preferential tax measures. Other Commission initiatives – proposals for directives on taxation on revenue from savings and on payment of interest and fees between companies – were still not agreed by the end of the year.

Growth, Competitiveness and Employment

The EU continued to develop its employment policy in 1998, albeit still arguably with more rhetoric than substance. In June, the Member States submitted their National Employment Plans (NEPs) to the European Council which, whilst superficially impressive, were subject to criticism from the Commission itself:

- The plans are vague in places or amount to a mere list of initiatives, with little evidence of an integrated strategy.
- The budgetary and resource implications are not clearly specified.
- There is a lack of precise and quantifiable policy objectives and related statistical indicators.

The practical implementation of the plans is to be examined at the Cologne summit in mid-1999.

At the European Council in December, the 1999 Guidelines for Employment were submitted and approved. They emphasized the four pillars identified by the Commission in 1997: the promotion of employability (upgrading skills), entrepreneurship (including the role of SMEs), adaptability and equal opportunities. Whilst generally accepting the guidelines, some Member States emphasized the need to develop measurable objectives for the future. Finally, the Council agreed to take steps to create a European Employment Pact.

The progress of the trans-European networks (TENs) continued to cause some concern. A Commission progress report in June showed that only three of the 14 priority transport TENs – the Cork–Dublin–Belfast–Larne conventional rail link, Malpensa airport, and the Øresund fixed link – were near completion. A further six were expected to be completed by around 2005, but the remaining five had longer (beyond 2005) and uncertain time scales and were still not fully financed.

Structural Funds and Regional Policy

Negotiations for the future of the structural funds (SFs) continued as part of *Agenda 2000*, with the Commission publishing formal proposals in June for a seven-year (2000–06) budget of 275bn ECU (1997 prices), of which 210bn ECU would be allocated to the SFs for the present EU membership, 20bn ECU to the Cohesion Fund and 45bn ECU to the prospective members from central and eastern Europe. The proposals reflect the Commission's basic principles of concentrating funds to reduce coverage from 51 per cent to 35–40 per cent of the EU's population, and simplifying procedures. More concentration means that the new Objective 1 will replace past flexibility by strict application of the qualifying criterion of GDP per capita less than 75 per cent of the EU average. Consequently, 11 regions will cease to be eligible for assistance including two in Britain (Northern Ireland and the Highlands and Islands of Scotland), although the UK will be the only country to experience an increase in terms of population coverage because Cornwall and the Scilly Isles, South Yorkshire and parts of West Wales will become eligible. The principal losers would be the Irish: unless they are successful in dividing Ireland into two regions, then the entire country will cease to be eligible for Objective 1 funding. Of course, this is all subject to agreement in the Council in 1999. The response of the Member States to the proposals has been predictably welcoming in general, but questioning and tenacious in the pursuit of their own self-interest. Thus the contributor countries, led by Germany, are calling for more budgetary discipline; the beneficiary countries, led by Spain, are demanding the opposite – greater financial support; and those countries like the UK, which face a potential net loss in their share of funding, are asking for more transitional assistance to cushion the effect. Furthermore, the British are also disputing the choice of criteria for the selection of Objective 2 regions, favouring national GDP over the Commission's preference for unemployment rates.

Finally, Italy began to use its SF receipts more quickly and more effectively. This was achieved in part by the Italians diverting funding from less efficient parts of the Mezzogiorno to other areas or programmes in southern Italy which were performing rather better. Encouragement to improve was provided by an agreement between the Commission and Italy of expenditure targets (in the shape of a percentage of available funds, initially 38 per cent but rising to 55 per cent, over a given period).

Industrial and Competition Policies

The Commission continued its efforts to promote restructuring and to enhance competitiveness in a number of industries:

- It sought to progress the restructuring of the aerospace industry by proposing a forum for consultation and dialogue between interested parties.
- In May, the Industry Council agreed to abolish operational aid for shipyards in the EU on 31 December 2000 and on stricter rules for other

aids for the shipbuilding industry, thereby effectively bringing it under the same rules as other sectors with regard to state aid.

• Also in May, the Council gave its support to the Commission's action plan to promote competitiveness in the textile and clothing industry which emphasized innovation, training and closer co-operation within the industry.

• In July, the Commission put forward proposals to address the problems confronting the EU's recycling industry.

However, it proved impossible for the Council to agree on a draft directive designed to speed up payments to SMEs by enforcing payment deadlines. Finally, the November Council identified what they considered to be the main problems faced by the industrial sector in the EU, specifically: an excessively rigid structure for company finance, an inability to absorb new technologies, and a heavy regulatory and administrative burden on companies in the EU.

In December, the Commission modified the legislative framework for examining competition policy cases, in order to simplify and modernize its procedures. More specifically, it tried, throughout 1998, to strengthen the rules on state aids by clarifying and tidying up existing practice, improving transparency, stepping up controls, and increasing the effectiveness and credibility of EU action by accelerating procedures. The Commission's proposals met with strong resistance from Member States, but a compromise was agreed with the Council in November which allowed the Commission to achieve some of its aims. Efforts were also made to build on the 1997 Green Paper on vertical competition restrictions. However, the new rules are unlikely to become effective until the year 2000.

In 1998, the Commission was notified of 225 planned mergers which were mostly cleared at the first stage (within one month); the ten that proceeded to the second stage (a further four months) were also authorized, in most cases subject to conditions. In addition, a merger notified in 1997 – between publishing firms Reed Elsevier and Wolters Kluwer (which would have created the world's largest publishing group) – was voluntarily abandoned in the face of objections raised by the EU (and the US anti-trust authority).

Finally, the Commission imposed particularly heavy fines on Volkswagen – 102m ECU (January) – for refusing to sell its cars in Italy to non-Italian customers (particularly Germans and Austrians) and on ABB (Asea Brown Boveri) – 70m ECU (October) – for its involvement in a district heating systems cartel.

Other Developments

In December, long-running negotiations with Switzerland finally culminated in a bilateral road *transport* agreement which gradually increases the size of EU lorries allowed to pass through Switzerland but requires the payment of a substantial 'transit tax'. At the same Council meeting, a common position was agreed on the 'Euro tax disk' or 'Eurovignette'; this authorizes six Member States (Benelux, Denmark, Germany and Sweden) to levy a (common) tax on HGVs, related to the degree of pollution caused, on certain motorways (where there are no road tolls). The Commission's ambitions to negotiate an 'open skies' agreement with the USA continued to be thwarted by the Council; the Commission responded by pressing on with infringement proceedings against those Member States which negotiated their own bilateral deals. Finally, the Commission published a White Paper on transport infrastructure charging in July. It proposed harmonizing the disparate national systems and rates over a ten-year period to create a transparent EU system based on the 'user pays' principle.

In November, the Council agreed to reorganize the EU's *energy* policy by setting up a multi-annual framework programme (1998–2002) with a budget of 170m ECU, incorporating the following individual programmes:

- ETAP (studies and forecasts)
- SYNERGY (international co-operation)
- CARNOT (promoting clean, efficient use of solid fuels)
- SURE (nuclear safety)
- SAVE (enhancing energy efficiency)
- ALTENER (promoting renewable energy sources).

The framework programme seeks to promote greater coherence, transparency, co-ordination and efficiency.

In May, it was finally agreed to begin the (gradual) liberalization of the natural gas market with a minimum opening of 20 per cent of annual consumption in the year 2000, rising to 33 per cent in 2010. Also in May, the Council approved a resolution on renewable energy sources which adopted the Commission's objective – of increasing the market share of renewable energy from the present 6 to 12 per cent of the EU market by 2010 – although it was made clear that this was regarded as a 'useful guideline' rather than a target.

Efforts to finalize the details of *Fifth Framework Programme for Research and Development* (1999–2002) continued. The main problem was the budget which was blocked by a protracted disagreement between the Council and Parliament; the latter sought to reinstate the Commission's original budget of 16.3bn ECU which the former had reduced to 14bn ECU. A compromise figure of 14.96bn ECU was not agreed until November. The programme now has four themes: quality of life and management of living resources; creating a user-friendly information society; promoting competitiveness and sustainable growth; energy, environment and sustainable development.

In July, the Commission announced changes to the EU's Joint Research Centre (JRC), designed to facilitate a greater focus on European policies and to improve the management of the JRC. Finally, in October, allegations began to emerge that Edith Cresson, the Commissioner for Research, had arranged for a dentist from the village where she was mayor to be employed by the Commission as a 'visiting scientist' in areas unrelated to dentistry.

The Jean Monnet Project supported 202 actions in *education* in 1998, including 45 new chairs and – a new initiative – 25 Jean Monnet Centres of Excellence. In December, Socrates II (education) and Leonardo II (vocational training) were agreed; they are to run for seven years (2000–06), with budgets of 1.55m ECU and 1.15m ECU, respectively. Tempus will also be extended to 2006 and continue to be funded by the general support programmes for eastern Europe.

The Commission proposed establishing a framework programme (2000–04) for *culture*, with a budget of 167m ECU (a considerable increase), which grouped together the three EU cultural programmes – Kaleidoscope (living arts), Ariane (literature) and Raphael (heritage). However, this was blocked by the Netherlands which would not accept a budget greater than 90m ECU in the absence of an agreed financial perspective post-1999.

In November, the Council approved the Commission's plans to develop an action programme for public *health* (focusing on information, prevention, and rapid reaction to epidemics). The directive banning tobacco advertising was adopted by the Council in June but is subject to separate legal challenges from the tobacco industry and Germany.

The Philoxenia programme for *tourism* remained blocked. However, the Commission did succeed in setting up a High Level Group on Tourism and Employment in March. The Parliament further criticized the Commission for financial irregularities in its tourism policy activities.

III. EU Finances

There was increasing concern over fraud in 1998. In April, the Parliament postponed the discharge of the Commission on its implementation of the 1996 budget, largely because of fraud-related issues and, in May, the Commission adopted its Annual Report on fraud which found an increase in the number of cases detected. There were allegations of fraudulent management of ECHO (which deals with food aid) and, in November, the Court of Auditors expressed concern about the 1997 budget. The Commission finally reacted in December by proposing the creation of OLAF, an independent fraud investigation unit, responsible for monitoring EU expenditure in all EU institutions and Member States; it will eventually replace UCLAF, an internal Commission body, which

© Blackwell Publishers Ltd 1999

Table 1: European Community Budget, 1998 and 1999, Appropriations for Commitment

	1998 Budget (m ECU)	1999 Budget (m euros)	1999 Budget (% of total)	% Change 1999 over 1998
1. COMMON AGRICULTURAL POLICY				
Markets (price support)	37,977.0	37,823.0	39.0	−0.4
Accompanying measures	1,960.0	2,617.0	2.7	+33.5
TOTAL 1	39,937.0	40,440.0	41.7	+1.3
2. STRUCTURAL OPERATIONS				
EAGGF guidance	4,183.1	5,164.0	5.3	+23.5
FIFG (Fisheries guidance)	464.2	808.0	0.8	+74.1
ERDF	14,000.4	15,646.0	16.11	+11.8
ESF	8,628.1	9,611.0	9.9	+11.4
Community initiatives	2,856.1	4,256.0	4.4	+49.0
Transnational/innovation/anti−fraud measures	350.2	417.0	0.4	+19.1
Cohesion fund	2,871.0	3,118.0	3.2	+8.6
EEA financial mechanism	108.0	5.0	−	−95.4
TOTAL 2	33,461.0	39,025.0	40.2	+16.6
3. INTERNAL POLICIES				
Research	3,491.0	3,450.0	3.6	−1.1
Other agricultural operations	145.9	147.8	0.2	+1.3
Other regional operations	17.0	17.0	−	0
Transport	19.1	21.2	−	+11.3
Fisheries and the sea	48.1	49.0	0.1	+1.6
Education, vocational training, youth	410.7	441.7	0.5	+7.6
Culture and audio−visual media	104.2	106.7	0.1	+2.5
Information and communication	102.5	107.6	0.1	+4.9
Other social operations	159.5	156.0	0.2	−2.2
Energy	33.0	40.6	−	+23.0
Euratom nuclear safeguards	16.0	16.4	−	+2.5
Environment	140.5	178.5	0.2	+27.0
Consumer protection	20.9	23.9	−	+14.2
Aid for reconstruction	3.0	2.2	−	−24.9
Internal market	157.3	152.2	0.2	−3.2
Industry	84.1	92.0	0.1	+9.4
Employment market and innovation	191.0	209.3	0.2	+9.5
Statistical information	29.8	30.7	−	+3.1
Trans−European networks	559.9	585.2	0.6	+4.5
Co−operation − justice/home affairs	25.8	27.0	−	+4.8
Measures to combat fraud	5.4	6.6	−	+22.2
TOTAL 3	5,764.5	5,861.6	6.0	+1.7
4. EXTERNAL ACTION				
Food and humanitarian aid	855.1	835.9	0.9	−2.2
Co−operation − Asia	440.8	438.5	0.5	−0.5
Co−operation − Latin America	299.1	314.1	0.3	+5.0
Co−operation − southern Africa	127.5	127.5	0.1	0
Co−operation − Mediterranean countries	1,148.7	1,094.0	1.1	−4.8
Co−operation − central/eastern Europe	1,124.8	1,444.4	1.5	+28.4
Co−operation − former Soviet Union	547.0	485.9	0.5	−11.2
Co−operation − former Yugoslavia	259.0	251.0	0.3	−3.1
EBRD	33.8	33.8	−	0
Other co−operation measures	373.8	359.7	0.4	−3.8
Human rights and democracy	97.4	98.0	0.1	+0.6
International fisheries agreements	295.7	283.7	0.3	−4.1
Other external aspects	88.1	111.5	0.1	+26.6
Common foreign and security policy	30.0	30.0	−	0
TOTAL 4	5,720.8	5,907.8	6.1	+3.3

Table 1: (Contd)

	1998 Budget (m ECU)	1999 Budget (m euros)	1999 Budget (% of total)	% Change 1999 over 1998
5. ADMINISTRATION				
Commission	2,377.5	2,425.4	2.5	+2.0
Other Institutions	1,660.3	1,579.3	1.6	–4.9
Pensions	466.8	497.6	0.5	+6.6
TOTAL 5	4,504.7	4,502.3	4.6	–0.1
6. RESERVES				
Monetary reserve	500.0	500.0	0.5	0
Guarantee reserve	338.0	346.0	0.3	+2.4
Emergency aid reserve	338.0	346.0	0.3	+2.4
TOTAL 6	1,176.0	1,192.0	1.2	+1.4
7. COMPENSATION				
Compensation	99.0	–	–	–100.0
TOTAL 7	99.0	–	–	–100.0
TOTAL APPROPRIATIONS FOR COMMITMENT	90,663.0	96,928.7	100.0	+6.9
of which:				
Compulsory	41,924.3	42,319.0	43.7	+0.9
Non–compulsory	48,738.7	54,609.7	56.3	+12.1
TOTAL APPROPRIATIONS FOR PAYMENTS	83,529.2	85,557.7	100.0	+2.4
of which :				
Compulsory	41,988.5	42,393.4	49.5	+1.0
Non–compulsory	41,540.7	43,164.3	50.5	+3.9

Source: Commission (1999) *General Report on the Activities of the European Union in 1998* (Luxembourg: CEC), Table 23, pp. 365–6.

Table 2 : Budget Revenue (% of Total)

	1998 (Outturns)	1999 (Estimates)
VAT	38.3	34.9
Customs duties	15.8	15.2
GNP-based own resources	40.3	45.1
Agricultural levies	1.3	1.2
Sugar and isoglucose levies	1.2	1.2
Budget balance from previous years	2.3	1.6
Other	0.8	0.8
Actually assigned own resources (%GDP)	1.130	1.090
Maximum assigned own resources (%GDP)	1.260	1.270

Source: Commission (1999) *General Report on the Activities of the European Union in 1998* (Luxembourg: CEC), Table 22, p. 362.

only has the powers to investigate the activities of the Commission. However, difficulties continued, and the year ended with calls in the Parliament for the resignations of two Commissioners (Marín and Cresson).

The debate on the financial aspects of *Agenda 2000* (the 2000–06 financial perspective) continued. The Commission presented detailed proposals in March. These respected the current 1.27 per cent (of GNP) ceiling and anticipated that it would not be reached until 2006 (1.13 per cent for current policies in Member States, 0.11 per cent to fund enlargement and 0.03 per cent to provide a 'margin of manoeuvre'); expenditure would initially rise in 2000–01 but then fall back. This met with contradictory reactions: Germany and the other main net-contributor states (Austria, Sweden and the Netherlands) accepted this in the main and were more interested in the prospect of a general 'corrective mechanism'; Spain, on the other hand, opposed the setting of a ceiling so early, given the unpredictable costs of enlargement.

In October, the Commission presented its report on the reform of the 'own resource' system. Three options (which are not mutually exclusive) were identified:

(1) A more 'unified and simplified' system, involving basing own resources mainly or completely on Member States' GNP (and abandoning other own resources). The existing correction mechanism could be eliminated.
(2) A ceiling on Member States' net contribution (0.2–0.4 per cent of GNP), made effective by the introduction of a generalized correction mechanism.
(3) A 'correction on the expenditure side', specifically through the introduction of EU–Member State co-financing of parts of the CAP.

The response from Member States was predictable with, for example, Britain opposing (1) and France (3).

The Commission's *Preliminary Draft Budget for 1999* envisaged only a modest increase over 1998, with commitment appropriations increasing by 6.5 per cent (to 96.9bn euros) and payments by 3.4 per cent (to 86.35bn euros), mostly accounted for by the structural funds with increases elsewhere averaging just 0.5 per cent. The draft budget – at 1.11 per cent of GNP – was 13bn euros below the own resources ceiling (1.27 per cent). The Council consequently made only modest cuts (of approximately 400m euros) but the Parliament substantially increased the budget to 98.6bn/89.6bn euros (commitments/payments); this was partly due to a 'strategic reserve', inserted by the Parliament as a negotiating tool in the 2000–06 financial perspectives debate. However, the Parliament, dropped its reserve in return for a declaration that there would be some flexibility in the interinstitutional agreement on the new financial perspective, the Council accepted some of the Parliament's amendments and a budget was finally adopted of 96.9bn euros (commitments) and 85.5bn euros (payments). Perhaps more importantly, the 1999 budget introduced two new elements: it was the first budget to be denominated in euros; and it was accompanied by a declaration which could significantly enhance the Parliament's role in the determination of compulsory expenditure.

The value of loans granted by the European Investment Bank (EIB) was 29.5bn ECU in 1998 (an increase of 13 per cent on 1997), of which 25.1bn ECU was advanced within the EU and the rest externally. Germany's share continued to increase (to 17.5 per cent), followed by Italy (15 per cent) and Spain, the UK and France (around 10 per cent each). The loans within the EU were provided for regional development (18.1bn ECU), trans-European networks (8.2bn ECU), environmental projects (6.2bn ECU), industry and services (4.6bn ECU), SMEs (2.4bn ECU) and energy projects (2.2bn ECU). (The total exceeds 25.1bn ECU because some projects fall into two categories.)

IV. Agriculture and Fisheries

Agriculture

The efforts to reform the CAP in the context of *Agenda 2000* continued. The Commission's proposals were finalized in March and, basically, sought to reduce guaranteed prices but increase (compensatory) direct support for farmers. Prices would fall for cereals (by 20 per cent), beef (30 per cent, in three phases) and dairy products (15 per cent in four stages). As part of or in addition to the main reform package, the Commission proposed new or revised policies in 1998 for:

- tobacco (January): the new policy was designed to improve the quality but reduce the quantity produced;
- olive oil (February): the new measures should combat the structural surpluses and fraud in this sector;
- wine (July): the focus here is not so much on quantitative restrictions but on improving quality.

The general *Agenda 2000* reform package met with the usual barrage of criticism in the Council and from agricultural organizations. The option of co-financing agricultural policy by the EU and its Member States – strongly opposed by France, Spain and the other cohesion countries – was perhaps the most controversial element of the debate. The reform of the olive oil sector was approved on a transitional basis until October 2001 (with definitive reforms to become effective thereafter) and a broadly similar arrangement was agreed for tobacco from 1999. However, negotiations over reforming the wine sector will continue as part of the negotiations of the overall *Agenda 2000* agricultural package.

The BSE saga appeared concluded in 1998 (at least for the British). Early in the year, the Commission proposed lifting the embargo on beef from certified BSE-free herds originating in Northern Ireland. This was approved by the Council in March and implemented in June. Then, in November, backed by ten Member States (but with four abstaining and Germany voting against), the Commission introduced measures to allow the (gradual) resumption of beef exports from the whole of the UK (but only de-boned beef from animals born after 1 August 1996, and after thorough checking by EU inspectors of the registration system and other controls), thereby effectively bringing the ban on UK beef exports to an end. This should become effective in 1999. The Commission's proposal to relax its decision to ban specified (beef-related) risk material fared less well and a decision was postponed. Towards the end of the year, concern began to be expressed about BSE in Portugal, culminating in Spain introducing an embargo on Portuguese beef and veal and the Commission introducing emergency measures (in November).

The 1998–99 price package put forward by the Commission amounted essentially to a continuation of the 1997–98 provisions. There were changes across a range of sectors (hemp, beef, wine, arable crops and sugar) but these were sufficiently minor to allow the package to survive the June Council more or less intact (it was approved by majority – only France and the Netherlands voting against).

The arrival of the euro heralded the beginning of the end of the agrimonetary system at the end of the year: 'green currencies' were abolished for all 15 Member States and a (simplified) compensation system retained on a transitional basis for the Euro-11 and on a diminishing basis for the four non-Euro-zone countries (disappearing completely in 2002). This will lead to significant savings, estimated at 2.7bn ECU over the 1999–2002 period.

Finally, the row over the 'banana regime' continued. The Commission's proposed reforms in response to the WTO's finding (against the EU) were considered inadequate by the US and the Latin American producer countries, and the year ended with the Americans publishing a list of EU products which would be subject to retaliatory customs duties from March 1999.

Fisheries

A number of significant conservation measures were introduced in 1998:

• In March, total allowable catches (TACs) and national quotas were introduced for the first time, as a precautionary measure, for six fish stocks in the North Sea: anglerfish; dab and flounder; lemon sole; megrim; skate and ray; and turbot.

- In June, the Council finally decided, by majority vote, to ban the use of driftnets by the end of 2001 (except for in the Baltic Sea). An aid package was also agreed for the affected fishermen (which did not discourage some French fishermen from appealing to the ECJ).
- In July, the Commission announced aid of 39.4m ECU for the introduction of satellite surveillance systems and the study of the use of new technologies to improve monitoring of fishing activities.

However, the Commission's analysis in February of the performance of the monitoring system introduced in 1993 concluded that even more urgent action was required. The Commission therefore put forward a three-year action plan to improve and extend the scope of monitoring, in particular after catches have been landed right up to the final phase of marketing. This was accepted by the Council (in a modified form) in December.

The TACs and quotas proposed for 1999 involved some reductions but the Commission argued that these would, for most species, not introduce further constraints on fishermen because many catches were below quota in 1998. As happened in 1997, the December Council partially offset the proposed cuts, but the end result was not too far from the Commission's original proposals. In fact, the main disagreement centred on bluefin tuna from the Mediterranean, for which the EU was allocating quotas for the first time. Indeed, the Italians and Greeks voted against the final compromise allocation, despite the fact that they received a higher quota than they would have got without EU involvement. This was because they had incurred penalties due to past overfishing which, in a spirit of 'solidarity' that some Member States found objectionable, the EU had partly transferred to France, Spain and Portugal.

V. Social Policy

In April, the Commission adopted a three-year *Social Action Programme for 1998–2000* which placed the issue of employment at the centre of social policy. It highlighted three areas: jobs, skills and mobility; the changing world of work; and the development of an inclusive society; and emphasized the external dimension of social policy, especially with regard to enlargement. The programme included a range of specific proposals in areas such as the modernization of the organization of work, increasing adaptability, embracing the information society, and guaranteeing health and safety in the workplace.

The Commission also unveiled plans for a major reform of the European Social Fund (ESF) to make it – in effect – the financial arm of the EU's strategy for employment. As such its activities should reflect the national action plans of Member States and the EU's annual guidelines on employment. Its central objective should be to facilitate the reform of labour market policies and practices through:

- setting up active labour market policies;
- combating social exclusion;
- promoting equal opportunities and participation of women in the labour market;
- developing a system of lifelong education and training;
- encouraging adaptability, innovation, entrepreneurship and job creation.

While pursuing the above, the ESF is expected to focus on local development and projects in particular.

There was extended discussion during the year of the EU's efforts to promote equal opportunities for men and women. Three reports were published which essentially identified substantial progress but emphasized that much still needed to be done, and an informal Social Policy Council was devoted to the subject in July. The third report adopted 'gender mainstreaming' as its guiding principle. Finally, in May, the Commission proposed a five-year programme (2000–04) to combat violence against women and children (Daphne) with an annual budget of 5m ECU. This is intended to promote the exchange of information, best practice and co-operation at the EU level, and to raise public awareness.

VI. Environmental Policy

In 1998, the main general development in environmental policy was the growing recognition of the need to take environmental concerns into account in other policy areas. The European Council in June identified transport, energy and agriculture as the three areas that should initially begin to do this. In fact, there had already been a joint Environment/Transport Council in April. This marked an important first step, advocating an integrated approach and indicating some priorities, but it was criticized for not making any specific commitments.

As a first step towards implementing the agreement reached at the December 1997 Kyoto conference on climate change, the EU signed the Kyoto Protocol in April, thereby committing itself to an 8 per cent reduction in emissions of six greenhouse gases by the 2008–12 period. The Commission adopted a communication in June containing proposals as to how the EU should proceed to meet this target but, not surprisingly, the key sticking point was the sharing out of the reductions amongst the Member States which was agreed only with difficulty. Policy in this area was dominated in the second half of the year by the fourth conference on climate change at Buenos Aires in November (and the preparations for it). However, the conference was beset by disagreements and was widely condemned as producing little of substance. Nevertheless, the policy process continues and the year closed with a lengthy debate on climate change in the Environment Council.

The Auto-Oil programme, intended to reduce air pollution caused by road vehicles significantly by 2010, made some progress in 1998. Two directives were adopted in September relating firstly, to emissions from cars and light commercial vehicles and, secondly, to the quality of petrol and diesel fuels; these directives set binding standards for fuel quality and limit values for polluting emissions. A common position was also agreed in the Council in December on a third directive on emissions from diesel-engine heavy commercial vehicles.

The LIFE programme – the EU's financial instrument for the environment – funded 201 projects in 1998, providing co-funding totalling 96.6m ECU. The funds were divided more or less equally between LIFE-Environment (the incorporation of environmental concerns into industrial and land-planning activities) and LIFE-Nature (nature conservation). In December, the Commission proposed LIFE III for the 2000–04 period which would have a total budget of 613m ECU. A third strand is proposed, LIFE-Third Countries, to co-fund technical assistance and environmental demonstration projects in third countries.

The four-year transition period during which Austria, Finland and Sweden were allowed to maintain their higher environmental and health standards ended on 31 December. However, the Commission was able to report that, in many cases, the EU had 'caught up' or had reached an agreement to do so in the future; where this was not so, it was agreed that a two-year extension could be granted on a case-by-case basis.

More negatively, the year was punctuated (like 1997) by frequent infringement proceedings, initiated by the Commission across a number of areas; all Member States failed to transpose at least some EU environmental measures into national legislation. Finally, the proposal for a CO_2/ Energy Tax remained firmly blocked in the Council.

References

Agence Europe (1998) *Europe Documents*, No. 2090/2091, 10 June.
Agence Europe (1998) *Europe Documents*, No. 2093, 17 June.
Agence Europe (1998) *Europe Documents*, No. 2101, 16 October.
Agence Europe (1998) *Europe Documents*, No. 2116, 23 December.

Journal of Common Market Studies

Volume 37, Annual Review
September 1999

External Policy Developments

DAVID ALLEN

and

MICHAEL SMITH

Loughborough University

I. General Themes

Introduction

1998 began and ended with the EU divided once again over an appropriate response to the activities of Saddam Hussein. It was this issue that presented some difficulties for the British, as they were forced to juggle their special relationship with the United States with their Presidency of the EU Council in the first half of the year. In Former Yugoslavia (FYR), Kosovo began to dominate the agenda and, as the EU Member States and the US worked uneasily together on this issue, they found themselves, at the same time, embroiled in a series of trade disputes with one another. Little real progress was made with the prepara-tions for implementing the Common Foreign and Security Policy (CFSP) provisions of the Treaty of Amsterdam in anticipation of its ratification. However, late in the year, British proposals for giving the EU a more effective defence dimension were seen by some as a significant breakthrough.

On the institutional front, the European Council considered proposals to improve the working of the General Affairs Council (GAC), including one to distinguish more clearly between the overall EU co-ordinating role of the GAC and its specialist management of relations with third countries. It was also suggested that the troika might relieve the Council as a whole of the increasingly burdensome task of participation in the numerous bilateral and multilateral political dialogues to which the EU is now committed.

In July, the European Commission convened a meeting of all its heads of overseas delegations, apparently to discuss the external representation of the euro, but also clearly to further its overall ambitions for its external services. The Commission never ceases to point out that it has the fourth largest network of overseas representatives in the EU – a comparison which is usually dismissed as irrelevant by the larger Member States, who show no great enthusiasm for transferring the work of their foreign ministries to the Commission. Indeed, the Commission is also under some pressure, internally and from the Member States, to distinguish better between its policy-making and policy-implementation procedures. The establishment of a Project Management Service was viewed with some trepidation by officials in DGVIII, who were concerned that they might become isolated from policy-makers.

At the end of the year, the Commission was represented in 123 countries and five international organizations. There are currently 165 foreign missions in Brussels accredited to the European Communities, with the Bosnian and Herzegovinian head of mission finally being given the rank of that country's first ever ambassador to the EC. In 1998 the Commission downgraded its Suriname delegation to an office and reorganized its offices in Antigua and Barbuda, Tonga and Vanuatu.

Foreign and Security Policy

On balance, the Member States would probably view 1998 as a year of cautious progress for the CFSP. While there were once again differences on Iraq and Turkey, limited progress was made on China, Algeria, the Middle East, Iran and on a number of aspects of policy towards the Former Yugoslavia. No great institutional decisions were taken, although again some progress was made towards establishing the participants in the proposed Policy Planning and Early Warning Unit. It was agreed that this would consist of 20 A-grade officials, 15 of whom would be drawn from the Member States, three from the Council Secretariat and one each from the Commission and Western European Union (WEU). No agreement was reached on the appointment of the new Secretary-General of the Council and High Representative for the CFSP, or indeed how the person who is eventually appointed will relate to the Council Presidency, the Special EU Envoys, WEU or the Council Secretariat. But it was at least established that the person in question would have a 'strong political personality'.

During 1998 the EU adopted 20 joint actions and defined 22 common positions, as well as issuing over 100 declarations. Under the British Presidency, the EU adopted a code of conduct for the export of arms from the EU. Although criticized by a number of NGOs, the Anglo-French inspired code is designed to ensure that EU arms exporters share information with one another and to prevent them either undermining or exploiting each others' individual arms export decisions. In anticipation of the ratification of the Treaty of Amsterdam in 1999, the EU agreed that the first common strategy would be towards Russia and that others would concern relations with the Ukraine, the western Balkans and the Mediterranean. The joint actions included ten towards the former Yugoslavia (three relating to Bosnia, five to FYR and one to Albania), one on the Middle East peace process, three on Africa and six on various aspects of arms control including the proliferation of small arms, land mines (the EU no longer exports land mines and in 1998 allocated 50m ECU for their continuing clearance) and the proliferation of nuclear weapons (the EU continues to try to persuade states that are not yet party to the Non-proliferation Treaty (NPT) that they should take part in the 2000 NPT review conference). The common positions related to former Yugoslavia (eight), Belarus (one), Asia (five) and Africa (six). Details of the numerous declarations on almost every conceivable international issue can be found in the detailed reports issued by the two 1998 Council Presidencies (the UK and Austria) and in the European Commission's *1998 General Report on the Activities of the European Union* (points 676–87).

The highlights of the year are probably the first attempt to mark the EU's concern about developments in Algeria, the renewed attempt to fill the vacuum in the Middle East peace process caused by the domestic and judicial distraction of President Clinton, the reopening of the dialogue with Iran and agreement on a broader approach to relations with China. The EU continued to make use of its special envoys to the Middle East, Central Africa and the Balkans (Wolfgang Petritsch being appointed as the EU's special envoy for Kosovo), and of the long-established troika of past, present and future Presidency representatives. The British government, during its Presidency, did much to try to extend its own concept of an ethical foreign policy to the EU level. This involved a new emphasis on the promotion of respect for human rights, democratic principles, the rule of law and good governance in all the EU's external dealings – especially those with African countries. The British Presidency was, on occasions, hampered by the concern of other Member States that the British position, on issues such as Iraq, was isolated in its close relationship to that of the United States. Commissioner Van den Broek on one occasion accused the British of 'neglecting their duties in pursuit of their own national objectives!'

Perhaps the most interesting development of the year came during the Austrian Presidency, when the British Prime Minister, Tony Blair, launched his defence initiative at an Anglo–French bilateral meeting in St Malo. In proposing that the EU should, indeed, develop a defence dimension (within NATO and courtesy of the Combined Joint Task Force (CJTF) concept). Blair appeared to be dropping previous British objections to such a development and, in so doing, he was enthusiastically supported by the French. While some accused the British of merely seeking a distraction from EMU and of highlighting an issue on which they could demonstrate 'leadership' within the EU, others were more willing to accept that this did represent a major new initiative. In any case, the first ever meeting of EU defence ministers was convened (albeit on an ad hoc basis) in Vienna in early November. Following this meeting, there was much speculation about whether defence would be integrated into the second (CFSP) pillar or form the basis of a separate fourth pillar of the EU Treaty. On the other hand, several British firms, by deciding either to merge with one another or to co-operate with the US, did much to undermine government efforts to create a European armaments industry capable of rivalling the US.

On the institutional front, we drew attention last year to the process of 'Brusselsization', by which the Member States, anxious to resist the Commission's ambitions to create a European foreign service, have begun more seriously to develop their joint activity in Brussels. The make-up of the new planning cell, dominated as it is by officials drawn from the Member States, will enhance this development, as will the various co-operative schemes proposed in 1998 by national foreign ministries. Britain and France, for example, seem prepared to reverse many years of rivalry in Africa, in order to gain the advantages of co-operation in their previous privileged spheres of influence. Similarly, plans to station deputy political directors in Brussels and more general plans by national foreign ministries to work more closely together would appear to be building up the potential for a clash of external competence between the Commission and the Member States. It will be interesting to see how the new Commission President chooses to reorganize the Commission for handling external relations. The pressure from the Member States to reform the practices of the Commission might just backfire on them if a revitalized and more independent body evolves from the crisis. A European Commission, relieved of some of the burdens of implementation and better co-ordinated by one senior external relations Commissioner, might prove to be a more effective participant in the European foreign policy process than the Member States might desire.

External Trade and the Common Commercial Policy

The EU's external trade relations during 1998 were dominated increasingly by the effects of the Asian and wider financial crises. The collapse of currencies first in the Pacific Rim, then in Latin America and Russia, meant that the international economic environment was increasingly unstable, and that the dangers of trade imbalances and consequent protectionist pressures were bound to grow. Although 1998 saw EC external trade in surplus, by the end of the year there were worrying trends towards surges in imports in commodities such as steel and products such as automobiles. This did not mean, though, that there were no moves towards further international trade reform; in previous years the EC had increasingly asserted itself in the shaping of the international trade agenda, and 1998 presented further opportunities for such activism. Meanwhile, the internal politics of EC trade policies were apparent in a number of highly sensitive sectors.

At the level of the multilateral system, and particularly the World Trade Organization (WTO), the key formal focus was the 50th anniversary of the General Agreement on Tariffs and Trade (GATT) in May, and the accompanying ministerial meeting. For some time, Sir Leon Brittan, the EC's Commissioner for External Trade Relations, had been suggesting a new round of trade negotiations (the so-called Millennium Round). The Americans, however, were less enthusiastic, preferring sectoral to comprehensive negotiations; other groups, such as the Cairns Group of agricultural exporting countries, harboured deep suspicions about the EC's willingness to negotiate on agricultural issues. Nonetheless, the ministerial meeting and a subsequent meeting of the 'Quad Group' (the USA, the EC, Japan and Canada) gave impetus to the preparations for a new round, with the emphasis on a comprehensive approach. A number of significant sectoral negotiations continued or were initiated during 1998: for example, in the areas of information technology trade (building on the 1997 Information Technology Agreement), environment and development (where the Community proposed a set of comprehensive studies) and electronic commerce or 'e-commerce', where the Community was in the forefront of proposing a WTO action plan.

The Community was also active in putting forward ideas on the development of the WTO's dispute settlement process; something of an irony in the light of the fact that disputes, particularly between the Community and the US, were at times seen as threatening the entire multilateral system. Brussels in general supported the candidacies of both China and Russia for WTO membership, although, as with other items on the trade agenda, these were put in a new perspective by the financial crises in the global economy. Finally, the Community found itself engaged in the early stages of the search for a successor to Renato Ruggiero as Director-General of the WTO.

The key area in the development of Community policies and instruments was that of anti-dumping. Always a matter of contention, this policy area was thrown into harsher relief by the impact of the Asian crisis in particular, which led to important shifts in the terms of trade for products such as steel. Early in 1998, the French proposed a reform of the Community's procedures to establish an independent agency for anti-dumping investigations; this met with a less than enthusiastic response from free-trading members of the Community who saw it as a potentially protectionist device. During the year, the Community published 24 notices of initiation of anti-dumping proceedings. It made definitive 11 sets of provisional measures, and it imposed provisional duties in a further 12 cases. The most persistent *cause célèbre* in anti-dumping, though, was one that had emerged during 1997: the attempts to impose anti-dumping penalties on the suppliers of unbleached cotton. Previously, the Commission had imposed provisional anti-dumping duties on imports of this material despite opposition from the majority of Member States, who had then overturned attempts to make the duties definitive. During spring 1998, the Commission again ignored its advisory committee and proceeded to impose provisional duties of up to 32.5 per cent on imports. Once again, when it came to making the duties definitive six months later, the majority of Member States in the Council of Ministers came out against it, despite attempts to buy some off by, for example, leaving Turkey off the list of those to be punished. In the meantime, India – one of the targets – had brought the case to the notice of the WTO. Besides this major area of contention, by the autumn there was pressure from EC producers to investigate imports of various steel products. There were also a number of 'examination procedures' initiated under the Community's Trade Barriers Regulation, the most exotic of which related to the transhipment of swordfish in Chile!

Elsewhere, the Community continued to try to systematize a number of areas of its external relations. Efforts to enhance customs co-operation continued under the 'Customs 2000' programme, including a path-breaking agreement with Hong Kong. The growth of a network of mutual recognition agreements for conformity assessment continued rapidly: new agreements were initialled, signed or concluded with Canada, the USA, Australia and New Zealand. As in 1997, the development of greater Community co-ordination in export credit featured on the agenda: in 1998, there were also moves to bring Community practices in line with the Organization for Economic Co-operation and Development (OECD) Consolidated Arrangement on Official Export Credits.

Development Co-operation Policy

The most important event of the year was undoubtedly the opening of negotiations between the EU and the African, Caribbean and Pacific (ACP) countries for a new agreement to replace the Lomé Convention after the year 2000. The EU, under pressure from the WTO, and aware of the fact that the successive Lomé regimes have not really achieved their objectives *vis-à-vis* the development of the ACP countries, is keen to negotiate a new 'partnership'. The stated objective is a series of interregional free trade agreements designed to combine a political dialogue on issues such as good governance and conditionality, with free trade arrangements aimed at eventually (by 2015) integrating the ACP countries into the global economy. While the EU accepts the need for continued development assistance, it is keen to focus it more specifically on the problems of poverty eradication and economic adjustment. It has conceded, though, that those very poor states, which do not feel that they can yet contemplate an equal partnership with the EU within a free trade regime, may, if they wish, continue with traditional arrangements that will leave them no worse off than before.

The ACP response was not wholly enthusiastic. They have argued that the Lomé arrangements need to be improved in order to offset the fall in Africa's share of EU imports from 11 per cent in 1965 to just 4.35 per cent in 1997, rather than dismantled. And they are uncertain about both the feasibility and desirability of being 'grouped' into regions (the EU has proposed east, west, south and central Africa, Nigeria, the Caribbean and the Pacific as suitable 'partners'). Many of them fear the conditionality that is built in and perceive the EU proposals to be more about opening up Africa for the EU than the EU for Africa. The negotiations clearly have a long way to go, but the EU seems determined to bring about a transformation of its relations with the Lomé states. This desire for change arises partly because of the EU's recent negative experiences in the WTO with some aspects of the present agreement and partly because of the importance attached to the evolving relationships with eastern Europe, the former Soviet Union and the Mediterranean. Many of the NGOs concerned with Lomé claim that it is being squeezed of funds because of the costs involved in the *Agenda 2000* programme and the planned increases in aid to the EU's more direct neighbours. Cuba's search for membership of Lomé, or whatever replaces it, took a further step forward during the year when it was given 'observer status' at the negotiations discussed above.

The EU's development and humanitarian programmes both came under quite strong attack during 1998. A series of scandals and instances of incompetence, highlighted by protests from a number of NGOs and by an adverse report from the Court of Auditors, cast doubt on the actions of individual Commission employees and consultants, on the EU's implementation practices and on its financial procedures. The European Community Humanitarian Office (ECHO) came under particular attack, but there was much general criticism of the EU's management. In its defence, the Commission highlighted both the tacit complicity of the Member States in some of the practices under scrutiny and its critical lack of staff. ECHO, for instance, has just 108 full-time officials and 80 fieldworkers but has been responsible for spending some 3.8bn ECU since 1992. In 1998 alone, ECHO was responsible for dispersing 517m ECU worth of humanitarian aid to states in every continent. The bulk of this aid went to Former Yugoslavia (123.1m ECU), the Great Lakes region of Africa (76m ECU) and the former Soviet Union (33 m ECU).

More positively, the EU has been able to reach agreement with the United Nations and the World Bank to set up a joint steering group to co-ordinate their joint aid programmes, leaving just the US and Japan of the major aid givers outside such arrangements. The EU and the UN together account for aid worth over 8 bn ECU. The first instance of active EU–UN co-operation came with their joint scheme for the development of the Great Lakes region of Central Africa.

II. Regional Themes

EFTA, the EEA and Northern Europe

In general, relations with the European Free Trade Association (EFTA) and non-EU members of the European Economic Area (EEA) were quiet during 1998. An interesting feature was the development of a more active trade diplomacy by EFTA itself, leading to the conclusion of free trade agreements with Canada among others; an achievement not yet managed by the Community itself. The EEA Council met in June and September, on both occasions in Luxembourg, while the Joint Parliamentary Committee met in May (in Vaduz) and in November (in Luxembourg). Practical work focused still on the incorporation of the EC *acquis* into the EEA, with 650 instruments incorporated in the veterinary field alone. For Norway and Iceland, who are members not only of the EEA but also of the Schengen area for free movement, there was additional work to be done on the Schengen *acquis* and its development in the wake of the Amsterdam Treaty.

The most significant activity in respect of non-EU members was undoubtedly the final resolution of the long-running negotiations with Switzerland. When the Swiss had rejected not only an application for EU membership but also the prospect of EEA membership in 1992, this had left a 'gap' in the Community's external agreements. For several years, negotiations had proceeded on the key issues: freedom of movement and establishment, research, public procurement, agriculture, transport and mutual recognition of conformity assessment procedures. In early 1998, an apparent breakthrough was made on the thorniest issue, that of transport and especially of transit through Switzerland by large trucks. This did not mean instant agreement, since the agreement included provisions on road-pricing and lorry weights which were the subject of competing interests within the EU itself. By the autumn, most of the issues were sorted out, and the overall EU–Switzerland 'package' was finally approved by the Council of Ministers on 10 December – in time for it to be welcomed at the Vienna European Council and to form one of the major achievements of the Austrian Presidency. The agreement means that, within five years, Swiss and EU nationals will share freedom of movement and establishment; it also includes provision for Swiss participation in the Framework Five research programme, for phased increases in lorry tonnages on Swiss roads, and for an extension of the EU's 'open skies' regime to Switzerland.

Central Europe

Most of the EU's dealings with the countries of central Europe come under the heading of enlargement and are covered in the section by Christopher Preston (see his 'Enlargement Update', pp. 109–11, this issue). Nevertheless, there are one or two specific issues worth noting. Changes of government in Slovakia, where Vladimir Meciar was replaced by Mikulas Dzarinda, and in Romania, where Victor Ciorbea was forced to resign, have clearly eased those countries' relations with the EU. The coalition in Poland found itself divided over the management of EU business, in particular over a Commission suggestion that the central European applicants establish special units to handle EU funds within their finance ministries. In Poland, this caused a bureaucratic battle between the finance ministry and the Committee for European Integration (KIE). At stake is the Polish PHARE allocation for 1998 and 1999, as well as future payments due to run at 500m ECU per year from 2000. The problem has been exacerbated by the fact that the finance ministry is controlled by the Freedom Union (the junior partner in the governing coalition), while a member of the Christian National Union (part of the Solidarity Electoral Action, the dominant coalition partner) heads the KIE. Similar problems of relating central European governmental practice to that desired by the EU, are likely to proliferate in the next few years.

In 1998, the total PHARE budget for central Europe rose to 1.38bn ECU, of which 579m ECU million went to national programmes, 180m ECU to cross-border co-operation, 349bn ECU to multi-country programmes and 150m ECU to Former Yugoslavia. All PHARE activities in the applicant countries are now linked to the pre-accession requirements laid out in the accession partnerships, with 30 per cent of the aid going to institution-building and 70 per cent going to reduce sectoral, regional and structural imbalances. The money for institution-building is clearly going to be very important as the EU Commission seeks to transfer more and more of its implementation responsibilities to the countries involved.

The EU concluded some difficult negotiations with Poland over steel, following a dispute over Poland's import tariffs. The result is that Poland is to cut its tariffs, whilst at the same time restructuring the steel industry, so as to lose 40,000 of the 90,000 currently employed. It remains to be seen what impact this will have on the popularity of the EU and EU membership within Poland. The EU estimates that in central Europe as a whole, some 250,000 jobs in steel will have to go over the next ten years. The EU also agreed to lift its ban on Polish dairy products following a Polish agreement to limit its exports to the EU to production from just five of its dairy plants, creating in effect a two-class dairy industry – one for export to the EU and one, with lower health standards, for domestic consumption.

The EU engaged in a minor skirmish with the Czech Republic over the apparent dumping of EU apples the previous year, in which it threatened to retaliate against reduced Czech apple quotas by suspending preferential import tariffs on Czech pigment, poultry and fruit juice. The issue was reported in Czech newspapers as an example of the 'Empire striking back' and it is symptomatic of the EU's continued determination to protect its agricultural producers however insignificant the threat to their business. Perhaps more serious was the concern the EU voiced about growing evidence that Commission funds, specifically allocated to improve nuclear safety, were in fact being used to upgrade rather than decommission nuclear plants which have been identified as unsafe, i.e. the Bohunice plant in Slovakia, and the Ignalina plant in Lithuania.

Russia and the Soviet Successor States

The EU made some progress in 1998 in developing its network of relations with those former Soviet states that are not presently being considered for EU membership. A new Partnership and Co-operation Agreement (PCA) was signed with Turkmenistan, and the first co-operation councils under similar agreements were held between the EU and Russia, Ukraine and Moldova. There were two summits between the EU and Russia in Birmingham and in Vienna (where Yevgenni Primakov stood in for an incapacitated Boris Yeltsin). A highlight of the Birmingham summit was the removal of Russia from the list of countries classified as 'non-market economies'. This decision should make it ultimately easier for Russia to join the WTO. It should also make Russia less vulnerable to EU anti-dumping measures. However, during the year, a number of old and new trade disputes arose to complicate relations, in particular over EU carpets, Russian fertilizers and Siberian overflying charges. Nevertheless, the PCA was seen as a useful framework for getting down to substantive work in the first instance on Russian investment laws, accounting standards, environmental regulations and intellectual property laws.

The crisis in the Russian economy led to renewed calls within the EU for the taming of 'hyena capitalism', but there was also a clear resistance to what was seen as the danger of throwing 'bad money after good'. However, in December, for the first time since the early 1990s, the EU agreed to send 400m ECU worth of food aid to Russia. This policy was criticized by some aid organizations who claimed that it amounted to nothing more than French-inspired dumping of EU surpluses and that it would do nothing to encourage Russia to introduce the necessary agricultural reforms. The worsening situation in Russia also encouraged a major rethink by the EU of its TACIS programme, which in 1998 devoted some 500m ECU to the former Soviet states. The Commission decided that its new TACIS programme, to run from 2000–06, would be more focused on fewer, and therefore bigger, projects designed to enhance trade and development within a 'zone of stability'. Whereas since 1992 3bn ECU had been spread over 1000 individual projects, from 2000 onwards it was proposed to devote 4bn ECU to no more than 100 projects.

Relations between the EU and Belarus were disrupted in 1998 when the EU was forced to withdraw its ambassadors from Minsk when the government of Belarus violated the Vienna Convention on diplomatic relations by evicting the EU ambassadors from their residences in Drozdy. No further progress with a PCA was possible and, even though the EU ambassadors eventually returned to Minsk, officials from Belarus were denied visas for entry into the EU.

The EU held a summit with Ukraine in the course of which further microeconomic aid of 150m ECU was promised, but relations were soured a little by a dispute over the Ukrainian decision to ban the importation of used cars from the EU. Interestingly, this was at the insistence of the Korean car manufacturer Daewoo, who made it a condition of its investment in a $1.3 billion car plant in Ukraine. Ukraine's relationship with Poland was disturbed by Poland's imposition of border controls resulting from its agreements with the EU. The difficult question of the final shutdown of the remaining reactors at Chernobyl, which has bedevilled EU–Ukrainian relations for many years, remains unresolved.

Finally, as well as seeking to encourage conflict resolution in the Caucasus by pushing for regional co-operation, the EU (Hans Van den Broek and Ritt Bjerregaard for the Commission and John Prescott for the Council Presidency) also accepted an invitation for the second year running to attend the meeting of Heads of State and Government of the Council of Baltic Sea States (CBSS) which took place in Denmark in June.

The Mediterranean and the Middle East

This was an area of high activity in 1998, with the EU seeking to underpin its political objectives, formulated within the CFSP, with the economic power of the EC. The Barcelona process continued multilaterally in a variety of fora and an ad hoc meeting of foreign ministers (with neither the Palestinian Authority nor Israel present), attempted to prepare for the third formal meeting of EU–Mediterranean foreign ministers, scheduled for 1999. The EU is anxious to maintain some momentum, despite the intrusive and disruptive nature of so many of the disputes in the area. Within the EU, Member States like France and Spain are keen to pursue the notion of an area of security and co-operation in the Mediterranean to counterbalance the German-dominated concern for a similar focus in central Europe. The problem is that these are also the Member States most anxious to protect their domestic agricultural interests and this often makes the development of Euro–Mediterranean relationships difficult. Co-operation proceeded only very slowly, despite the EU's determination to inject momentum into the Middle East peace process. The full implementation of EU expenditure under the MEDA regulation, for which 941m ECU was allocated for 1998, was once again frustrated by Greek hostility towards giving approval to funds for Turkey. In retaliation, Turkey hardened its position on Cyprus and the question of its own inclusion in EU enlargement considerations and, rather ominously, threatened to unify with Turkish-occupied Cyprus. Turkey has already begun to station Turkish Cypriots in various Turkish embassies in EU Member States and to include Turkish Cypriots in its external delegations.

The EU also continued the development of its various bilateral links within the overall framework of the Barcelona process. With the opening of what will certainly be long drawn out talks with Syria, the EU has at least begun the process of negotiating Euro–Mediterranean association agreements with all participants. Admittedly progress in the talks with Egypt were frustrated by squabbles over rice, flowers, potatoes and orange juice, and contact with Algeria was limited to the visit of a troika of EU ministers, which failed to reach agreement over the question of either UN or EU inspection of alleged atrocity sites. Nevertheless, the EU has plugged away, and where agreements have been made as, for instance, with Israel or Turkey, the EU has sought to use the terms of those agreements to induce its partners to behave in accordance with them. Thus, pressure was placed on Turkey over its treatment of Kurds and retaliation in the shape of a ban on the importation of hazelnuts (strongly resisted by EU confectioners like Ferrero-Rocher!) was used to force the Turks to lift their own ban on EU beef.

Israel too was forced in the end to modify its obstructive behaviour over the development of the Palestinian Territories. Israel was required by the EU to change its negative approach towards the opening of an airport in Gaza and to stop interfering with the development of Palestinian trade. Furthermore, the EU, despite the strong resistance of Benjamin Netanyahu to its attempts to play a role in the peace process, rallied around Council President Robin Cook when he was snubbed by the Israeli government. Despite the Israeli bluster, the EU success-fully insisted that Israel halt its practice of exporting goods to the EU that originated in occupied territory or settlements that the EU did not recognize as part of Israel. For its part, the EU remained determined, both within the CFSP and via its economic policies, to build a role in the peace process around its substantial investment in the Palestinian Territories. The EU has been responsi-ble for over 50 per cent of all the aid sent to the Palestinians (1.68bn ECU between 1993 and 1997) and it believes that it therefore has a right to remind Israel and the US of their Oslo commitments with regard to the Palestinian Territories.

In Former Yugoslavia, despite the war clouds gathering over Kosovo, the EU also sought to bring its economic power to bear. Additional aid was granted to Albania, and, in Bosnia, the EU granted extra assistance to Republika Srpska following the acceptance by a new government of the Dayton peace accord. The Croatian government was persuaded by the EU to honour its obligations with regard to the return of refugees and offered further assistance as a reward. On the other hand, the situation in Kosovo led to increased EU sanctions against the Federal Republic of Yugoslavia, including the freezing of funds held abroad, the prohibition of new investment in Serbia, and a ban on flights by Yugoslav airlines between the FYR and the EU. It was a ban which, momentarily, caused the UK some embarrassment, when it seemed as if it could not be imposed for a year because of an agreement between the UK and Yugoslavia that preceded Britain's membership of the EU.

Further afield, the EU states remained divided over how best to respond to Saddam Hussein's continued intransigence, but they were able to agree in 1998 that the time had come to lift some of the restrictions on a dialogue with Iran that had been imposed at the time of the *Mykonos* verdict in Germany. Following the election of President Mohammad Khatami, and despite protests from the US, the EU agreed to send the troika (although there was a dispute with Iran about the appropriate level of representation) to Tehran and in return extracted reassurances from the Iranian government concerning the author, Salman Rushdie. When the dialogue was resumed, a number of important issues such as terrorism, Afghanistan and nuclear non-proliferation were on the agenda.

Africa

The EU once again failed to conclude the long-awaited trade agreement with South Africa despite the assurance that was given to Nelson Mandela when he attended the Cardiff European Council that a deal would be completed 'by the autumn at the latest'. By December an agreement was virtually in place but the EU refused to settle until South Africa was prepared to accept that port and sherry were trade marks that could only be applied to products produced within the EU. Despite the urgency that the South African elections in May 1999 gave to the proceedings, the EU saw this agreement as an important precedent for future arrangements with all the ACP countries and was therefore unwilling to concede further ground. South Africa has proved stubborn over its own import restrictions on textiles and car components, but generally it is the EU that has been castigated for its 'meanness', 'pettiness' and refusal to reconsider its original negotiating mandate during the four-year negotiations. Trade between the EU and South Africa is already worth 17bn ECU per year, with the EU taking 27 per cent of South Africa's exports and providing 43 per cent of its imports. If the present negotiations are finally completed in 1999, the EU will abolish tariffs on 94 per cent of all its imports from South Africa and South Africa will lift 86 per cent of its tariffs on EU imports. Despite the fact that their growing seasons do not coincide, the EU has refused to lift all protection against the import of certain South African agricultural products. During the year, South Africa's partial accession to the Lomé Convention came into force and South Africa received a further 125m ECU via the European Programme for Reconstruction and Development. The South Africans awarded contracts for arms purchases worth $5.2 billion to a number of EU suppliers, in part because the US has been slow to lift its weapons embargo that was imposed during the apartheid period.

Whilst developments in Nigeria, the Great Lakes Region, Angola, the Sudan and Guinea-Bissau were mainly dealt with by CFSP declarations, irregularities during the elections in Togo led the EU to threaten to suspend activities under the Lomé Convention (Togo receives some 130m ECU per year from the European Development Fund). This is only the second time that such a threat has been made (Nigeria is the other case). Observers were puzzled by this apparent inconsistency in the treatment of African states by the EU, and the ACP group as a whole were highly critical of such unilateral action.

Asia

The influence of the Asian financial crisis on the EU's external policies was pervasive. Its effects (or anticipated effects) for trade policy, the likelihood of radical shifts in the terms of trade, meant that the costs to the EU had to be calculated and the resulting pressures for protection to be managed. In the area of international financial policy, the Union had no choice but to link the crisis with the moves for 11 of its members to Stage 3 of EMU at the beginning of 1999. The euro would be put to an early test, and could also be presented at least partly as an alternative to the US dollar in turbulent financial times.

The most obvious early focus of attention was the planned second Asia–Europe Meeting (ASEM 2), to be held in London during April. The first meeting, in Bangkok, in March 1996, had taken place in an atmosphere where the Asian participants were conscious of their economic achievements and weight, and the EU was aware of the need to finesse issues such as that of human rights in the context of economic needs. The London meeting was different, in the sense that the EU was keen on reassuring Asian participants of its support – the phrase of the 'fair-weather-friends' was coined here – while the Asians were anxious that the EU's words should be backed up with some hard resources. Among the most tangible outcomes were the establishment of a 'trust fund' for Asian countries under the auspices of the World Bank, the setting up of a network of experts to work on financial reform, and the establishment of a 'vision group' to develop long-term plans for co-operation. In addition, an action plan for trade and investment was propounded, and a number of other meetings dealing with business issues took place over the year. For many observers, this still left the feeling that, despite all the figures showing that the EU and its citizens were doing as much in many areas as the Americans, there was a credibility gap in the EU's Asia strategy.

While the 'big picture' of economic crisis was largely handled through the ASEM process, the EU's relations with the Association of Southeast Asian Nations (ASEAN) tended to be more specific and focused more on political issues. The continuing issue of human rights in Burma (Myanmar) led the Council of Ministers to extend its common position of 1996, and with it the diplomatic and other sanctions taken against the regime in Rangoon. As a consequence, the EU–ASEAN Joint Committee supposed to meet under the Co-operation Agreement was postponed yet again, since the ASEAN members insisted on including Burma (now an ASEAN member). Links were maintained under the longer-standing arrangements whereby the troika and the Commission attended the ASEAN post-Ministerial Conference and the meeting of the ASEAN Regional Forum, both of which were held in Manila during July. Another cause for EU concern was the turbulence and instability in Indonesia that led to the replacement of the Suharto regime by President Habibie, which were considered in the context of the CFSP, along with issues such as East Timor, an area in which the EU has consistently been concerned. The ambassadors of the troika countries visited East Timor in June.

The EU was also associated with the elections held in Cambodia during July 1998. Indeed, 200 observers were sent, and significant financial and logistical support was provided. As a result, the EU observers declared the elections to be broadly free and fair – a judgement not shared by all of those in Cambodia or in the broader region. An important general issue of EU credibility was thereby raised, since one of the key activities in the CFSP has been precisely the authoritative evaluation of electoral processes in the post-Cold War era.

Relations with South Asia during 1998 contained the same kind of mixture as those with Southeast Asia: continuation of established contacts, such as those with the South Asian Association for Regional Co-operation (SAARC), further development of partnerships (for example through the signature of a co-operation agreement with Pakistan in April, and meetings with Indian and Sri Lankan leaderships), accompanied by specific conflicts and tensions. In partic-ular, the India–Pakistan confrontation over nuclear testing drew the attention of EU foreign ministers, who initially condemned the tests and later (in October) adopted a common position on non-proliferation and confidence-building. The CFSP was also engaged by the activities of the Taliban regime in Afghanistan, leading to the adoption of a common position on 26 January. Finally, in the area of trade policies, the EC's relations with India came under some strain. Partly this was the result of the long-running anti-dumping procedures related to unbleached cotton (see above); partly it reflected disputes over market access in India (particularly over car parts and investment in the automobile industry, where the EC referred its concerns to the WTO).

The year was a significant one in the development of relations between the EU and China. To a large extent, the tone was set by a new Commission Communication published in March ('Building a Comprehensive Partnership with China', *COM*(1998)181). This established five central priorities for EU policies: fostering the integration of China into the international community through political dialogue; supporting China's transition to an 'open society'; making China an integral part of the world economy; improving the effectiveness of European financing; and improving the EU's image. The publication of the Communication was closely followed by the first EU–China summit, held in London before ASEM 2; again, the final communiqué from this summit stressed the need for political dialogue and for Chinese entry into the WTO. It is notable that the new EU stance places less emphasis on the specification of Chinese human rights violations (for example) and more on the positive aspects of building partnership and democracy. In the spirit of the new partnership, the EU–China Joint Committee met in Brussels during June. In late October/early November Jacques Santer paid the first official visit by a Commission President to China since 1986.

Other parts of East Asia saw relatively little EU attention during 1998. Relations with Japan were centred on two formal events: the annual EU–Japan summit took place in January, when the primary focus was on the impact of the Asian crisis and the implied need for reform in Japan; and the theme continued at the EU–Japan ministerial meeting in October, where the EU put forward detailed proposals for deregulation including 200 specific reforms. Otherwise there was broad agreement in this context on political issues and on approaches to the Millennium Round of proposed trade negotiations. Taiwan concluded a new trade agreement with the Community in July, offering some concessions in the context of Taiwanese hopes for EU support in its application for WTO membership. In December, the Commission published a new Communication on relations with Seoul (*COM*(1998)714), full of good intentions about the development of a fuller partnership with Korea, now a member of the OECD. There was some friction over shipbuilding, given the fact that Korea's capacity in the industry now exceeds the capacity of the EU in total and that there are suspicions of subsidization. Finally, completing the circle on an earlier policy issue, the agreements providing for Euratom participation in the Korean Peninsular Energy Development Organization (KEDO) entered into force during September.

Latin America

Latin America, alongside Asia, is one of the key targets for the EU's interregional diplomacy, reflecting the desire not only for market access but also for a kind of 'parity' with the United States. During 1998, there were important developments in the EU's relations with the region, but also indications of the limitations to which they are subject. There is by now a well-established cycle of routine interregional contacts, which was maintained during 1998 with meetings with the San José Group, the Rio Group and the Andean Group of Latin American countries. The tone was generally positive, with the EU concerned to emphasize the need for progress on human rights issues and to explain the benefits of changes in its generalized system of preferences. During April, Sir Leon Brittan visited three Latin American countries – Argentina, Uruguay and Brazil – with the aim of garnering support for the proposed Millennium Round of trade negotiations, and (as some argued) of offsetting the United States' push for progress on the Free Trade Area of the Americas. In the longer term, it was agreed in all of the fora noted above that the EU and its partners in Latin America and the Caribbean should push on with preparations for an interregional summit, to be held in Brussels in June 1999. Such a summit should in principle form the centrepiece of a partnership such as that expressed in the ASEM (see above), but it may also suffer from the constraints already noted. Later in the year, the specific challenge posed by Hurricane Mitch and its impact on Central America led to a rapid response by the EU and to funding in the amount of 8.2m ECU for longer-term reconstruction.

The most significant development in group-to-group relations during 1998 was between the EU and MERCOSUR. For some years, there had been pressures and preparations for a new type of interregional agreement, in principle leading to a free trade area. Following the EU–MERCOSUR ministerial meeting in Panama in February, the Commission continued to put forward negotiating directives, and in July recommended that the Council authorize it to open negotiations. While the majority of the Commission favoured this step, it was significant that some Commissioners, including the Agriculture Commissioner, Franz Fischler, were opposed. Given that the opening of negotiations requires unanimity in the Council, this was not a good sign. Sure enough, the French, especially, opposed the proposals from the Commission, arguing that since a free trade area had to include at least 90 per cent of all trade between the regions, it would be impossible to insulate sensitive areas of agriculture from its effects. A study carried out by the Commission indicated that a free trade agreement could cost 14.3bn ECU in compensation to farmers for lost markets; given that the EU was starting on the fraught process of renegotiating the CAP in the autumn of 1998, the prospects for EU–MERCOSUR negotiations were not good at all. Indeed, the response of the MERCOSUR Heads of State and Government was instant and predictable: any negotiation that excluded major areas of agriculture would not be worthwhile.

More substantial results could be reported from negotiations with Mexico, although a number of the same complications were present. In March 1998, the

Commission adopted proposed negotiating directives, and in July the interim agreement on trade and trade-related measures (negotiated during 1997) came into force. Meanwhile, in May, the Council had authorized the Commission to negotiate a 'trade liberalization agreement', to cover trade in goods and services, public procurement, capital movements, competition rules and matters of intellectual property. On 14 July, the first meeting took place of the EU–Mexico Joint Council, and already the atmosphere was one of negotiation, although the first formal negotiation session did not take place until November, in Mexico City. Whereas with MERCOSUR, agriculture is a major obstacle to agreement, with Mexico it is a relatively minor issue; in addition, both the EC and Mexico have important incentives to offset the predominance of the United States and the North American Free Trade Area (NAFTA) in Mexico's external trade.

The United States and Other Industrial Countries

The institutionalization of EU–US relations has occurred partly at the transatlantic level, and partly in the context provided by other international bodies. During early 1998, the focus was particularly on the transatlantic level: in March, Sir Leon Brittan launched his proposals for the establishment of a New Transatlantic Marketplace. These proposals embodied, among other ideas, the notion that trade in services across the Atlantic could be totally free, and that trade in industrial goods could equally be subject to sweeping cuts in tariffs. Alongside this, existing moves towards mutual recognition in a variety of areas could be accelerated, and a process of continual improvement could be introduced. In essence, this plan drew upon the established infrastructure of the New Transatlantic Agenda, The Transatlantic Action Plan and the Transatlantic Business Dialogue, which had been set up in 1995. But in many ways it went further in proposing an integrated economic area encompassing the enlarging EU and the USA, and offering an estimated $166 billion of trade gains. Significantly, though, the plan excluded agriculture and audio-visual products, both subject to fierce protectionist feelings on the part of the French and others.

A cautious welcome from the US administration could not conceal their frustration at these limitations or their awareness that Congress would not wear such an agreement, even if the White House could. A process of attrition during the spring and summer of 1998 meant that by the time of the EU–US summit in London in May, there could be agreement only on a more limited set of proposals, embodied in the Transatlantic Economic Partnership. The autumn of 1998 saw the development of an action plan around this idea, and particularly around a number of key issues: agriculture regulatory policy and biotechnology, intellectual property rights, government procurement, electronic commerce, services trade, standards and mutual recognition agreements, and what were called 'civil society issues' (the environment, labour standards).

Alongside this transatlantic process, there were a series of EU–US encounters in various multilateral institutions, most importantly, the Group of Seven industrial countries (G7) and the WTO, the two main arenas in which the financial and trading implications of the international economic turbulence took effect. If the EU had suffered from a certain credibility gap in the Asian crisis, the need to establish its future credentials – or those of 'Euroland' – was a significant part of discussions in the G7. Apart from their general importance, these discussions could not help but acquire an EU–US tinge. In many international fora, the Americans see the EU as having multiple representation, and as 1998 wore on, they began to make clear their view that EMU could not mean a massive increase in the numbers of European representatives at every table. While welcoming EMU in principle, as in other phases of European integration, the Americans reserved their right to point out its adverse implications.

At the same time as EMU approached, so did the prospect of a new European-sponsored round of trade negotiations (see above). Although the Clinton administration was reluctantly converted to the idea of a wide-ranging round during the summer of 1998, it seemed rather clear that trouble might be in store, especially as the effects of the Asian crisis were felt in sensitive US industries. The Americans felt, rightly or wrongly, that the EU needed to show that it would actively share the burden of absorbing Asian, Russian or other imports rather than putting up the shutters.

The attempts by the US Congress to impose sanctions through the use of extra-territorial legislation on those trading with or investing in Cuba, Iran or Libya had caused a great deal of friction in the EU–US relationship during 1996 and 1997. In a way, these frictions had demonstrated the capacity of the EU to stand up to US pressures, since by mobilizing the threat of counteractions through the WTO and by demonstrating solidarity, the EU and its Member States had brought the White House to the negotiating table. Through late 1997, the aim had been to move towards a resolution, or at least a suspension of the conflict, but there remained a significant risk of open hostilities, for example as the result of French oil companies' investments in Iran. By April 1998, a draft text existed on which negotiations between the Commission and the US administration continued; for some EU Member States, no progress was possible on such issues as the New Transatlantic Marketplace until the extra-territoriality issue was decided. The negotiations went on until the very last minute, against the deadline of the EU–US summit in May, but eventually a text was agreed.

This was not the end of the story, since the amendment of the US legislation was subject to Congressional approval (by no means a foregone conclusion), and some of it at least also depended upon definitions of what was or was not a qualifying investment for the purposes of the agreement. By the autumn, there was evidence that Congress was unwilling just to acquiesce in the process, and

President Clinton had (as in previous years) to waive parts of the legislation for another six months. In addition, further complications arose because some of the legislation applied at the sub-federal level, beyond the control of both the White House and Congress. The Community had been made aware of this issue by the existence of Massachusetts legislation excluding from public contracts those who dealt with Burma (Myanmar), and this state legislation itself was the subject of a running battle during 1998. The Commission itself was involved in the litigation, and, along with Japan, in a reference to the WTO. Eventually a US federal court overturned the law, but again this was not the end of the affair.

Trade disputes of the more traditional type claimed a great deal of attention in EU–US relations during 1998, although even these had novel aspects to them. The most threatening of the disputes, and the one that occupied the most time for negotiators on both sides of the Atlantic, was the conflict over the EC's regime for trade in bananas. The need to apply a Community-wide set of rules for trade in bananas, while also catering for the historical patterns of trade between some members of the EU and their former colonies, had led to a system in which a complex mixture of quotas, tariffs and licences was deployed. This had led to complaints from Central American banana producers – and more significantly, from the distributors who were predominantly American – that the regime was unfair and illegal. A WTO panel found it to be so, and, in 1998, the EC produced its proposals for change to make the regime 'WTO-legal'. From the moment its proposals became public, if not even before, US companies and the US government were convinced that they did little but dress up the existing illegal arrangements. As a result, the Americans spent most of the summer and autumn moving towards the imposition of sanctions on the EC, whilst the Community itself was arguing that the proposals had not been judged by the WTO. By November, the US had published a provisional list of sanctions to be imposed, and in December they narrowed this down to a definitive list to be imposed if the EC did nothing before 15 January 1999. Both sides claimed to be acting not only on behalf of their own interests, but also to protect the producers in Central America or the Caribbean, and also on behalf of the WTO itself, or rather the integrity of its dispute procedures.

Alongside the 'banana war', there was a set of other disputes or potential disputes centring on food or health issues. The long-running dispute over growth hormones in meat, which the EC had banned on health grounds, still festered. The WTO had found against the EC, but had allowed the Community to submit further scientific evidence, which some interpreted as giving Brussels years more to delay its compliance. Towards the end of the year, the EC banned antibiotics in a number of best-selling animal feeds – another possible recipe for conflict for the US, or at least US multinationals. For the longer term, it was also quite clear by the end of the year that the trade in genetically-modified organ-isms, or foods containing them, would be a major source of conflict, not only between the EU and the US but also within the EU itself as different interests made themselves felt. Since the Americans estimated those potential losses of trade through 'resistance' to genetically-modified products could add up to $200 million in 1998 alone, the stakes are considerable.

By the end of the year, it was also clear that the impact of the global financial crisis was beginning to make itself felt in EU–US relations. At the most general level, there was the pressure on the EU from Washington to 'open up' to imports of steel and other products from ailing economies (for example, Russia). This was resisted by the Commission, who were also alarmed at the increasingly protectionist attitude of steel producers and others in the USA. Such concerns, linked up with other issues in agricultural trade, or others mentioned earlier in textiles, to create a general impression that 1998 was only the start of further trade 'wars'. Not only this, but seemingly marginal issues, such as a proposed EC ban on aircraft using so-called 'hush kits', seemed likely to lead to retaliatory measures on the part of the US, to such an extent that Concorde could be banned from using US airports.

In addition to these (often far from) 'traditional' trade issues, EU–US relations reflected the impact of problems emerging from industrial restructuring and regulation. Some of these were of long standing: for example, the disputes associated with airline alliances and the allocation of air routes, which had raised issues of competition policy and also of EC transport policy competence, rumbled on during 1998. The French among others succumbed to the appeal of an 'open skies' agreement with the USA, while the British tried but failed to agree; in each case, the agreements were linked to approval of strategic alliances, between Air France, Delta and Continental on the one hand, and British Airways and American Airlines on the other. In turn, these alliances linked to issues such as the allocation of landing slots at major airports, which were again the subject of dispute between the Commission and Member States. Another industry engaged in frantic restructuring (or the emergence of any kind of structure) was what might be called the 'electronic marketplace', in which two issues had a specifically EU–US tinge. In the first place, projected EC legislation in the form of the Data Protection Directive, due for implementation in October 1998, threatened to withhold data from countries where it was held to be poorly protected, among them the USA, where protection is voluntary rather than statutory. Secondly, the need to provide a long-term structure for the manage-ment of the Internet, including the allocation and registration of domain names, led the Americans to propose a form of management which appeared to institutionalize their 'ownership' of the web. On both issues, negotiations continued through 1998; the former was still unresolved at the end of the year, while the latter had moved at least partly towards a balanced solution through the creation of a management body structured on a regional basis.

The restructuring of industries engaged in the provision of major services was accompanied in 1998 by moves towards restructuring some much more traditional producers. In the automobile sector, the creation of Daimler-Chrysler perpetuated a trend in which EU–US automobile manufacturing was becoming increasingly globalized (although in this case the EU company was the dominant partner). In another strategic industry, defence and aerospace, there were significant moves towards the consolidation of the EU industry, explicitly as the basis for competition with the Americans. In this case, though, there were important tensions between national priorities in the EU, the case for a European champion, and the desire for a transatlantic dimension as opposed to a 'fortress Europe'.

Beyond economic relations, there were important indications during 1998 that the tension between European and Atlantic priorities in security and defence issues was alive and kicking. The British Presidency in the first half of the year provided the spectacle of the country leading the CFSP engaged in a policy of bombing Iraq which was opposed by many other EU Member States. As the year wore on, the tensions over Kosovo again saw the difficulties inseparable from the disparity between the EU's security aspirations and the reality of its dependence on the USA. Finally, the tangled question of Cyprus saw the United States taking an active role in trying to bring the Turks and the Greeks together and, when that failed, they sought to 'encourage' the EU to find a way of accommodating the Turks in the moves towards enlargement. In each of these cases, the internal tensions in the EU combined with perceptions of external dependence on the USA to provide that peculiar mix of ambition and resignation which is central to transatlantic relations.

Journal of Common Market Studies

Volume 37, Annual Review
September 1999

EU Enlargement: Developments in 1998

CHRISTOPHER PRESTON
British Know How Fund for Poland

The EU's pre-accession strategy has been based on two broad principles. The first is to maintain, wherever possible, the inclusivity of the process: all applicants, regardless of their circumstances, retain a notional equality, and are offered the promise of full membership at some point in the future. The second is to differentiate between applicants on the basis of their progress towards meeting the 1993 Copenhagen criteria.

As 1998 showed, these two principles are to a degree in conflict. The Luxembourg summit in December 1997 endorsed the view of the Commission that five applicants from central and eastern Europe – Poland, Hungary, the Czech Republic, Slovenia and Estonia (together with Cyprus) – met the Copenhagen criteria and could move to full accession negotiations. The UK Presidency then moved quickly to ensure that the formal process was opened in the first half of the year.

On 12 March, the European Standing Conference, to which all EU applicants were invited, met for the first time in London at the level of Heads of State or Government. The Conference met again in Luxembourg on 6 October at foreign minister level. On both occasions Turkey declined to attend, raising doubts about the value of such a conference framework.

Also in March, the Council finally endorsed the Accession Partnerships, negotiated with each applicant state. These partnerships identified the short- and medium-term sector priorities in each applicant for the adoption of the *acquis*.

The partnerships were used as the basis for accessing pre-accession aid, through the PHARE programme, and for detailed work in the national programmes for the adoption of the *acquis*, against which the Commission will judge progress in its annual progress reports.

Of the PHARE aid available to support pre-accession, 70 per cent will be allocated to infrastructure development, whilst 30 per cent will be allocated to institution-building. The majority of this component will go to supporting institutional twinning partnerships between the Member States and the applicants. The Commission's framework, developed during the course of the year, envisaged the secondment of officials from ministries in Member States to their equivalents in applicant states.

The formal accession process was opened in Brussels on 30 March, by a meeting of foreign ministers from EU Member States and the six first-wave applicants. The formal structure of negotiations adhered to the traditional method, in which a separate accession conference is convened with each applicant, who negotiates with the EU Member States. The Commission established an 'Enlargement Task Force', to co-ordinate the work of the EU side, and to facilitate the development of common positions.

The first stage of negotiations focused on a detailed analytical examination (screening) of the 31 chapters of the *acquis communautaire*. This involved a chapter-by-chapter examination of the *acquis*, in the first, multilateral stage between the Commission and all applicants together, in order to agree on a common understanding of the legislation and policies in each chapter. In the second, bilateral stage, each applicant separately examines with the Commission the transposition and implementation status of each directive in the chapter.

In order to be able to demonstrate some progress in the screening process, uncontroversial chapters were screened first. Thus the process opened with an examination of SME policy, research and development, education and science, statistics, culture and audio-visual policy, telecommunications and information technology, and the Common Foreign and Security Policy. Bilateral screening has been used for clarification and for the identification of where transition periods might be sought.

The Commission noted in its annual progress report of November 1998 that by the end of October the screening of 16 out of 31 chapters of the *acquis* had been completed for the six first wave applicants. The Commission's overall evaluation was positive, noting that 'the applicant countries showed that they were fully aware of the conditions for negotiations, declared willingness to take over the *acquis* and sought to limit transition periods'.

In order to maintain its inclusive approach, the Commission also opened screening, on 3 April, with the five countries – Bulgaria, Latvia Lithuania, Romania and Slovakia – which have not started negotiations. The Commission noted that the multilateral screening of 28 chapters of the *acquis* had been 'largely didactic', and that more precise issues will appear only when bilateral screening has opened in 1999.

A key issue under debate during 1998 was how and when to move beyond screening to substantive negotiations, in order to maintain the momentum of the process within such a diverse group of applicants. At the General Affairs Council of 5 October, the EU decided to proceed to first substantive negotiations with the six 'first-wave applicants' in the first seven chapters screened on the basis of the position papers submitted by them.

The applicants have used the target entry date of 1 January 2003, except for Hungary which has used 1 January 2002, as the basis of their position papers. By November, a small number of requests for transition periods in these chapters had been made. These requests do not pose major problems for the EU side. However, they do presage far more serious problems in the 'difficult' chapters, such as agriculture and environment, which will emerge in 1999.

Although the Commission was sanguine that the difference between the 'ins' and 'pre-ins' is not significant, by late 1998 the tension between the EU's desire for inclusion and differentiation had become more evident. Despite the EU's hope, if not its expectation, Turkish Cyprus had not participated in the negotiations. Turkey itself remained outside the accession process, though the subject of intensified measures aimed at deepening its customs union with the EU. Moreover, in its annual progress report, the Commission noted 'a worrying slowdown' in the pace of transposition of the *acquis* in Slovenia and the Czech Republic, previously regarded as leading candidates. However, they noted a new momentum of change in Latvia, and recommended that, if maintained, Latvia might be able to join the full negotiating process before the end of 1999. The Commission's progress reports and the overall strategy for enlargement were endorsed by the Vienna Council on 11–12 December.

Despite the progress made within the framework of the accession negotiations, overall enlargement remained hostage to the fortunes of *Agenda 2000*. Pre-accession aid depends on a budget deal, a point mentioned explicitly in the conclusions of the Vienna Council. Common negotiating positions on the EU side in financially sensitive chapters, such as agriculture, also remain dependent on the *Agenda 2000* blueprint. Furthermore, institutional questions remain unanswered, at least until the Cologne Council.

1999 will show how far it is possible to pursue the accession of such a large and diverse group of countries without a clear view on the side of the EU of how such an enlarged EU would operate.

Journal of Common Market Studies

Volume 37, Annual Review
September 1999

Legal Developments

NIGEL FOSTER

Cardiff Law School, University of Wales

I. Introduction

The general approach of this section continues to be to review the judicial developments of the European Court of Justice (ECJ) through cases which add to the body of Community law. It is not to consider the numerous cases concerned with the detailed interpretation of finer points of technical legislation. Some cases merely continue past developments but, by inclusion, confirm a line of development.

Delays in reaching the ECJ appear to have increased again with 2–3 years required for Art. 234 (old 177) references, 7–13 months for Art. 226 actions (old 169) and 26 months about the average for Art. 230 (173) direct actions.[1] Cases on appeal from the Court of First Instance (CFI) may expect to add from 18 months to 3 years and 6 months[2] to be heard before the ECJ and thus upwards of 3–4 years in total. Direct actions before the CFI took between 14 months and 2 years 7 months.[3] The total number of case in the pipeline[4] also gives rise to some serious concern about further delays. Further reform of the working practices of the CFI and ECJ may be necessary.[5]

---

[1] This is despite the optimism expressed last year, see *Annual Review 1997*, pp. 93–4.

[2] Case C-185/95 *P. Baustahlgewerbe GmbH* v. *Commission* [1988] ECR II-987 and considered below.

[3] Delay was one of the grounds for appeal against a CFI decision claimed in the *Baustahlgewerbe* case considered below.

[4] Over 300 before the ECJ and now over 1,000 before the CFI!

[5] See Sonelli (1998), pp. 871–900.

II. The Development of the Competence and the Powers of the EU and its Institutions

External Competence

Racke v. *Mainz* [6] confirmed previous case law[7] that provisions of Association Agreements between the EC and third nations could confer rights upon which individuals may directly rely before national courts, the direct effects of Community law. More important, however, is the clear statement from the Court of Justice that a regulation which sought to amend or alter such provisions giving rights may be attacked by reference to either rules of customary international law or, as in the case itself, the Vienna Convention of the Law of Treaties. Although not binding on the Community as a signatory, the ECJ has held that these reflect rules of international law which must be respected by the EC in the exercise of its powers. Thus, rules of customary international law concerning the termination and suspension of treaty relations by reason of a fundamental change of circumstances are binding on Community institutions and form part of the Community legal order by which the validity of a later Community regulation can be challenged. The case concerned a regulation suspending concessions of the Co-operation Agreement with the former Yugoslavia. No violation of international law was found.

There is a common organization of the market[8] in bananas which seeks to uphold a Community preference for bananas produced in ACP countries, and particularly former colonies of France and the UK, whilst allowing imports from other banana producing countries. Quite how much longer this will survive is a moot point in view of two cases decided in 1998 which added to the problems of this already beleaguered regime by the GATT agreements, the WTO decisions[9] and the staunch support of the Chiquita Company by the USA. In *Germany* v. *Council*[10] and considering the same matter, *T. Port* v. *Hauptzollamt Hamburg*,[11] the ECJ decided that Decision 94/800,[12] which discriminated against Colombia, Costa Rica, Nicaragua and Venezuela by requiring them to obtain export licences whereas operators importing ACP bananas were exempted, was invalid. Trade talks and WTO arbitration continued, with the latter due to report in March 1999.

---

[6] Case C-162/96 *Racke GmbH & Co* v. *Hauptzollamt Mainz* [1998] 3 CMLR 219.
[7] Cases 21-24/72 *International Fruit Company v. Produktschap voor Groenten en Fruit* [1972] ECR 27, [1975] 2 CMLR 1.
[8] At the time of writing that is! Regulation 404/93 *OJ* 1993 L47/1.
[9] For further details, see Enchelmaier (1998), pp. 708–10; Snyder (1996), pp. 744–7.
[10] Case C-122/95 *Federal Republic of Germany* v. *Council of the European Union* [1998] 3 CMLR 570.
[11] Cases C-364-5/95 *T. Port & GmbH* v. *Hauptzollamt Hamburg-Jonas* [1997] 2 CMLR 1.
[12] 1994 *OJ* L336/1.

In *Dorsch* v. *Council and Commission*,[13] the Court of First Instance considered the consequences of the UN embargo against Iraq following its invasion of Kuwait. A damages claim was made because the legislative action by the EC to embargo trade indirectly caused the applicant loss. Although the case was not a success for the applicant, it is nevertheless interesting from the point of view of the Court that it considered with some care the otherwise very obvious facts that the losses were a result of Iraqi economic retaliations following the imposition of UN sanctions. Its close consideration of damage, cause of damage and special damage hardly seemed necessary.

Internal Competence

In *UK* v. *Commission*,[14] the UK assumed the role of guardian of the Community purse. Despite the fact that the Council had decided not to support 'Poverty 4', a programme to combat poverty and social exclusion, the Commission decided to fund a number of projects amounting to an expenditure of 6m ECU and issued a press release[15] to advertise this. The ECJ held that the Commission lacked the competence to commit the expenditure and the decision was annulled. However, in view of the fact that much of the expenditure had already taken place, the ECJ decided in the interests of legal certainty to exercise the discretion given to it under Art. 231 (old 174) and rule in favour of the payments made or promised.

Interinstitutional Relations

Under the Treaty on European Union, the Court of Justice had only limited rights of jurisdiction over matters to be decided under Pillar III on Justice and Home Affairs. However, the Court has a review jurisdiction to ensure that such matters decided on by the Council under TEU are not ones which should have been decided under a provision of the EC Treaty. In *Commission* v. *Council*,[16] the Commission considered that a joint action on airport transit visas adopted by the Council on the basis of Art. 31 TEU (old K.3(2)(b)) should have been adopted under (old) Art. 100c EC. The ECJ does not have a direct role to play under this pillar, being restricted by Art. 46 (b) (old L (b)) to interpreting conventions decided on by the Member States but only when they request the ECJ to do so. However, the ECJ argued that, according to Art. 47 (old M) TEU, nothing in the TEU should affect the provisions of the EC, apart from agreed amendments, therefore the ECJ has the jurisdiction to determine whether acts within the scope of Art. 31 (old K.3) should instead have been based on Art. 100c (old). On the

[13] Case T-184/95 *Dorsch Consult Ingenieurgesellschaft mbH* v. *Council and Commission* [1998] 2 CMLR 958.
[14] Case C-106/96 *UK* v. *Commission* [1998] 2 CMLR 981.
[15] IP/96/97 of 23 January 1996.
[16] Case C-170/96 *Commission v. Council* [1998] 1 CMLR 1092.

facts, which concerned visas to allow access to airport international areas but not access to the internal area of the EU, the ECJ held this was not within the ambit of old Art. 100c and the Commission application failed. The case, however, clearly provides the justification for the power of review of the ECJ over sections of the TEU where it has no direct jurisdiction.

In *EP* v. *Council*,[17] the EP continues to challenge the Council for enacting legislation under the incorrect legal base.[18] In this case, the Council employed Art. 308 (old 235) which provides law-making power where no other is suitable and, in doing so, requires unanimity on the part of the Council of Ministers and only a requirement to consult the EP. The EP argued that Art. 156 (old 129d), the co-decision procedure which gives the EP greater participatory rights in the legislative process, should have been employed. This case dealt with the telematic interchange of data between administrations, but the substance was not in dispute. The ECJ annulled the decision but its effects were to carry on. It seems the Council is still offending, the EP is still pursuing actions, and the European taxpayer still picking up the bill.

III. Development of the Principles of Primary EC Law

Equality/No Discrimination

Art. 12 (old 6) which prohibits discrimination on the grounds of nationality continues to make its mark. In *Bickel and Franz*[19] it was held that where national rules allow for another language to be used in court than that of the state, the rule comes within Community law jurisdiction. It would be a breach of Art. 12 if that right was not also extended to nationals of other Member States, whose language it was. This occurred in Bolzano (south Tyrol) in Italy, where there are specific rules for the protection of the German-speaking minority.

In *Levez* v. *Jennings*,[20] the ECJ considered a UK procedural law which limited the period of claim for damages in sex discrimination cases to a period not exceeding two years running backward from the date of commencement of proceedings. The ECJ acknowledged that, in the absence of a Community regime on the matter, it was for Member States to determine procedural rules governing Community law rights providing they were equivalent to similar domestic actions and were effective. A limit of two years was not criticized. However, Ms Levez has been misinformed or deliberately misled by the employer as to the

---

[17] Case C-22/96 *EP* v. *Council* [1999] 1 CMLR 160.
[18] See *Annual Review 1997*, p. 95.
[19] Case C-274/96 *Bickel and Franz*, [1998] 1 CMLR, 348, *The Times*, 1 December 1998.
[20] Case C-326/96 *B. S. Levez* v. *T.H. Jennings (Harlow Pools)* [1999] All ER (EC) 1. The case is also relevant to the Sex Discrimination section below.

higher earnings of a male predecessor and had learnt the truth only on leaving her job. Under such circumstances the ECJ held that, if applied, the rule would serve to deprive an employee from effective enforcement of Community law because it would be almost impossible to obtain arrears of remuneration and enable employers to avoid paying damages by deceit. In such circumstances the rule would be manifestly incompatible with principles of EC law.

In *Ibiyinka Awoyemi*[21] the ECJ confirmed the favoured status of EC citizens or, in this case, the non-favoured status of non-EC nationals. A Nigerian national who held a Community model driving licence issued in the UK, moved to Belgium. After two years he was stopped and prosecuted for not having a Belgian driving licence. The ECJ was asked whether Mr Awoyemi was protected from the high fine by EC law. The ECJ held that the Driving Licence Directive[22] applies to all persons holding driving licences in the EC irrespective of nationality and EC case law states that penalties for breaching EC rules, i.e. not changing to a national licence after 12 months' residence, are acceptable, providing that they are not disproportionate so as to become an obstacle to free movement of persons. However, the rules did not apply to Mr Awoyemi, because they arose in the context of the free movement of persons intended only for Community nationals. The ECJ held there is nothing in EC law to prevent Member States from applying the full measure of national sanctions, even if including imprisonment for the failure to hold a national driving licence. This may be accurate in the facts, but is there any real need for such a stark contrast to be drawn? The offence remains a minor offence. It is a pity a more sympathetic judgment could not have been reached.

Articles 30–36 (non-tariff barriers to the free movement of goods including intellectual property considerations)

Art. 28 (old 30) EC prohibits Member States introducing measures having equivalent effect to a ban on imports. Art. 30 (old 36) provides certain grounds by which Member States may prevent imports, health protection often being claimed. Case law[23] has provided further grounds whereby Member States may introduce rules to protect certain interests such as worker protection (Sunday trading) or the environment. However, these rules must be indistinctly applicable, which means they must apply to imports and domestic products. They must also be proportionate and not a disguised restriction on trade or an arbitrary discrimination. If, however, a particular product has satisfied standards in another Member State, it should be accepted under the second principle to arise from the case law and known as the principle of equivalence.

[21] Case C-230/97 *Ibiyinka Awoyemi, Weekly Proceedings of the Court of Justice*, 26/98, p.17.
[22] Directive 91/439 (*OJ* 1991 L1/237) as amended by Directive 97/26 (*OJ* 1997 L150/41).
[23] Notably *Cassis de Dijon*, see *Annual Review 1997.*

In *Aher-Waggon* v. *Germany* [24] a national provision which ignored standards in other Member States has been accepted by the ECJ, with good reason. Germany refused to register propeller driven aircraft previously registered in Denmark because they did not meet German noise standards. Levels, stricter than those of the EC are allowed under Directive 80/51. The same type of aircraft registered before the new standards came into force in Germany, could continue to be registered and used. It was claimed the provision was contrary to Art. 28 (old 30) but the ECJ held it could be justified by public health considerations or environmental protection. The ECJ concluded standards applied to new registrations only and the fact that older aircraft could continue to be used, if either registered previously in Germany or registered in another Member State to EC standards but below German standards. The provision was held to be acceptable and not disproportionate despite its seeming divergence from previous case law. The environmental argument seems to have won the day!

A Community directive [25] sets outs standards of care for animals including the protection of calves during rearing and fattening. Member States are allowed to impose stricter standards in their own territories. There is also a 1988 recommendation on the rearing of cattle from a Community standing committee established to put into effect the European Convention on the Protection of Animals kept for Farming Purposes which is approved by the Community. [26] The UK had higher standards than the directive and observed the latter, especially in respect of the ban of the use of veal calf crates. However, after export, the calves were reared in single calf veal crates as the importing states did not observe the same standards. This practice and the export of live veal calves attracted much criticism and consequent publicity. The RSPCA and Compassion in World Farming asked the UK Agriculture Minister not to export. He refused and the case *R* v. *Minister of Agriculture, Fisheries and Food, ex parte: CIWF* [27] arose as a challenge to that refusal in the UK courts. A question about the compatibility of a ban with Art. 28 (old 30) was referred to the ECJ, which held the exceptions in Art. 30 (old 36) did not allow the UK to ban the export of veal calves on the grounds of danger to the health of animals because it has adopted stricter provisions for the rearing of veal calves than the importing states. The directive did not conform to the Convention but was nevertheless held to be valid, and the recommendation of the Committee was not binding on the Member States or on the Community. Hence, a ban would be contrary to Community law and the UK Agriculture Minister was supported in his refusal to stop the export of live veal calves to be raised in crates.

[24] Case C-389/96 *Aher-Waggon GmbH* v. *Bundesrepublik Deutschland, Weekly Proceedings of the Court of Justice*, 19/98, p. 13.
[25] Directive 91/629 (1991 *OJ* L340/28).
[26] By Article 1 of Council Decision 78/923 (1978 *OJ* L323/12).
[27] Case C-1/96 *R* v. *Minister of Agriculture, Fisheries and Food, ex parte: CIWF Ltd* [1998] 2 CMLR 661.

It might have been thought on the facts alone that the *Decker*[28] case would be decided under the freedom to receive services as with the *Kohll* case noted under services below. It concerned the refusal of the Belgian social security fund to reimburse Mr Decker the cost of prescription spectacles bought in Luxembourg because he had not received prior authorization. Mr Decker asserted this was in breach of the free movement of goods. Spectacles bought in Belgium were not subject to prior authorization. The ECJ held that these rules must be categorized as a barrier to the free movement of goods and since based on economic motives were not justified on public health grounds as the professions are regulated by EC law. Hence then the rule was held to be contrary to Art. 28 (old 30).

There have been more cases in the complex area of intellectual property rights and the internal market. In *Silhouette* v. *Hartlauer*,[29] the ECJ was asked to consider whether national rules which allowed for the exhaustion of right principle should also apply in the situation where goods were exported and marketed outside the European Economic Area (EEA) to allow an importer to buy products outside the EEA and lawfully import and distribute them in the EC without infringing the trade mark of the manufacturer.[30] If a manufacturer has not exhausted his or her rights in a product, they are able to protect their exclusive right to distribute a product under their trademark in the EEA according to Directive 89/104. The ECJ held that under the Community regime, exhaustion of rights applies only to the EEA and there is no international exhaustion of rights. Hence, out-of-fashion quality spectacle frames, made by Silhouette and sold cheaply outside the EEA but bought there and reimported into the EEA by Hartlauer, could not be marketed in the EEA under the Silhouette trademark.[31]

It was held in *Metronome Musik GmbH* v. *Music Point Hokamp GmbH*[32] and *Foreningen af danske Videogramdistributorer* v. *Laserdisken*[33] that the exclusive rental rights introduced by Directive 92/100 are unlike sale rights and are not exhausted after first rental approval or distribution. Thus, the prohibition or restriction on offered copies for rental in one Member State by the holder of an exclusive rental right where copies have already been offered for rent in another Member State does not infringe Art. 28 (old 30) EC Treaty. Rental rights cannot therefore be exhausted in the same way as distribution for sale rights. The Court reasoned that this was justified in any event by the protection of artistic and literary property afforded by Art. 30 (old 36) EC Treaty.

[28] Case C-120/95 *Decker* v. *Caisse de maladie des employés privés* [1998] 2 CMLR 879. See the *Kohll* case at n. 42 below.
[29] Case C-355/96 *Silhouette* v. *Hartlauer* [1998] 2 CMLR 953.
[30] Thus presenting the argument that the manufacturer's rights had been exhausted. See also on this point *Annual Review 1996*, p. 100 and *Annual Review 1997*, p. 96.
[31] See, generally, on exhaustion of trade marks: Alexander (1999), pp. 56–76.
[32] Case C-200/96 *Metronome Musik GmbH* v. *Music Point Hokamp* [1997] ECC 325.
[33] Case C-61/97 *Foreningen af danske Videogramdistributorer* v. *Laserdisken*, [1999] 1 CMLR 1297, [1999] All ER (EC) 366.

The free movement (or not) of bees! It was held in *Ditlev Bluhme*[34] that Danish legislation which prevented the keeping of any other bees than the subspecies *Apis mellifera mellifera* (Laeso brown bee) on the island of Laeso was a measure having equivalent effect to a quantitative restriction contrary to Art. 28 (old 30). It was, however, justified under Art. 30 (old 36) to protect the health and life of animals, in this case to preserve the biological diversity of the subspecies from other genetically dominant species of bee and thus an acceptable reason to resist free movement.

Article 95

In confirmation of past case law[35] comparing the application of tax regimes to imported and domestic products, the ECJ held in *Outokumpu Oy*[36] that a flat rate tax on imported electricity from Sweden would infringe Art. 90 (old 95) because the tax rate on domestic electricity was calculated according to the product used in its manufacture for environmental reasons. The fact that only in limited circumstances would the rate of imported tax be higher was immaterial to the ECJ. The ease of administration in setting up a general system and that it was extremely difficult to determine precisely the method of manufacture of imported electricity were not accepted as grounds justifying the system adopted. I would assume that, following the case, the Finnish importer would have to find out from what product the electricity was made in Sweden to be able to determine the appropriate rate.

Article 48 (free movement of workers)

In *Kalliope Schöning-Kougebetopoulou* v. *Hamburg*,[37] a public service collective agreement required eight years' employment to qualify for seniority promotion but would not count time served in the public service of another Member State. This was held to be in breach of Art. 39 (old 48) and Arts. 7(1) and (4) of Regulation 1612/68 because of detriment to migrant workers. The ECJ did not accept the arguments that public service is organized differently in the different Member States and that some employees of the German public service might encounter the same situation as migrant workers. Art. 39 (old 48) (4) exempts public service employment from the application of the rest of the article but, in

---

[34] C-67/97 *Ditlev Bluhme*, [1999] 1 CMLR 612.
[35] Case 132/78 *Denkavit* v. *France* [1979] ECR 1923, [1979] 3 CMLR 605.
[36] Case C-213/96 *Outokumpu Oy, Weekly Proceedings of the Court of Justice*, 10/98 p. 21.
[37] Case 15/96 *Kalliope Schöning-Kougebetopoulou* v. *Hamburg* [1998] 1 CMLR 931. In support of this judgment is Case C-187/96 *Commission* v. *Greece, Weekly Proceedings of the Court of Justice*, 8/98 p. 9 which extends the judgment to cover an administrative regulation or practice which does not take into account periods of employment in the public service of other Member State when determining seniority increments and salary grading.

line with previous case law,[38] the ECJ held that the position could not be excluded from the application of Community law. The occupation in question, of specialized doctor, involved no direct or indirect participation in the exercise of powers conferred by public law, nor, indeed, was the case concerned with access to public service but with conditions. Hence, unless objectively justified and proportionate to its aim, a provision of national law must be regarded as indirectly discriminatory if it is intrinsically liable to affect migrant workers more than national workers. The ECJ stressed that the national courts must apply the same rules to members of the group discriminated against, without waiting for the offending clauses to be removed by negotiation or other means.

In *Clean Car Autoservice*,[39] an employer was forbidden from appointing a manager, who did not reside in Austria, from managing a car hire and leasing company. The ECJ held that Art. 39 (old 48) enables employers to engage managers without indirect discrimination. It further confirmed that, as in services,[40] a residence requirement cannot be imposed on workers, confirming too, that managers are workers.

Articles 52 and 59 (freedom of establishment and free movement of services)

Raymond Kohll v. *Union des caisses de maladie*[41] concerns the right of a Luxembourg national to receive the services of a German orthodontist in Trier. This right would be infringed contrary to Art. 46 (old 56) if prior authorization was necessary. The fear of the Member State that the social security system budget would be unbalanced was not sufficient to persuade the ECJ to decide otherwise, because in this case the refusal was not to pay in itself, but the refusal to pay if prior authorization was not given. The court stated, however, that it is open to Member States to justify objectively a prohibition on broader grounds.

Articles 85, 86 and 90 (Competition Law)

Oscar Bronner GmbH & Co KG v. *Mediaprint Zeitungs- und Zeitschriftenverlag GmbH & Co.*[42] helps define in a more positive way the boundaries of what may be regarded as the abuse of a dominant position, in that this was not found to be the legal position from the facts. A media undertaking holding a clear dominant

---

[38] Case 149/79 *Commission* v. *Belgium* [1980] ECR 3881, [1981] 2 CMLR 413. Case 307/84 *Commission* v. *French Republic* [1986] ECR 1734, [1987] 3 CMLR 555. Case 66/85 *Lawrie-Blum* v. *Land Baden-Würtemberg* [1986] ECR 2121, [1987] 3 CMLR 389. Case C-4/91 *Bleis* v. *Ministry of Education* [1991] ECR I-5627, [1994 1 CMLR 793.

[39] Case C-350/96 *Clean Car Autoservice* [1998] 2 CMLR 637.

[40] Case 2/74 *Reyners* v. *Belgium* [1974] ECR 631, [1974] 2 CMLR 305.

[41] Case C-158/96 *Raymond Kohll* v. *Union des caisses de maladie* [1998] 2 CMLR 928. See the *Decker* case at n. 29 above.

[42] Case C-7/97 *Oscar Bronner GmbH & Co KG* v. *Mediaprint Zeitungs- und Zeitschriftenverlag GmbH & Co.* [1999] 4 CMLR 112.

position (46.8 per cent circulation) in one market was not obliged to allow access to a home delivery scheme, the only one in the market, to a smaller rival newspaper who could not economically set up their own scheme. There was, in other words, no breach of Art. 82 (old 86) although there was a dominant position in the market. The case stresses that the exploitation of the advantages achieved by reaching a dominant position does not necessarily amount to unlawful abuse.

In *France* v. *Commission* and joined case *SCPA & EMC* v. *Commission*,[43] the ECJ determined that the merger regulation[44] applies also to collective dominance. The case concerned a proposal that potash companies in Germany be concentrated, thus creating a *de facto* monopoly in the German market and a dominant position with the French company SCPA in the Community market. To obtain Commission approval, the parties agreed to certain conditions relating to co-operation between the dominant firms and the distribution of products in the markets identified. France objected to the Commission decision before the ECJ, and SCPA, before the CFI. As they both concerned the same decision, the CFI declined jurisdiction and the whole matter was referred to the ECJ. The decision is important because it is the first time the ECJ has clearly stated the merger regulation to be applicable to collective dominance, despite the lack of express words to that effect in the regulation and the doubts of the Member States when the regulation was enacted that it would apply to oligopolies. The ECJ, on the other hand, thought that there was nothing in the regulation to exclude its application. That collective dominance was not sufficiently established by the Commission in the case itself does nothing to upset this.

Silvano Raso[45] concerned statutory monopoly positions. Previously[46] it had been held that a Member State may breach Art. 86 (old 90) (1) if it creates a monopoly which has no choice but to infringe Art. 82 (old 86) (1) by abusing its dominant position. The ECJ held that a statutory monopoly may need only to be led to abuse its dominant position by the legal framework established by the Member State rather than being unable to avoid a breach. In this case, the right to supply temporary labour to undertakings operating in a port was reserved to a dock company also operating in that port. It was held that the company was a statutory monopoly which, in view of the importance of the port (La Spezia) in Mediterranean trade, held a dominant position in a substantial part of the EC. The fact that the company concerned could supply labour and operate its own labour in competition led to an abuse of its dominant position contrary to the EC Treaty.

---

[43] Joined cases C-68/94 *France* v. *Commission* and C-30/95 *Société Commerciale des Potasses et de l'Azote (SCPA)* v. *Commission* [1998] 4 CMLR 829, *Weekly Proceedings of the Court of Justice*, 10/98 p. 6. See also case note (1998) 23 EL Rev pp. 475–80 and Venit (1998), pp. 1101–34.

[44] Council Regulation 4064/89 1990 *OJ* L257/14.

[45] Case C-163/96 *Silvano Raso et al* [1998] 4 CMLR 737. See also a full case note on this (1998) 23 EL Rev pp. 364–70.

[46] See, *inter alia*, the cases of C-41/90 *Höfner and Elser* [1991] ECR I-1797, [1993] 4 CMLR 306.

Hence the inevitability of an abuse is not necessary, but the creation of a situation where the monopoly might be led to abuse its position will suffice.

Article 119 and Related Directives (equal pay and sex equality)

As ever, it has been a busy time in the area of social policy. Sex discrimination cases feature significantly and particularly those concerned with rights relating to pregnancy. The first case draws the line at the scope of the protection afforded by EC law as outlined in *P* v. *S and Cornwall County Council*.[47]

In *Grant* v. *South West Trains*,[48] South West Trains' regulations specifically restricted rail travel facilities to opposite sex partners (it was not necessary to be married but a stable relationship had to be established), whereas same sex partners were denied rail travel benefits. It was argued the rules were contrary to Art. 141 (119) and Directive 75/117. Whilst there was clearly discrimination in the case it was not, in the view of the ECJ, the type of discrimination covered by the agreed EC law so far established by the Member States. This was not discrimination based on sex; the rule would apply equally to same sex male partnerships. This was, instead, discrimination based on sexual orientation, which, the ECJ stated, was not prohibited by EC law. In reaching this conclusion, the ECJ considered a number of points, including: the EP deplores such discrimination; in some Member States such a relationship would be treated the same as an opposite sex relationship but only for a limited range of rights whereas in other states such rights would not be recognized in any particular way; the ECHR has not yet gone as far as to recognizing it for the purposes of Art. 8 (family life), Art. 14 (discrimination on the grounds of sex) or Art. 12 (marriage); and the present state of law in the EC does not equate same sex relationships with opposite sex ones. The discrimination, although present, is therefore lawful. The ECJ also referred to the new Art. 13 (old Art. 6a) by which the Member States can legislate to prohibit sexual orientation discrimination and concluded it should leave the Member States to prohibit this form of discrimination under that new ability.

The well-established case law in respect of part-time workers and indirect discrimination[49] is applied in a more modern day form. *Hill and Stapleton* v. *Revenue Commissioners*[50] confirms that it would be unlawful discrimination to appoint job sharers who transfer to full-time work to a lower salary scale point than they enjoyed previously, when based on the actual time worked, and where a majority of women are job sharers. The usual proviso applies that such a rule

---

[47] See *Annual Review 1996*, p. 104.
[48] Case C-249/96 *Grant* v. *South West Trains* [1998] 1 CMLR 993.
[49] Case 96/80 *Jenkins* v. *Kingsgate* [1981] ECR 911, [1981] 2 CMLR 241 Case 170/84 *Bilka Kaufhaus* v. *Karin Weber Van Harz* [1986] ECR 1607, [1986] 2 CMLR 701.
[50] Case C-243/95 *Hill and Stapleton* v. *Revenue Commissioners* [1998] 3 CMLR 81.

can be justified by objective criteria unrelated to any discrimination on grounds of sex.

Coote v. *Granada*[51] is interesting for two reasons. Ms Coote settled a sex discrimination claim with Granada and the employment relationship was terminated by mutual consent. She found it difficult, however, to obtain another job due to Granada's refusal to supply an employment agency with a reference. It was claimed this was contrary to Art. 6 of Directive 76/207 (the equal treatment directive) under which Member States should take measures to achieve the aims of the directive and must ensure that the rights can be enforced by individuals before the national courts. This right of recourse to the courts is a general principle of Community law reflected in the Member States' constitutions and Art. 6 ECHR. The ECJ held that Art. 6 of the Directive also covers measures an employer might take as a reaction against legal proceedings of a former employee *outside of dismissal.*This extends the scope of EC protection beyond the protection against dismissal.[52] The second point is that although the judgment appears to be directed at the Member State to take the necessary measures, it was given in a preliminary ruling procedure between two individual parties obliging the private employer to comply.[53]

CNAVTS v. *E. Thibault*[54] held that a condition for promotion should be that the person to be assessed must have been at work in the previous six months was contrary to Arts. 2(3) and 5(1) of Directive 76/207 when applied to Mrs Thibault because she was on maternity leave for some of the relevant period of assessment.

Despite thinking initially *Boyle et al* v. *Equal Opportunities Commission*[55] was contrived to test typical civil service contractual clauses, nothing I have read thus far confirms this suspicion. It therefore appears to be genuine, although surprising that the EOC, set up to promote and defend equal rights, should be accused of unlawful discrimination. The case was also one of the first cases to consider Directive 92/85.[56] *Boyle* and five colleagues raised questions about the maternity scheme run by the EOC, which reflected the civil service maternity scheme. It had been agreed in the Industrial Tribunal, and accepted by the ECJ, that for the purposes of direct effects of the directives, the EOC was an emanation of the state. The ECJ decided as follows:

---

[51] Case C-185/97 *Coote* v. *Granada* [1998] All ER (EC) 865.
[52] In reality this, more often than not, amounts to compensation for unlawful dismissal.
[53] As with other cases in this review, this looks like horizontal direct effects.
[54] Case 136/95 *CNAVTS* v. *E. Thibault* [1998] 2 CMLR 516.
[55] C-411/96 *Boyle et al* v. *Equal Opportunities Commission* [1998] 3 CMLR 1155. See also *The Times* 'Law Report' 29 October 1998, *Financial Times*, 3 November 1998.
[56] 1992 *OJ* L348/1 as well as Art. 141 (old 119), Directive 75/117 (1995 *OJ* L45/19) and Directive 76/207 (1996 L39/40).

- A clause requiring repayment of maternity payments over and above the statutory minimum if a woman did not return to work following maternity leave when she had undertaken to return, was not contrary to the directive. Although there was no similar clause applying to those receiving higher rate sick leave payments, this was not discrimination against women, according to the Court, as maternity leave under Directive 92/85 was a special provision not to be compared with that of a man or woman on sick leave. Higher rate sick leave pay would apply to both women and men.
- In answer to a question about the commencement of maternity leave, the directive specified only the minimum number of weeks to be granted and left it to Member States to lay down provision as to when it should commence.
- A clause prohibiting a woman from taking sick leave during the minimum period of 14 weeks' maternity leave under Art. 8 (1) of Directive 92/85, unless she elected to return to work and thus terminate her maternity leave, was contrary to EC law. However, a similar clause in respect of supplementary maternity leave is compatible with Directives 76/207 and 92/85 as EC law does not apply to supplementary maternity leave. Thus a woman can be restricted to maternity or sick leave but not both.
- Directive 92/85 Art. 11 (2)(a) requires maternity leave rights in the 14-week minimum period to be at least the same as minimum statutory rights when on sick leave. A clause which limited the period during which annual leave accrues to that 14-week period was compatible with EC law. Outside of that period no annual leave would accrue. There was no discrimination, direct or indirect, according to the ECJ, as all employees on unpaid leave accrued no annual leave entitlement. A right to supplementary leave over and above the protection provided by the directive and which was available to women only could not constitute less favourable treatment.
- In contrast, in answer to the fifth question, a clause which restricted the accrual of pension rights to the 14-week period and denied it during the supplementary unpaid period of leave was held to be contrary to Directive 92/85. Although, under Art. 11 (4), entitlement to benefits could be subject to workers satisfying national legislation, this was not possible where the pension scheme was wholly occupational and governed by the employment contract. Therefore, accrual of pensions rights was not dependent on receiving pay during the supplementary period.

This meant a part success for the applicants. Moreover, the offending clauses cannot now be enforced either by the EOC or other employers with the same clauses. Given the complexity and length of the case, it is difficult to do it justice in a review of this nature. It is recommended therefore that reference be made to the case itself or longer reviews.[57]

Directive 92/85 was also considered in *Pedersen et al.*[58] Danish law provided that women who were unfit for work as a result of the pregnancy before or after the maternity leave period could not receive full pay but rather benefits instead from the local authority.[59] Workers who were medically attested ill, received full pay from their employers. Secondly, employers were also permitted not to provide employment for a pregnant employee, even if not unfit, if they considered there was no work available. With regard to the first provision, it should be of no surprise that the ECJ held that the discriminatory treatment based on the pregnancy was contrary to Art. 119 and Directive 75/117, and that the second provision led to unequal treatment of women in breach of Art. 5 of Directive 76/207. The argument that the rule was for the protection of pregnant women in line with Art. 2 (3) of 76/207 and Directive 92/85 was rejected by the ECJ which considered it to preserve the interests of the employer. The failure to pay in full when the employee was sent home was thus contrary to those directives.

Worker Protection

Two cases help clarify the scope of Directive 77/187.[60] Previously, it was held that the directive does not apply to transfers of undertakings in the course of insolvency proceedings when it was anticipated that a company would cease trading. In *Jules Dethier Equipment SA* v. *Jules Dassy,*[61] the question was whether this included judicial winding-up. The undertaking was allowed to continue to trade for the purposes of ensuring continuity of business for the benefit of a transferee company, therefore the ECJ was able to distinguish judicial winding-up from insolvency proceedings and extend the protection of the directive to employees who were dismissed during the course of the winding up. Workers who were unlawfully dismissed[62] before the transfer retain rights against the transferee company who had not taken them on. *Europieces and Sanderson*[63] confirms the extension of the scope of the directive to cover voluntary liquidation which was equated to winding-up by the Court. A further interesting aspect of these cases is that they are between two individual parties,

---

[57] *Emp. Law* (1998), 13, pp. 10–12; E.O.R. (1999), 83, pp. 39–42.
[58] Full name: Case C-66/96 *Handels- og Kontorfunktionaererernes Forbund I Danmark* v. *Faellesforeningen for Danmarks Brugforeninger (Pedersen et al)* [199] IRLR 55, [1999] CEC 26.
[59] Administrative Instruction 191 of 27/10/1994.
[60] Which is designed to safeguard employees' rights in the event of transfers of undertaking and is the one which featured in the *Francovich* litigation. See *Annual Review 1997*, p. 103.
[61] Case C-319/94 *Jules Dethier Equipment SA* v. *Jules Dassy* [1998] 2 CMLR 611.
[62] I.e. not for the reasons allowed by the directive for economic, technical or organizational reasons.
[63] Case C-399/96 *Europieces and Sanderson, Weekly Proceedings of the Court of Justice*, 27/98, p. 4.

but a solution was found on the basis of the directive. In other words, the interpretation of the directive has provided rights which one individual can uphold against another in a national court – another example of implicit horizontal direct effects of directives.

The case of *Dusseldorp*[64] concerns an interesting mix of the topics involving Arts. 29, 30, 82, 86 and 176 (old 34, 36, 86, 90 and 130t). It was questioned whether a Member State could hinder the export of waste products for recovery because of Community law principles for the export of waste for disposal.[65] The national authorities required it to be processed by a national undertaking with exclusive rights unless the processing of waste in another Member State was of a higher quality. Waste for disposal should satisfy the principles of self-sufficiency and proximity designed to prevent unnecessary transportation of waste. The Dutch authorities prevented the export of the waste for recovery contrary to Art. 29 (old 34). The grounds of protection of the health and life of humans did not apply, as it was plain to the ECJ that the object of the Dutch provision was to restrict exports and provide a particular advantage for national enterprise. Waste for recovery should move freely so as to encourage the best technologies, and thus aid the environmental policy of recovery unless a threat is imposed to the environment by movement. The Dutch created a national monopoly which had a dominant position and allowed abuse of the position by the rules which favoured the national undertaking and increased its dominant position contrary to Art. 82 (old 86).

IV. Enforcement and Effectiveness of Community Law

Individual Enforcement

Brinkmann v. *Danish Skatteministeriet*[66] concerns state liability under the *Francovich* doctrine and appears to bring this more in line with Community institution liability for damage caused as a result of error.[67] The ECJ held that liability is not incurred due to error in classifying a tobacco product as a cigarette. Although the failure by the Member State to transpose into national law the relevant EC directive was itself a serious breach of Community law, as was the subsequent erroneous definition of a product into a higher tax rate, and even the subsequent refusal to suspend the decision, these errors did not give rise to liability when more than one interpretation was possible. It was held that there was not a sufficiently serious breach and thus no liability.

---

[64] Case C-203/96 *Dusseldorp BV et al* v. *Minister van Volkshuisvesting* [1999] All ER (EC) 25.
[65] Directive 75/442 as amended by Directive 91/156 and Regulation 259/93.
[66] Case C-319/96 *Brinkmann* v. *Danish Skatteministeriet*, [1998] 3 CMLR 673.
[67] See, on this topic, Steiner and Woods (1998), pp. 512–14; Craig and de Burca (1998), pp. 236–54.

V. Protection of Individual Rights

General Principles of Law and Fundamental Rights

Articles of the European Convention on Human Rights have over the history of the European Community increasingly been the inspiration for and indirect provider of general principles of Community law. In this case, Art. 6 (1) ECHR is the focus of attention, providing a right to a fair and public hearing within a reasonable period. This was a right acknowledged by the ECJ to be one of the general principles of Community law, namely, the right to fair legal process in a reasonable period. In *Baustahlgewerbe* v. *Commission*,[68] the victory achieved in asserting this right was for the party a pyrrhic one, however. The company appealed to the CFI against a fine levied by the Commission in August 1989 for a breach of Art. 81 (old 85) (1). In reaching its judgment to reduce the fine from 4.5.m ECU to 3m ECU, the CFI took 5 and a half years.[69] *Baustahlgewerbe* appealed against this judgment, partly on the basis of the excessive duration of proceedings. In determining whether the delay was reasonable or excessive, the ECJ considered the criteria of the importance of the case for the person concerned, the complexity of the case, the conduct of the applicant and the competent authorities. According to the ECJ, nothing in the case relieved the CFI of the obligation to observe reasonable time limits, which it had not done. A reduction of the fine by 50,000 to 2.95m ECU (a 1.66 per cent reduction!) was considered reasonable satisfaction by the ECJ. Not incidentally, *Baustahlgewerbe*, who were required to pay their own costs and three-quarters of the costs of the Commission. They did fail on five other grounds of appeal. The appeal process took 3 and a half years!

Good faith received support as a general principle of Community law in a case[70] concerned with the recovery of exports refunds which had been found to have been unduly paid. The export company were not responsible for the breach of rules and had acted in good faith. Under national law and also in view of the time elapsed, the refunds should not be recoverable. The ECJ held this to be the position under EC law also.

Individual Rights of Redress against Community Institutions (Transparency Decisions)

It is clear that the transparency decision[71] is helping to provide information to individuals to enable them to seek redress against Community institutions before

---

[68] Case C-185/95 *P. Baustahlgewerbe GmbH* v. *Commission, Weekly Proceedings of the Court of Justice,* 32/98 p. 1.
[69] From 20/10/1989 to 6/4/1995.
[70] Case C-366/95 *Landbrugsministeriet – EF-Direktoratet* v. *Steff-houlberg Export I/S et al, Weekly Proceedings of the Court of Justice,* 13/98 p. 17.
[71] See *Annual Review 1997*, p. 107.

the ECJ, but it is also its own source of case law to determine the scope of the right of access to documents.

In *Interporc Im- and Export GmbH* v. *Commission*,[72] Interporc was the subject of an action to recover import duties by the German authorities and requested certain documents from the Commission. According to Decision 94/90 on public access to Commission documents, the applicants need not state reasons, and requests may be refused only on the grounds set out in the code of conduct, issued under Art. 1 of the decision. The grounds include the protection of public interest (which includes court proceedings) and was the grounds given by the Commission for its refusal. The CFI held that access to documents assists individuals to protect their rights, therefore a refusal to supply the documents under the exhaustive grounds provided in the code of conduct should be reasoned and subject to the same strict legal requirements as in the legislative process. Thus, the requirements of Art. 253 (old 190) apply by analogy to the Access to Documents decision. Hence, the refusal to furnish documents should contain specific reasons why disclosure of the documents requested is precluded by one of the exceptions. These were not present in the case and the Commission decision refusing access was annulled.

By contrast, in *Wal* v. *Commission*,[73] the refusal on the ground that the Commission considered the release would be detrimental to the protection of the public interest as they related to court proceedings, was upheld by the ECJ. This was held to be a sufficient explanation for the purposes of the legal requirements of Community law to refuse the release of correspondence between the Commission and national courts.

A case which considered the *Access to the Council Documents Decision*[74] was *Svenska Journalistförbundet* v. *Council*.[75] This involved a deliberate test conducted by the Swedish Journalists' Union to see how access to Council Documents compared with access to the same documents from the Swedish authorities involved in Council deliberations. The Swedish authorities allowed access to 18 out of 20 documents, the Council initially only two, and after a further written application by the applicant, another two. By letter, the Council rejected the application for the remaining 16 documents. The applicant then lodged an action under Art. 230 (old 173) before the CFI. During the process, however, the Journalists' Union published the Council position on the Internet. This led to the suspension of the written procedure and the ruling by the CFI that

---

[72] Case T-124/96 *Interporc Im-and Export GmbH* v. *Commission of the European Communities* [1998] 2 CMLR 82.
[73] Case T-83/96 *Gerard van der Wal* v. *Commission*, [1998] 4 CMLR 954; [1998] AllER (EC) 289.
[74] Directive 93/731 (*OJ* 1993 L340/43).
[75] Case T-174/95 *Svenska Journalistförbundet* v. *Council of the European Union, Weekly Proceedings of the Court of Justice*, 16/98, p. 33, [1998] All ER (EC) 545. See generally on this topic, Österdahl (1998), pp. 336–56.

this constituted an abuse of procedure, leading in judgment to a reduction in costs awarded to the Journalists' Union who were successful.

Considering admissibility first, the CFI held that, as the right to documents was intended for everyone, no interest need be established to satisfy admissibility, when a request for documents is made, but rejected. On the findings, the CFI reiterated the position that any person entitled to ask for access does not need to provide reasons for the request. As with the Commission access decision, there are grounds by which access may be refused by the Council, particularly Art. 4 (1) where disclosure would undermine the protection of public interest (public security being one sub-ground) and Art. 4 (2), confidentiality. There is, however, a duty to state reasons. The Council simply referred to these grounds in respect of all the documents without specifying which ones individually. The CFI held that the terms of the contested decision did not allow the applicant or the Court to check whether the Council has complied with its duty to carry out a genuine balancing of interests, hence then the Decision did not comply with the requirements for reasoning laid down in Art. 253 (old 190) and was annulled.

*Judicial Review (*Locus standi *of the non-privileged applicants under Art. 173 EC)*

Dreyfus v. *Commission*,[76] considered the admissibility of an Art. 230 (old 173) action to annul an act of the Commission. In order to cross the threshold of admissibility, applicants have to satisfy the ECJ that where an act of an Institution it is not addressed to them but to another individual, they have been individually and directly affected. To be directly affected, the act must leave no discretion to the addressees of the measure who must implement it automatically without intervention. The ECJ held that directly extends to the situation where the possibility for addressees not to give effect to the Community measure is purely theoretical and their intention to act in conformity is not in doubt.[77]

In *Greenpeace*[78] the question of direct and individual concern was considered and it was held that neither Greenpeace as an association nor other individuals had *locus standi* to challenge a Commission subsidy decision in respect of two power stations in the Canary Islands because the Commission decision affected them in a general and abstract fashion like any other person in the same situation and not individually. The ECJ suggested that the environmental effect on the applicants, if any, would be best pleaded against the directive authorizing construction of the stations before the national courts rather than seeking to

[76] Case C-386/96 *Dreyfus* v. *Commission* (and associated cases C-403-404/96), [1999] 1 CMLR 481.
[77] Thus confirming the earlier case of Case 11/82 *AE Piraiki-Patraiki* v. *Commission* [1985] ECR 207, [1985] 2 CMLR 4.
[78] Case C-321/95P *Stichting Greenpeace Council (Greenpeace International) et al* v. *Commission* [1998] 3 CMLR 1.

challenge the decision to subsidize them before the ECJ. Any challenge to Community law could be then referred to the ECJ. The ruling of the CFI was upheld.

Actions under Article 232 (old 175): Failure to Act

Gestevision Telecinco v. *Commission*[79] was a rare success under Art. 232 (old 175). A private television company complained to the Commission about state and regional subsidies to public broadcasters. At first the Commission did nothing. However, when *Gestevision* formally complained to the Commission under Art. 232 (175), it commenced an investigation but made no decision. *Gestevision* then took matter to court. As with Art. 230, applications under Art. 232 require that if not the potential addressees, then applicants must be directly and individually concerned. There was no dispute by the Commission that the applicant was a concerned party. Hence the failure to take a decision directly and individually affected the applicants. It was questioned whether there was a duty to act when the applicant called upon the Commission to act. The CFI held that, since the Commission has the exclusive right of investigating state aid breaches, in the interests of sound administration and state aid rules, it must examine such complaints and act within a reasonable time. The Commission took close on four years. The CFI thought that was time enough. A letter of response saying that action was being taken was not sufficient to define the position of the Commission, hence the Commission failed to act, in breach of Art. 232.

Damages Actions under Article 215 EC

Successful actions under Art. 288 (215) are rare enough, therefore *Embassy* v. *EP*[80] was novel for that reason alone. The EP was seeking tenders for chauffeur driven vehicles for MEPs and whilst doing so an official of the EP had led Embassy to believe it would be awarded the contract without, however, the award being made to them nor a contract concluded. As a result, the company incurred considerable expenditure in preparation of the contract which was not then forthcoming, being awarded elsewhere. Embassy were not informed. This was enough for the CFI to conclude that the EP had breached Embassy's legitimate expectations and caused the damage suffered by it. The EP was ordered to pay damages.

The case of *Coldiretti* v. *Council*[81] *concerned* individual rights but, more importantly for the purposes of this review, the ability of trade associations to

---

[79] Case T-95/96 *Gestevision Telecinco* v. Commission, *Weekly Proceedings of the Court of Justice*, 20/98, p. 40 [1998] All ER (EC) 918.
[80] Case T-203/96 *Embassy Limousines & Services* v. *EP*, [1999] 1 CMLR 667.
[81] Case T-149/96 *Coldiretti* v. *Council, Weekly Proceedings of the Court of Justice*, 22/98, p. 36.

bring representative actions on behalf of members. There is no general right in Community law for representative actions, although individual directives provide for it.[82] In the present case, the CFI held that the application for damages by *Coldiretti* on behalf of farmers was inadmissible. An association has the right to bring proceedings for damages only where it is able to assert in law either a particular interest of its own, which is distinct from that of its members, or a right to compensation which has been assigned to it by others.[83]

And finally, the case of *Lemmens*[84] was a clever attempt to get around a breathalyser test. Previously in the *CIA Security* case,[85] the ECJ held that a Member State could not rely on national regulations in court proceedings where it was under a duty under Directive 83/189 to notify to Commission how technical regulations had been implemented, but had failed to do so.[86] The ruling sought to protect the free movement of goods by not allowing Member States to rely on regulations which prevent or hinder free movement. In *Lemmens*, the regulations related to breathalysers and had not been notified. Lemmens, who had failed a breath test, claimed they were unenforceable under the previous ruling and that the results of the breath test could not be used by the state in Court. Whilst the ECJ agreed that the regulations should have been notified but had not, it held that the failure to notify did not have the effect of making it unlawful for evidence obtained by means of such apparatus to be used. Lemmens' attempt thus quite rightly failed.

VI. Overall Evaluation and Conclusion

Whilst not providing any sensational cases in 1998, the ECJ and CFI have moved things along gently with general rights of equality and other areas of law. Discrimination cases continue to provide some of the most interesting developments in EC law, this time, though, it might be argued that the ECJ has been very conservative in its *Grant* ruling. Paradoxically, it may be because the Member States equipped themselves with the ability to prohibit discrimination on the grounds of sexual orientation under the new Art. 13, that the Court was not inclined to extend Community law itself.

[82] See Directive 86/ 450 (1984 *OJ* L250/17) Misleading Advertising and Directive 93/13 (1993 *OJ* L95/29) Unfair Terms in Consumer Contracts.
[32] For a further brief consideration of representative actions in EC law, see Steiner (1995), pp. 77–8 and 111–12.
[84] C-226/97 *Lemmens, Weekly Proceedings of the Court of Justice,* 16/98, p. 7 [1998] All ER (EC) 604. For slightly more detail refer to Weatherill (1998), pp. 217–19.
[85] Case C-194/94 *CIA Security International S.A* v. *Signalson S.A. and Securitel SPRL* [1996] ECR I-2201, [1996] CMLR 781.
[86] Notification allows the Commission to consider whether the proposed national regulation conforms with the law on the free movement of goods.

The extension of the Mergers Regulation to positions of collective dominance will provide the Commission with a green light to consider the further application of this to situations of collective dominance.

The access to documents decisions relating to both the Council and Commission has already provided individuals with the ability to challenge the decisions not to furnish documents. For the moment, we will have to wait to see whether some of these documents will assist individuals in challenging either national or Community acts affecting their rights.

References

Alexander, W. (1999) 'Exhaustion of Trade Marks Rights in the EEA'. 24 EL Rev, pp. 56–76.

Berkey, J.O. (1998) 'The European Court of Justice and Direct Effect of GATT: A Question Worth Revisiting'. *European Journal of International Law*, Vol. 9, pp. 626–57.

Cardiff University of Wales European Access: «http://www.cf.ac.uk/uwcc/liby/edc/euracc/»

Case Law of the EC: «http://europa.eu.int/jurisp/cgi-bin/form.pl?lang=en»

Cottier, T. (1998) 'Dispute Settlement in the WTO: Characteristics and Structural implications for the EU'. *Common Market Law Review*, Vol. 35, pp. 325–78.

Craig, P. and de Burca, G. (1998) *EU Law: Text, Cases and Materials,* 2nd edn (Oxford: Oxford University Press), pp. 236–54.

de Groot, C. (1998) 'The Council Directive on the Safeguarding of Employees' Rights in the Event of Transfers of Undertakings: An Overview of Recent Case Law'. *Commmon Market Law Review*, Vol. 35, pp. 707–29.

Ellis, E. (1998) 'Recent Developments in European Community Sex Equality Law'. *Common Market Law Review*, Vol. 35, pp. 379–408.

Enchelmaier, S. (1998) 'Agriculture, Fisheries and Environment'. 47 ICLQ 706, pp. 708–10.

European Court of Justice Home Page: «http://europa.eu.int/cj/en/index.htm»

Legislation in force at: «http://europa.eu.int/eur-lex/en/lif/index.html»

Official Journal for legislation at: «http://europa.eu.int/eur-lex/en/oj/index.html»

Österdahl, I. (1998) 'Openness v. Secrecy: Public Access to Documents in Sweden and the EU'. 23 EL Rev., pp. 336–56.

Snyder, F. (1996) 45 ICLQ pp. 744–7.

Sonelli, S. (1998) 'Appeal on Points of Law in the Community System – A Review'. 53 CMLR, pp. 871–900.

Steiner, J. (1995) *Enforcing EC Law* (London: Blackstone Press), pp. 77–8 and 111–12.

Steiner, J. and Woods, L. (1998) *Textbook on EC Law*, 6th edn (London: Blackstone Press), pp. 512–14.

Venit J. (1998) 'Two Steps Forward and No Steps Back: Economic Analysis and
    Oligopolistic Dominance after *Kali & Salz*'. 35 CML Rev, pp. 1101–134.
Weatherill, S. (1998) *Free Movement of Goods*. 47 ICLQ, pp. 217–19.

Journal of Common Market Studies

Volume 37, Annual Review
September 1999

Developments in the Economies of the European Union

NIGEL GRIMWADE
South Bank University

I. Overview

According to the European Commission (Commission, 1999a), in 1998 output in the European Union (EU) grew at an estimated rate of 2.9 per cent. This compares favourably with a rate of 2.7 per cent in the previous year and was the best performance since 1990. Thus, the recovery which began in 1994, following the recession of 1992–93, and which suffered a brief pause in late 1995 and early 1996, was both maintained and strengthened. This was despite an adverse change in the global economic climate caused by the financial crisis centred on emerging markets in the Asian region, Russia and, to a lesser extent, Latin America. Although this will result in some decline in EU growth in 1999, the crisis has thus far had no serious impact on growth in the EU. The main reason has been the relatively low dependence of the EU on external markets for economic growth. Exports account for only 9.7 per cent of the GDP of the Fifteen and 13.7 per cent of the GDP of the Euro-11.

At the same time, the deterioration in the global economic situation has, thus far, had no adverse effect on private investment and consumption, the domestic components of the aggregate demand for goods and services. In 1998, both private consumption and gross fixed capital formation were the main generators of economic growth, increasing, respectively, by 2.6 per cent and 4.7 per cent. This outcome was better than any previous year since 1990. However, the risk remains that the global financial crisis could spill over into private investment and consumption in 1999. Clearly, this would be the case if a serious decline in equity prices took place or if the financial crisis were to create difficulties for financial institutions within the EU. On the other hand, EU consumption is less vulnerable to any adverse wealth effect initiated by a collapse of equity prices than in the United States because EU households keep proportionately less of their wealth in this form. EU financial institutions may also be less exposed to emerging markets and better able to withstand any deterioration in their asset positions. A more serious situation, however, could arise if business confidence was upset by an intensification of the global financial crisis.

The expansion of domestic demand in the EU in 1998 was the result of a variety of factors. Rising real disposable incomes led the increase in private consumption. This, in turn, was helped by a declining rate of inflation and an increase in employment, resulting in a small reduction in the rate of unemployment. High and increasing profitability contributed to the increased willingness of firms to invest. A relatively moderate rate of nominal wage growth, only slightly faster than the rate of increase in labour productivity, ensured that unit wage costs rose only modestly. This, in turn, contributed to a further decline in the EU inflation rate. In 1998, inflation dropped to only 1.6 per cent, the slowest rate of price increase for over 40 years.

Declining short- and long-term rates of interest also served to improve business and consumer confidence further. Long-term interest rates in the EU have been declining fast in the EU since 1996 and currently stand at around 4 per cent. With the reduction in inflationary expectations, that implies a real long-term rate of interest of roughly 2 per cent, which is much the same as the long-run rate of growth of productive potential in the EU. At the same time, there has been a significant convergence of long-run rates of interest rates in the countries which joined the single currency on 1 January of this year. Short-term interest rates within the EU also fell over the course of last year. Although short-term interest rates in several countries remained within the range of 3–3.5 per cent for much of the year, significant reductions took place in several Member States (notably, Spain, Ireland, Italy and Portugal) towards the end of the year with the build-up to the launch of the euro. However, given the sharp drop in inflation, the level of short-term interest rates prevailing at the end of 1998 still implied a real rate of between 2–3 per cent. The fact that short-term rates were at much the same level as long-term rates (i.e. the yield curve was virtually flat) suggests that monetary conditions within the EU can be expected to ease further during 1999.

If falling interest rates imply an easing of the monetary policy stance within the EU during the course of 1998, the same cannot be said of budgetary policy. For the EU as a whole, the government deficit fell in 1998 to 1.5 per cent of GDP, its lowest level for several decades. In 1993, it reached a peak of over 6 per cent of GDP. As part of the convergence criteria for qualifying to join the single currency, Member States were required to reduce their budget deficits to a level no greater than 3 per cent of GDP. In addition, they were expected to reduce the ratio of government debt to GDP to a level no greater than 60 per cent of GDP. In 1998, for the EU as a whole, the debt to GDP ratio reached 69.7 per cent, a small reduction from 71.7 per cent in the previous year. However, this improvement was almost entirely due to higher growth (which boosted tax revenues and reduced spending on unemployment benefit) and lower interest rates (which reduced interest charges on outstanding debt). In fact, in 1998, the cyclically adjusted deficit rose somewhat as a share of GDP. On the other hand, the forecasts of the Commission (Commission, 1999a) anticipate that this year will see a reduction in both the actual and the cyclically adjusted borrowing ratio. Thus, after a pause in 1998, the process of budget consolidation, which has been taking place since 1993, has been resumed.

The major deficiency in the performance of the EU economy in 1998, however, has been the continuing high level of unemployment. During 1998, the unemployment rate fell from 10.6 to 10.0 per cent, a modest improvement. However, this remains high in comparison with both other advanced industrialized regions and with the EU's own past historical levels: the unemployment rate averaged 4.5 per cent in the United States and 4.1 per cent in Japan. Moreover, even this figure is only an average, which disguises disturbingly higher rates in certain Member States (notably, Spain at 18.8 per cent, Italy 12.2 per cent, France 11.9 per cent and Finland 11.4 per cent). On the other hand, the strong performance of output in 1998 did result in the EU's biggest increase in employment for several years. In 1998, employment grew by 1.1 per cent, a rate not achieved since 1990. However, with an expanding labour force, enhanced by higher rates of participation (more people being drawn back into the workforce), the growth in the number of jobs available remains inadequate to bring about a significant reduction in the unemployment rate. A particular concern for the EU is that the employment rate, which measures the number of employed relative to the population of working age, is well below that of other advanced industrialized countries. At 61 per cent, it is well below the level in the United States and Japan (roughly 74 per cent in both cases) and well below the rate existing in the EU in previous decades.

Clearly, the current high levels of unemployment within the EU are, in part, the consequence of several years of unsatisfactory growth. Over the period 1991–98, GDP grew at a rate of only 1.9 per cent a year on average. Partly as a consequence of this, employment actually fell at an average rate of 0.1 per cent a year. The average unemployment rate rose from 8.3 per cent in 1991 to a high of 10.9 per cent in 1996, before falling to 10 per cent last year. By way of contrast, over the same period, the real GDP of the US grew by 2.6 per cent a year, resulting in the creation of new jobs at a rate of 1.5 per cent every year. The explanation for this difference lies, at least partly, in the macroeconomic policies being pursued in the two regions. Both regions experienced a recession in the early 1990s as efforts were made to bring down inflation. However, the US economy recovered more rapidly.

One reason was that the US entered the recession with a much reduced budget deficit, which provided room for a fiscal stimulus to the economy. At the same time, the monetary authorities engineered a series of reductions in real short-term interest rates, which reinforced the expansionary effects of fiscal policy. By way of contrast, the Member States of the EU all faced much larger budget deficits, such that budgetary policy could not provide the necessary support to the economy to permit as early and rapid a recovery as in the United States. Indeed, the requirement to reduce their level of borrowing in order to meet the convergence criteria laid down by the Treaty on European Union (TEU) necessitated budget consolidation at a time when their economies were stagnant or, at best, growing slowly. In addition, because the EU lacked a common monetary policy analogous to that of the United States, there was no mechanism for bringing about the necessary reduction in short-term interest rates. Rather, because of the currency turmoil within the Exchange Rate Mechanism (ERM), several Member States were forced to maintain extremely high levels of short-term rates in order to give credibility to their declared parities within the ERM.

What is less clear is the extent to which the EU's high unemployment rate reflects structural as opposed to macroeconomic factors. Without doubt, the performance of the US economy has been impressive in this respect when contrasted with that of the EU. Since 1990, unemployment in the US has been nearly half the rate applying in the EU, while at the same time inflation has, until now, been lower. This might suggest that the US economy is able to grow at a faster rate without encountering inflationary bottlenecks by virtue of greater supply-side flexibility. Much attention has been focused in recent years on so-called supply-side rigidities and costs, which hold back growth and hinder job creation in Europe. The single market programme (SMP) has sought to address many of the impediments which exist in the markets for goods and services, hold back growth and reduce the competitiveness of EU industries. However, similar impediments in the labour market may be a further factor contributing to the EU's high unemployment rate. These include taxes that impose high non-wage costs on employers who take on additional workers, regulations that restrict the ability of employers to dismiss workers and thereby discourage them from hiring new workers, high marginal tax rates on low incomes which discourage low-skilled workers from seeking work and wage-rate rigidities that prevent labour markets from clearing. Further labour market reforms may be needed if the EU is to achieve desired long-term rates of growth without running into inflationary bottlenecks.

On the external front, the EU enjoyed a current account surplus with the rest of the world equal to 1.2 per cent of GDP, slightly below the 1.5 per cent of GDP recorded for 1997. Taking the Euro-11 alone, the surplus was slightly higher at 1.7 per cent of GDP. The surplus for the EU as a whole compares with a deficit equal to 0.3 per cent of GDP for the period 1991–95. As the EU's current account has moved into surplus during the decade, the US current account deficit has increased from 1.0 per cent of GDP between 1991–95 to 2.5 per cent of GDP in 1998. In part, this may reflect the faster pace of growth in the US economy relative to that of the EU. In part, too, it is the result of a modest rise in the value of the dollar relative to the EU currencies measured in real terms since 1995.

II. Main Economic Indicators

Economic Growth

Table 1 shows the rate of real GDP growth in individual EU Member States for various years and the forecast rate of growth for this year and the next.

Table 1: Gross Domestic Product, Annual Average % Change, 1961–2000

	1961–1973	1974–1985	1986–1990	1991–1995	1996	1997	1998 Estimate	1999 Forecast	2000 Assuming Unchanged Policies
Austria	4.9	2.3	3.2	1.9	2.0	2.5	3.3	2.3	2.7
Belgium	4.9	1.8	3.0	1.3	1.3	3.0	2.9	1.9	2.5
Denmark	4.3	2.0	1.3	2.5	3.2	3.3	2.7	1.7	2.0
Finland	5.0	2.7	3.4	–0.5	4.1	5.6	5.3	3.7	3.9
France	5.4	2.2	3.2	1.1	1.6	2.3	3.2	2.3	2.7
Germany	4.3	1.7	3.4	2.0	1.3	2.2	2.8	1.7	2.4
Greece	8.5	1.7	1.2	1.2	2.4	3.2	3.7	3.4	3.6
Ireland	4.4	3.8	4.6	6.2	8.3	10.6	11.9	9.3	8.6
Italy	5.3	2.7	3.0	1.1	0.7	1.5	1.4	1.6	2.3
Luxembourg	4.0	1.8	6.4	5.4	3.0	3.7	5.7	3.2	4.1
Netherlands	4.9	1.9	3.1	2.1	3.1	3.6	3.7	2.3	2.7
Portugal	6.9	2.2	5.5	1.8	3.2	3.1	4.0	3.2	3.3
Spain	7.2	1.9	4.5	1.3	2.4	3.5	3.8	3.3	3.5
Sweden	4.1	1.8	2.3	0.5	1.3	1.8	2.9	2.2	2.7
UK	3.2	1.4	3.3	1.6	2.6	3.5	2.3	1.1	2.3
EUR 11	5.2	2.1	3.4	1.5	1.6	2.5	3.0	2.2	2.7
EUR 15	4.8	2.0	3.3	1.5	1.8	2.7	2.9	2.1	2.7

Source: Commission (1999b).

Not since 1991 has the EU enjoyed a growth rate faster than in 1998. The fastest rate of economic growth (11.9 per cent) occurred in Ireland. Indeed, throughout the 1990s, Ireland's growth rate has been significantly above that of other Member States. Luxembourg, Finland and Portugal all achieved growth rates in excess of 4 per cent. At the other end of the spectrum, Italy, for the third year running, was the most sluggish economy. By way of contrast, the acceleration of growth in Germany and, to a greater extent, in France did much to lift the EU economy on to a plateau of faster growth. Disappointing output figures for the fourth quarter, however, suggest that growth in Germany may have weakened significantly towards the end of the year.

In its latest forecast, the Commission predicts a reduction in the growth of output to 2.1 per cent in 1999, rising to 2.7 per cent in 2000 (Commission, 1999b). As in 1998, the main contributor to slower growth will be external trade. In 1998, net exports contributed –0.1 per cent to GDP growth. The Commission forecasts a negative contribution of 0.3 per cent in 1999. The export sector could potentially exert a more damaging effect on EU growth if the next 12 months were to witness a strong rise in the external value of the euro. On the other hand, private domestic demand is expected to remain strong. Clearly, however, this depends crucially on consumer and business confidence remaining high. On the negative side, confidence could be upset if the global financial crisis were to worsen. Equity prices on all the world's major stock markets are thought grossly to overvalue the true worth of companies. Should this result in a sudden and sharp decline in stock market prices, there would be an adverse wealth effect on consumers which could have a harmful effect on confidence.

On a more positive note, the Commission expects the slowdown in growth to be short lived and growth to pick up in 2000, assuming unchanged policies. The economic fundamentals are regarded as sound and there are grounds for expecting some improvement in the international environment. At the same time, the launching of the euro is expected to have a positive effect on business confidence and to yield an important stimulus to fixed investment. However, should the drop in growth turn out deeper than forecast or more protracted, monetary policy may need to play a role in stimulating demand. With budgetary policy constrained by the need for Member States to fulfil the requirements of the Stability and Growth Pact, some further reduction in short-term interest rates would then be necessary.

Unemployment

Table 2 shows that the average level of unemployment continued to fall in all Member States, bringing the EU average to 10 per cent. However, unemployment has yet to fall to the levels reached just before the recession of 1992–93. Also, as noted above, unemployment remains well above rates in other advanced

Table 2: Annual Average Rates of Unemployment, % of the Civilian Labour Force

	1961–1973	1974–1985	1986–1990	1991–1995	1996	1997	1998 Estimate	1999 Forecast	2000 Assuming Unchanged Policies
Austria	1.4	2.5	3.4	3.7	4.3	4.4	4.4	4.3	4.2
Belgium	2.0	7.7	8.7	8.5	9.7	9.2	8.8	8.3	7.8
Denmark	0.9	6.4	6.4	8.6	6.8	5.6	5.1	4.6	4.8
Finland	2.3	4.8	4.2	13.5	14.8	12.7	11.4	10.1	9.4
France	2.2	6.4	9.7	11.1	12.4	12.4	11.9	11.5	11.0
Germany	0.7	4.2	5.9	7.3	8.9	9.9	9.4	9.0	8.7
Greece	4.2	3.8	6.6	8.3	9.6	9.6	9.6	9.4	9.2
Ireland	5.7	10.6	15.5	14.5	11.6	9.8	7.8	6.0	4.7
Italy	5.2	7.0	9.6	10.3	12.0	12.1	12.2	12.2	11.9
Luxembourg	0.0	1.7	2.1	2.5	3.0	2.8	2.8	2.7	2.5
Netherlands	1.3	7.1	7.4	6.4	6.3	5.2	4.0	3.6	3.3
Portugal	2.5	6.9	6.1	5.6	7.3	6.8	4.9	4.7	4.6
Spain	2.8	11.3	18.9	20.9	22.2	20.8	18.8	17.3	15.8
Sweden	2.0	2.4	2.0	7.2	9.6	9.9	8.2	7.8	7.6
UK	2.0	6.9	9.0	9.5	8.2	7.0	6.3	6.5	6.6
EUR 11	2.5	6.6	9.4	10.4	11.8	11.8	10.9	10.4	9.9
EUR 15	2.4	6.4	8.9	10.0	10.9	10.6	10.0	9.6	9.2

Source: Commission (1999b.)

industrialized countries. The highest rates of unemployment within the EU are to be found in Spain (18.8 per cent), Italy (12.2 per cent), France (11.9 per cent) and Finland (11.4 per cent). In the case of Finland, this appears to be directly the result of the severity of the drop in output experienced in the first half of the decade. However, the recovery from a maximum rate of 19 per cent has been very rapid. In the case of Italy, unemployment has risen because output has been growing too slowly and employment decreasing. France also failed to achieve a sufficiently rapid increase in employment to effect any reduction in the unemployment rate. In Spain, growth slowed down markedly in the first half of the decade. As a consequence, the rate of unemployment more than trebled from only 6 per cent in 1991 to 24.1 per cent in 1994. Although in recent years output has risen strongly, the unemployment rate has been slow to fall.

Even in those Member States with lower rates of unemployment, the average is generally above that of other advanced industrialized countries. Only in Luxembourg, the Netherlands and Austria is the unemployment rate below that of the United States. Although these three countries did enjoy above average growth in 1998, they were by no means the fastest growing economies. Indeed, it is noteworthy that Ireland, which enjoyed the fastest growth of any Member

State throughout the 1990s, still faced an unemployment rate almost twice that of the United States. On the other hand, Ireland began the decade with an unemployment rate significantly above that of other Member States (14.5 per cent). Whereas most other Member States experienced a rise in unemployment during this period, Ireland's unemployment fell. (The Netherlands and the UK also succeeded in cutting unemployment, although from a lower starting point.)

Whereas total employment increased at a rate of 1.3 per cent a year in the United States between 1991–95, it fell by 0.5 per cent a year in the EU. Only in Luxembourg and Ireland did employment expand at a rate equal to or in excess of that of the US. In more recent years, net employment has increased in the EU as growth has picked up. Last year, employment rose by 1.1 per cent, only a little below that of the US (1.5 per cent). In Germany, however, there was no rise in employment. The Commission forecasts a further decline in the unemployment rate to 9.6 per cent in 1999 and 9.2 per cent in 2000, despite a small reduction in output growth. Falls in the unemployment rate tend to lag increases in output, so some of this improvement reflects growth currently being enjoyed. However so long as output growth of 2.1 per cent in 1999 and 2.7 per cent in 2000 is achieved, this should be sufficient to permit some further reduction in the unemployment rate for the region as a whole. The Commission expects productivity growth of 1.5 per cent in 1999 and 1.8 per cent in 2000, while the labour force is predicted to grow by 0.4 per cent and 0.5 per cent respectively (Commission, 1999a). It follows that output growth of between 1.9 and 2.3 per cent will be needed simply to prevent unemployment from rising. Anything in excess of this should lead to a fall in the unemployment rate.

Inflation

One of the factors, which may provide scope for the monetary authorities to bring about a further reduction in short-term interest rates, is the very positive situation on the inflation front. The EU's implicit deflator of private consumption estimates the EU's rate of inflation at 1.5 per cent, the lowest rate for 40 years. In part this reflects global factors, in particular the recession in East Asia induced by the global financial crisis, the fall in oil and non-oil commodity prices and the depreciation of the dollar. In the course of 1998, the average price of a barrel of Brent crude oil dipped briefly below $12, a figure not witnessed since 1986. However, domestic factors were also important. The rate of increase in nominal wage rates was modest relative to the growth in labour productivity. As a consequence, unit wage costs rose at a very modest rate. Another reason why inflation remained subdued was the existence of a substantial output gap (broadly, the difference between what the EU economy is physically capable of producing and actual output) estimated by the Commission at 1.5 per cent. The EU estimates that, currently, the trend rate of growth in the EU is between 2.25

Table 3: Inflation Rates, Annual % Change in the Deflator of Private Consumption

	1961–1973	1974–1985	1986–1990	1991–1995	1996	1997	1998 Estimate	1999 Forecast	2000 Assuming Unchanged Policies
Austria	4.1	5.8	2.0	3.0	2.8	2.0	0.9	1.1	1.3
Belgium	3.7	7.4	2.4	2.7	2.3	1.8	1.0	1.0	1.3
Denmark	6.6	9.6	3.8	1.7	1.7	2.2	1.9	2.3	2.2
Finland	5.7	10.8	4.5	3.0	1.6	2.5	1.4	1.0	1.1
France	4.7	10.5	2.9	2.3	1.8	1.1	0.4	0.5	1.1
Germany	3.5	4.3	1.5	3.5	1.7	1.7	1.0	0.7	1.3
Greece	3.6	18.2	17.6	13.8	8.3	5.6	4.7	2.5	2.2
Ireland	6.3	13.8	3.2	2.5	1.4	0.9	2.5	2.2	2.7
Italy	4.9	15.9	6.1	5.7	4.3	2.5	2.4	1.8	1.9
Luxembourg	3.0	7.4	2.4	3.0	1.6	0.9	1.0	0.7	1.2
Netherlands	5.1	5.7	0.9	2.5	1.6	2.0	1.9	1.8	1.8
Portugal	3.9	22.2	12.2	7.7	3.6	2.5	2.8	2.2	2.1
Spain	6.5	15.4	6.6	5.6	3.4	2.5	2.0	1.8	1.9
Sweden	4.8	10.3	6.7	4.7	1.2	2.2	1.1	0.7	1.0
UK	4.8	11.9	5.4	4.2	3.1	2.6	1.9	2.0	2.0
EUR 11	4.6	10.3	3.7	3.9	2.5	1.9	1.4	1.2	1.5
EUR 15	4.6	10.7	4.4	4.1	2.7	2.1	1.5	1.3	1.6

Source: Commission (1999b).

and 2.5 per cent, which suggests that actual output is growing at a slower rate than productive potential. This suggests that there may exist some scope for output growing faster within the EU without the danger of encountering inflationary bottlenecks.

Table 3 shows the rates of inflation for individual Member States. The highest rates of inflation were apparent in Greece (4.7 per cent) who remains outside the euro and Ireland (2.5 per cent), Spain (2.0 per cent) and Portugal (2.8 per cent), all of whom have joined. At the other extreme, France enjoyed something very close to stable prices. Within the Euro-zone, despite a low average rate of inflation, there was a small tendency for inflation differentials to widen during 1998. Whereas Germany, France and Belgium all enjoyed a significant fall in their inflation rates, Ireland and Portugal witnessed a small increase. For 1999, the Commission expects a further decline in the rate of inflation to 1.3 per cent before picking up to 1.6 per cent in 2000 as growth accelerates (Commission, 1999b). Austria, France and the UK will experience some modest increase in inflation. All other countries, including those with above average rates of inflation, will see inflation fall further.

Public Finances

In 1998, the Member States made further progress in reducing their public sector deficits. General government borrowing declined to 1.5 per cent of GDP for the Fifteen (2.3 per cent for the Euro-11). This compares with a level of government borrowing equal to 6.5 per cent of GDP in 1993. Table 4 shows the level of government borrowing in individual Member States.

All of the Member States succeeded in reducing government borrowing below the maximum of 3 per cent of GDP needed to achieve the convergence criteria set out in the Maastricht Treaty. In the previous year, Greece had a deficit equivalent to 3.9 per cent of GDP and France of 3 per cent. A determined effort was, therefore, necessary if these two countries were to keep below 3 per cent in 1998. The average level of government borrowing for the Fifteen of 1.5 per cent of GDP compares favourably with 5.2 per cent of GDP in the first half of the decade. This illustrates the degree of fiscal consolidation that has taken place in the Member States in preparation for monetary union.

Table 4: General Government Net Lending (+) or Borrowing (−) as a % of GDP

	1970–1973	1974–1985	1986–1990	1991–1995	1996	1997	1998 Estimate	1999 Forecast	2000 Assuming Unchanged Policies
Austria	1.5	−2.3	−3.2	−3.9	−3.7	−1.9	−2.1	−2.0	−1.9
Belgium	−3.4	−7.9	−7.1	−5.9	−3.1	−1.9	−1.3	−0.9	−0.6
Denmark	4.2	−2.7	1.3	−2.6	−0.9	0.4	0.8	2.8	2.9
Finland	4.5	3.7	4.0	−4.9	−3.1	−1.2	1.0	2.5	2.7
France	0.7	−1.7	−1.8	−4.5	−4.1	−3.0	−2.9	−2.4	−2.0
Germany[a]	0.2	−2.8	−1.5	−3.1	−3.4	−2.7	−2.1	−2.2	−2.1
Greece	0.2	−5.0	−12.1	−11.7	−7.5	−3.9	−2.4	−2.1	−1.9
Ireland	−4.1	−10.4	−5.4	−2.1	−0.3	1.1	2.3	2.5	3.1
Italy	−5.4	−9.6	−10.9	−9.2	−6.6	−2.7	−2.7	−2.3	−2.1
Luxembourg	2.7	1.9	−	1.8	2.8	2.9	2.1	1.5	1.4
Netherlands	−0.5	−3.6	−5.1	−3.6	−2.0	−0.9	−0.9	−1.6	−1.3
Portugal	2.0	−6.9	−4.5	−5.4	−3.3	−2.5	−2.3	−2.0	−1.7
Spain	0.4	−2.7	−4.1	−5.7	−4.5	−2.6	−1.8	−1.6	−1.3
Sweden	4.5	−1.7	3.2	−7.7	−3.5	−0.7	2.0	0.3	1.8
UK	0.1	−3.6	−0.8	−6.1	−4.4	−1.9	0.6	−0.1	−0.1
EUR 11	−0.7	−3.9	−4.1	−5.0	−4.1	−2.5	−2.1	−1.9	−1.7
EUR 15	−0.3	−3.7	−3.4	−5.2	−4.1	−2.3	−1.5	−1.5	−1.3

Source: Commission (1999b).
Note: [a] Not including unification-related debt and asset assumptions by the federal government in 1985 (Treuhand, eastern housing companies and Deutsche Kreditbank) equal to DEM 227.5 bn.

However, less success was achieved in bringing the ratio of government debt to GDP below the 60 per cent level stipulated in the Maastricht Treaty. For the Fifteen, the ratio of government debt to GDP stood at 69.7 per cent, only marginally down on the previous year. (For the Euro 11, the ratio was 73.4 per cent.) Table 5 shows the position for individual Member States. Three Member States – Italy, Belgium and Greece – had debt to GDP ratios of over 100 per cent. A further five countries – Germany, Spain, Netherlands, Austria and Sweden – had debt to GDP ratios in excess of 60 per cent. Although all of these countries managed to reduce the level of public sector indebtedness during 1998, it was insufficient to bring about any significant improvement in public finances.

Moreover, much of the improvement reflected the faster rates of growth that these economies enjoyed, combined with the effects of lower interest rates. Because this year should see only a modest reduction in growth, while interest rates should remain low, it is reasonable to expect some further reduction in budget deficits. However, the requirements of the Stability and Growth Pact are that budget deficits in the Euro-zone should not exceed 3 per cent in any year 'in normal circumstances' and should be close to balance over the duration of the

Table 5: General Government Gross Debt as a % of GDP

	1980	1985	1990	1994	1995	1996	1997	1998 Estimate	1999 Forecast	2000 Assuming Unchanged Policies
Austria	36.6	49.8	58.0	65.6	69.4	69.8	64.3	63.1	62.7	62.0
Belgium	77.1	120.2	126.0	135.1	132.2	128.0	123.4	117.3	113.4	109.7
Denmark[a]	37.6	70.4	59.7	76.5	72.1	67.4	63.6	58.1	54.7	50.4
Finland	11.6	16.4	14.5	59.6	58.1	57.8	54.9	49.6	46.2	43.1
France	20.1	31.0	35.5	48.6	52.8	55.7	58.1	58.5	59.3	59.2
Germany	31.7	41.7	43.8	49.9	58.3	60.8	61.5	61.0	61.2	61.2
Greece	23.9	51.5	90.1	109.3	110.1	112.2	109.4	106.5	105.4	103.8
Ireland	70.3	102.4	93.3	86.5	78.9	69.4	61.3	52.1	42.6	34.5
Italy	58.1	82.3	98.5	125.7	125.3	124.6	122.4	118.7	116.0	112.6
Luxembourg	12.5	13.0	4.6	5.5	5.8	6.3	6.4	6.7	7.6	8.1
Netherlands	46.9	71.5	79.1	77.8	79.0	77.0	71.2	67.7	67.0	65.4
Portugal	32.4	61.9	65.4	63.8	65.9	64.9	61.7	57.8	55.8	54.2
Spain	17.5	43.7	43.9	61.3	64.2	68.6	67.5	65.6	64.7	62.4
Sweden	41.0	63.8	43.5	79.3	78.0	77.2	76.9	75.2	69.7	65.2
UK	54.7	54.1	35.6	50.6	53.0	53.6	52.1	49.4	47.7	45.7
EUR 11	35.3	52.6	58.7	69.5	72.9	75.3	75.1	73.4	72.6	71.2
EUR 15	38.4	53.6	55.2	67.8	70.9	72.8	71.7	69.7	68.6	67.0

Source: Commission (1999b).
Note: [a] Government deposits with the central bank, government holdings of non-government bonds and public enterprise related debt amounted to some 11.7 per cent of GDP in 1998.

business cycle. The latter necessitates attainment of a budget surplus in the upswing years of the cycle. In 1998, only six Member States achieved this, three of which are outside the Euro-zone (the UK, Sweden and Denmark). Not only does this mean that fiscal policy in the EU must assume a contractionary stance at a time when output growth may, arguably, need a stimulus, it also means that very few Member States within the Euro-zone have any scope for using fiscal policy in a countercyclical manner to combat any asymmetric shocks that they might experience.

Of particular concern must be the degree of budget consolidation, which is planned to take place in Member States already experiencing high unemployment and below average rates of economic growth. Spain has the highest unemployment rate within the Union, yet is faced with one of the most demanding tasks of turning a budget deficit of just under 2 per cent of GDP into a budget surplus. Italy faces a similar dilemma. A budget deficit of 2.7 per cent of GDP must be converted in to a surplus over the same period if any inroads are to be made into the debt to GDP ratio, which is the highest of all the Member States. France is similarly constrained, while Finland has only a little more room for adjustment. Of the four countries currently outside the euro, Denmark and the UK currently meet the convergence criteria for government borrowing. However, Greece and Sweden have ratios of debt to GDP in excess of 60 per cent, although, in both cases, the ratio is falling.

It is clear that most of the reduction in public sector deficits will have to take place through cuts in public consumption spending. The share of public investment in GDP has been declining in all Member States over several decades. At about 47 per cent of GDP in the Euro-zone as a whole, the level of taxation is high in comparison with other advanced industrialized countries. Any attempt to raise the tax level, therefore, is likely to have damaging effects on economic growth and competitiveness. In particular, any increase in direct taxes is likely to reduce the incentive to invest and to impose costs on work at a time when the need is to boost employment. Member States will, therefore, need to find ways of increasing the efficiency of public expenditure and making significant savings in costs.

III. Economic Developments in the Member States

Germany

The first half of 1998 saw a noticeable acceleration of economic growth, after several years of disappointing performance. However, by the second half of the year, it was clear that growth was beginning to peter out. The final quarter actually saw a 0.4 per cent reduction in GDP. Other indicators appear to confirm a worrying drop in business confidence. Forecasts for growth next year have been widely lowered downwards. The Commission's latest forecast predicts only 1.7 per cent increase in GDP in 1999 (Commission, 1999b). This is disturbing because, at 9.4 per cent, unemployment in Germany is high. What has gone wrong? The major factor has been the global crisis, which has badly affected some of Germany's most important export markets, namely, Japan, South East Asia and Russia. A sharp rise in the D-Mark against the US dollar during 1998 further aggravated the situation. The devaluation of the Brazilian real could further damage German's export prospects in 1999. Germany's exports fell dramatically in 1998 and it is more dependent for economic growth on exports to the rest of the world than are most other Member States. The heavy dependence of the German economy on manufacturing has left it more vulnerable to the global slowdown than other countries.

There must also be concern that, despite rapid growth in the first half of the year, total employment was stagnant. This follows seven years of more or less continuous employment decline. This would suggest that, although increased private sector demand for goods and services could help tackle Germany's unemployment problem, it is unlikely to be sufficient on its own. This is all the more the case because Germany's budget deficit leaves no room for fiscal expansion. Instead, the government must seek other ways of increasing employment, including measures to reduce taxes on employment, structural measures to create greater labour market flexibility and measures to boost business confidence. Another important issue will be to hold down wage increases. Some commentators have pointed to the Dutch example as an illustration of how agreement between social partners to contain the growth in real wage rates can contribute to rapid employment growth. (The Commission forecasts employment growth of 1.3 per cent in the Netherlands for 1996–2000 compared with 0.1 per cent for Germany.)

France

By way of contrast, the French economy enjoyed a healthy expansion in 1998. GDP grew by 3.2 per cent compared with 2.3 per cent in the previous year. Whereas exports played an important role in France's growth in 1997, the main stimulus in 1998 came from domestic demand and, in particular, private consumption spending. In 1998, private consumption grew at a rate of 3.6 per cent, with increased spending on housing a major contributory factor. Lower interest rates, rising disposable incomes and a lower rate of inflation were important factors. By way of contrast with Germany, France has benefited from an expanding service sector.

Unemployment remains France's major problem. At 11.9 per cent, France has the third highest unemployment rate in the EU. However, in 1998, it enjoyed a 1.3 per cent increase in employment, a faster rate than for several decades. A major factor was the government's youth employment scheme designed to create new public sector jobs for first-time job seekers. However, 1999 is likely to see somewhat slower growth in employment. The European Commission forecasts a reduction in the growth rate to 2.3 per cent with unemployment falling only modestly to 11.5 per cent (Commission, 1999b). A faltering of growth in the German economy would also have negative spillover effects on the French economy. With an inflation rate of only 0.4 per cent, France's biggest problem may be one of price deflation. The Commission predicts that the inflation rate will rise only very slightly to 0.5 per cent in 1999. With a central government borrowing level of 2.9 per cent of GDP, France has no flexibility to use fiscal policy to stimulate demand further.

Italy

With real GDP growth in 1998 of only 1.4 per cent, Italy remains the most sluggish economy in the EU. Moreover, output is forecast to increase only a little faster in 1999. With an unemployment rate of 12.2 per cent, Italy has the second highest unemployment rate in the EU. The slow growth of output in 1998 was due partly to a low rate of private consumption, and partly to poor export performance. Private consumption was depressed by the phasing out of tax incentives on car sales, the squeeze on personal disposable incomes and a fall in consumer confidence. In the past three years, short-term interest rates have fallen dramatically from 9 per cent to 3 per cent at the beginning of 1999. Yet, these reductions in interest rates have singularly failed to stimulate the economy. One reason is that the Italians have a high propensity to save and declining interest rates serve simply to reduce their income from savings. This serves to offset the beneficial effect of lower interest rates on the cost of borrowing.

Italy's problem is that slow growth has made it more difficult for the government to reduce the level of its borrowing. At 2.7 per cent of GDP, government borrowing in 1998 was comfortably below the 3 per cent threshold required to qualify for entry to the single currency. However, at 118.7 per cent the debt to GDP ratio is the highest in the EU. Hence, Italy must run a primary budget surplus (the difference between government spending and revenue excluding interest payments) in excess of GDP growth in order to reduce the level of outstanding debt relative to GDP. Falling interest rates have offset some of the adverse effects of slower growth on tax receipts. However, the stance of Italy's fiscal policy must remain contractionary for some years to come. Because of its exposure to the crisis in the Asian and Russian markets, Italy cannot rely upon export demand to boost growth. In addition, the traditional escape route of a lira devaluation is not available, although it will benefit from any decline in the external value of the euro which takes place. This means that it must rely on structural reforms to effect a major reduction in the unemployment rate.

United Kingdom

After a growth rate of 3.5 per cent in 1997, growth in the UK economy dropped to 2.3 per cent in 1998. The crisis in East Asia, combined with a sharp appreciation of sterling, were contributory factors. However, there were signs that the UK economy was beginning to turn downwards even before the deterioration in the global economic situation. The reason was the monetary and fiscal policy stance adopted by the authorities in response to evidence that the economy was growing too fast. Because the forecasts showed inflation set to rise above the official target of 2.5 per cent, monetary policy remained relatively tight throughout much of 1998. At over 7 per cent in September, 1998, UK short-term interest rates stood well above the level prevailing in any other major industrialized economy. At the same time, the budget moved from a deficit of 1.9 per cent of GDP to a surplus of 0.6 per cent. The Commission's latest forecast shows growth decelerating further to 1.1 per cent in 1999 before picking up to 2.3 per cent in 2000 (Commission, 1999b). With inflation forecast to rise to 2 per cent in 1999, the scope for further reductions in short-term interest rates may be limited. On the other hand, the healthy state of the public finances means that fiscal policy could be eased should growth turn out to be disappointing. The Commission forecast a budget surplus of 2 per cent of GDP by 2000. However, the government remains committed to the 'golden rule' that, over the economic cycle, tax revenues should not exceed current government spending. The main threat to the UK economy remains an overvalued pound in relation to both the euro and the US dollar.

Spain

In 1998, Spain's real GDP grew at a rate of 3.8 per cent, making Spain one of the fastest-growing economies in the EU. Moreover, the Commission forecasts only a slight reduction in output growth for 1999 (Commission, 1999b). The main contribution has come from rising private consumption and investment in equipment by companies. (Fixed investment grew by 12.7 per cent in 1998.) Increasing optimism about Spain's prospects under EMU has been an important factor. Higher employment and rising real incomes have also played a major role. Private domestic demand has been further encouraged by a fall in short-term interest rates from 8.75 per cent in 1996 to 3 per cent at the beginning of 1999. However, at 18.8 per cent, Spain's unemployment rate remains the highest in the EU, despite rapid employment growth in recent years.

The fall in the inflation rate to 2 per cent means that output can continue to grow quickly without the need to confront any inflationary constraints, providing wage settlements remain modest. However, growth will be hit by the downturn on the world market, especially in Latin America. Slower growth in other parts of the EU could also have an adverse effect on Spanish exports. The need to reduce the level of government borrowing further can be expected to exert an additional dampener on output growth. With a ratio of government borrowing to GDP of 1.8 per cent and debt to GDP ratio of 66 per cent, Spain has more fiscal flexibility than Italy. Moreover, fast growth and lower interest rates should enable Spain to achieve a more rapid reduction in borrowing than other Member States while, at the same time, applying a more moderate fiscal squeeze.

Other Member States

Austria grew at a rate of 3.3 per cent in 1998, slightly faster than 2.5 per cent in the previous year. Investment rose fast and consumer confidence was restored, after several years of fiscal squeeze required to satisfy the convergence criteria for joining the euro. A particular concern has been the absence of little growth in total employment, such that the unemployment rate, although low in comparison with other Member States, has been creeping upwards for several years in succession. On the other hand, at 0.9 per cent, Austria's inflation rate is among the lowest in the EU.

Belgium grew by 2.9 per cent in 1998, which made possible some further reduction in its unemployment rate to 8.8 per cent. Over the last two years, Belgium has made strenuous efforts to reduce the level of government indebtedness, which, at 117.3 per cent of GDP is the second highest in the EU. Despite this, output growth has held up moderately well. It is clear however that, if the level of indebtedness is to be reduced further, Belgium will need to run a primary budget surplus for several years to come. The Commission forecasts a deceleration in growth to 1.9 per cent in 1999, before recovering to 2.5 per cent in 2000 (Commission, 1999b).

Denmark experienced a small reduction in its growth rate to 2.7 per cent in 1998, after growing by 3.3 per cent in 1997. Growth of only 1.7 per cent is forecast for 1999. At 5.1 per cent, unemployment remained low, while inflation was moderate at 1.9 per cent. A particular concern for Denmark was the switch of the current account of the balance of payments from a surplus of 0.9 per cent to a deficit of 1.2 per cent, which suggests declining competitiveness.

Ireland remains Europe's 'miracle economy' with GDP growing at a rate of 11.9 per cent in 1998, compared with the EU average of 2.9 per cent. At the same time, employment grew by 6.1 per cent and the unemployment rate fell to 7.8 per cent. Foreign investment has continued to play a key role in this process with foreign companies attracted to Ireland by its low rate of corporation tax. Despite the phenomenal output growth, inflation remained relatively modest at 2.5 per cent. The social pact between unions and management, in which wage moderation by unions was exchanged for tax cuts promised by the government, is widely regarded as having been an important reason for this. However, although inflation is forecast to fall to 2.2 per cent in 1999, there are signs of overheating in the economy. Asset prices, particularly housing prices in the Dublin area, are rising fast. The fall in short-term interest rates from 7 per cent in 1997 to 3 per cent at the beginning of 1999 can be expected to add considerably to demand pressures. With a budget surplus of 2.3 per cent of GDP and forecast to rise to 2.5 per cent of GDP in 1999, fiscal policy is performing a valuable counter-cyclical role in restraining demand.

Finland enjoyed its seventh year of economic upswing in 1998 with GDP growing by 5.3 per cent, down slightly on 5.6 per cent in the previous year. Although, at 11.4 per cent, unemployment remained high in comparison with other Member States, the rate has been falling steadily since 1994. At the same time, inflation fell further to 1.4 per cent. A marked reduction in growth to 3.7 per cent is forecast for 1999, but this is not expected to prevent unemployment from coming down further. Finland's public finances were strong with a budget surplus of 1 per cent of GDP and a debt to GDP ratio of 49.6 per cent.

Greece made considerable progress in 1998 towards meeting the convergence criteria for entry to the third stage of EMU in 2001. Inflation fell to 4.7 per cent. Government borrowing was reduced to 2.4 per cent of GDP and the debt to GDP ratio to 106.5 per cent. At the same time, it managed a growth rate of 3.7 per cent. Unemployment was unchanged at 9.6 per cent. It is widely recognized that Greece's biggest challenge in the next two years will be to reduce inflation to within 1.5 percentage points of the three best performing Member States.

In 1998, *Luxembourg* continued to enjoy one of the fastest rates of growth in the EU. GDP grew by 5.7 per cent. At the same time, its unemployment rate of 2.8 was the lowest in the EU, while inflation also remained modest at 1 per cent. Its budget was in surplus at 2.1 per cent of GDP and the government debt to GDP ratio stood at a mere 6.7 per cent. In every sense, Luxembourg could be described as Europe's model economy.

The Netherlands enjoyed a GDP growth rate of 3.7 per cent and an unemployment rate of only 4 per cent. Only Luxembourg enjoyed a lower unemployment rate. The Netherlands' 'active labour market policy', with its emphasis on training people to be fit for work, is widely regarded as a cause of its success in reducing unemployment. An alternative view is that the low rate of unemployment is due to peculiar features of the Dutch labour market, such as a relatively low average number of hours worked, a low labour force participation rate and a relatively high number of workers on sickness or disability benefit (see Munchau and Cramb, 1997). An additional strength of the Dutch economy has been that fast growth has not resulted in accelerating inflation. In 1998, prices rose by only 1.9 per cent.

Like Spain, *Portugal* has enjoyed rapid growth in recent years. In 1998, its GDP grew by 4 per cent. The biggest problem has been one of overheating, with the inflation rate rising to 2.8 per cent. The downturn in world economic growth, however, is likely to have a benign effect on Portugal by reducing inflationary pressures, providing that it is not too severe. Portugal's main concern must be that euro-wide short-term interest rates will be lowered by too much. Budgetary policy, however, may be able to play a useful role in counteracting the effects of excessive monetary expansion. At 2.3 per cent of GDP, Portugal's budget deficit is excessive and needs to be reduced further to fulfil the objectives of the Growth and Stability Pact.

In 1998, *Sweden* grew at a rate of 2.9 per cent, compared with only 1.8 per cent in 1997. For the first time in six years, unemployment fell below 9 per cent to 8.2 per cent and should fall further to 7.8 per cent in 1999. A key factor was a boom in private sector fixed investment, which grew at an annual rate of 12.4 per cent. At the same time, inflation remained modest at 1.1 per cent and the budget in surplus at 2 per cent of GDP.

IV. Conclusion

Although 1999 will lead to weaker growth due to a deterioration in the global economic climate, the Commission remains optimistic that rapid growth will be resumed in 2000, assuming unchanged economic policies. The decision of the European Central Bank on 8 April to cut interest rates by 50 basis points to 2.5 per cent, the first cut since the launching of the euro, should help ease monetary conditions within the Euro-zone. The cut in UK interest rates, which took place on the same day, will provide some stimulus to weakening growth in the UK. However, the bigger problem is that not all the Member State economies are situated at the same point in the business cycle. While lower interest rates are needed in the slower growing large economies, such as Germany, France and Italy, they may create problems for the smaller, faster-growing economies, namely Ireland, Spain and Portugal (see Beattie, 1999). Fortunately, falling commodity prices and a moderate level of wage settlements have, so far, ensured a low inflation rate even in the fast-growing Member States. However, a fall in the euro in the first quarter of 1999 has added to import costs. Should the euro weaken further and the level of wage settlements point upwards, the European Central Bank will be restrained in making any further cuts in short-tern interest rates. The need to bring about a further reduction in levels of government indebtedness will mean that fiscal policy will continue to exert a deflationary impact. In this case, growth could prove more disappointing than has been predicted. Member States would, then, be obliged to place much greater reliance on supply-side measures to boost growth and reduce unemployment.

References

Beattie, A. (1999) 'The Deflationary Ogre Smiles'. *Financial Times*, 9 April.

Commission of the European Communities (1998) 'European Economy, Supplement A'. *Economic Trends,* No. 10, October.

Commission of the European Communities (1999a) *1999 Annual Economic Report, The EU Economy at the Arrival of the Euro: Promoting Growth, Employment and Stability,* Brussels, January, *COM*(1999) 7 final.

Commission of the European Communities (1999b) *Spring Economic Forecasts*, Brussels, 30 March.

Munchau, W. and Cramb, G. (1997) 'Debunking the Dutch Myth'. *Financial Times,* 18 August.

Journal of Common Market Studies

Volume 37, Annual Review
September 1999

Justice and Home Affairs

JÖRG MONAR
University of Leicester

I. Introduction

If 1997 had been the year of major, in some respects even dramatic treaty changes in the areas of Justice and Home Affairs (JHA), 1998 was the year in which the European Union had to prepare for the effective implementation of the whole set of reforms and new objectives. This meant achieving progress in individual policy areas and agreement on major structural questions. On both accounts, 1998 was not a year of spectacular developments. Yet, in spite of major difficulties in implementing some areas of the Treaty of Amsterdam, the Union was able to consolidate its basis for action in the areas of asylum and immigration policy, make some progress with the implementation of its Action Plan against organized crime and adopt two important conventions in the area of judicial co-operation. At the end of the year under review, the Member States also agreed on a range of significant principles and objectives for the next few years.

II. Developments in Individual Policy Areas

Asylum and Immigration

The streams of refugees generated by the continuing instability in Former Yugoslavia and the economic migratory pressure in the Mediterranean again highlighted the need for the EU to define common responses to the challenges of asylum and immigration policy. Both the Member States and the Commission gave clear signs that they wanted to move towards a more proactive attitude to common challenges in these areas.

On 26 January, the Council adopted an action plan on the growing problem of the influx of Kurdish migrants from northern Iraq and south eastern Turkey. This plan comprised a number of innovative elements of EU action. Instead of limiting itself to measures of restriction and control, the Council placed a major emphasis on combating the root causes of migratory movements inside the third countries concerned. It decided to improve the analysis of the underlying cause of these movements, to develop an action-oriented dialogue with Turkey and the United Nations Commission on Human Rights (UNHCR), to seek ways of making more effective use of humanitarian aid and to try to improve non-governmental organization (NGO) access to some of the Kurdish regions. On the internal side, measures were taken to counter illegal immigration more effectively. These focused on improving visa-issuing procedures, the speeding-up of expulsion of persons illegally present in the Member States' territories, and police co-operation in the fight against organized crime which plays a major role in illegal immigration.

Following a Dutch proposal launched at the Vienna European Council in October 1998, the General Affairs Council decided on 7 December to create a high level working group on asylum and migration. Its purpose is twofold: to provide the Council with a list and an assessment of countries of origin and transit from which the large majority of asylum seekers and migrants come, and to develop integrated action plans in respect of these countries. These action plans are to combine economic, humanitarian, political and diplomatic action. They include, for instance, exploration of the possibility of concluding readmission agreements and strengthening co-operation with the UNHCR and NGOs. The broad range of measures falling within the remit of the high level group marked a significant step forward towards an integrated approach to asylum and immigration issues which uses instruments from all three pillars to react to the increasing challenges.

In earlier years the Union had been frequently criticized for focusing on restrictive action rather than taking measures in favour of asylum seekers and refugees. During 1998, some important steps were to reduce this major deficit. On 27 April, the Council adopted two Joint Actions (98/304/JHA and 98/305/JHA) on the financing of specific projects in favour of displaced persons having found temporary protection, asylum-seekers and refugees. The joint actions made a total of 16,750m ECU available for the improvement of admission facilities for persons falling within these categories, and for projects on education facilities, vocational training and information measures assisting reintegra-

tion into their countries of origin. Although projects were described as of an
'experimental' nature only, they allowed the development of new co-operation
mechanisms between the Member States, the UNHCR and various NGOs and
procedures, and also represent a small step forward towards burden-sharing
among the Member States.

Building on its experiences with the pilot projects and on earlier requests by
the European Parliament, the Commission submitted, on 16 December, two
complementary proposals on a Community action programme to promote the
integration of refugees (*COM*(1998) 731) and on practical support in relation to
the reception and voluntary repatriation of refugees, displaced persons and
asylum applicants (*COM*(1998) 733). Both proposals focus on improving
reception conditions for asylum applicants and displaced persons whose status
has been recognized, and can therefore be regarded as suitable candidates for
integration into the society of the Member States. Throughout the year, the
European Commission tried to achieve progress on the difficult issue of establishing common principles for temporary protection regimes for refugees. On 24
June, under pressure from several Member States, the Commission submitted a
new proposal (*COM*(1998) 372), which restricts the circumstances in which
temporary protection regimes can be put in place to 'events of mass flight of
persons' and separates the provisions on the establishment of such regimes from
those on the special assistance to Member States particularly affected. Yet these
concessions were not sufficient to bridge the gap between the majority of the
Member States (which include Germany and Italy), according to which temporary protection and 'solidarity' in the sense of burden-sharing should be linked,
and a minority (including France and Spain) which continued to reject this point
of view. Different views also emerged on questions of whether decisions on
temporary protection should require unanimity and whether burden-sharing
should be of a financial nature or consist of an even distribution of refugees
among all Member States. After an inconclusive discussion at ministerial level
in December, the dossier had to be returned again to the expert level.

The final political agreement on the Eurodac Convention (establishing a
computerized system for the comparison of fingerprints of asylum seekers)
which is of crucial importance for the effective implementation of the Dublin
Convention, was delayed until December 1998 because of two issues: France
objected to the creation of Eurodac's central unit within the Commission and the
UK, Ireland and Denmark opposed the idea of granting a preliminary ruling
competence to the ECJ in a convention concluded on the basis of intergovernmental Title VI TEU. In the end, the Council agreed on reassuring France by
explicitly declaring that the management of Eurodac's central unit by the
Commission would not prejudice the management of the intergovernmental
Schengen Information System (which France wants not to leave to the Commis-

sion) and on satisfying the UK, Ireland and Denmark by temporarily 'freezing' the Eurodac Convention so that it could be established on the basis of a Community regulation following the entry into force of the Treaty of Amsterdam. The ministers also agreed on the desirability of extending electronic fingerprinting to illegal immigrants, a step on which negotiations were still under way at the end of the year.

On 3 December, the Council adopted a Joint Action (98/700/JHA) on setting up a European Image Archiving System (FADO). The system was designed to enable the Member States to exchange, by computerized means and within very short periods of time, images of false and forged as well as genuine documents, together with information about forgery and security techniques. It should serve as a supporting instrument for both immigration policy (where forged documents represent an increasing problem) and police co-operation.

Police Co-operation and the Fight against Organized Crime

More than two years after its signing, the Convention on the establishment of Europol entered into force on 1 October. It had been delayed not only by lengthy national ratification procedures but also by difficulties and disagreements over some of the aspects of the implementation of the Convention. Germany, for instance, raised objections to the immunity from legal process granted to members of bodies and staff of Europol in respect to any acts performed in the exercise of their duties. At the beginning of the year this immunity was still criticized in Germany as being uncomfortably close to the principles of an authoritarian police state. In the end, the German government accepted the Protocol on Privileges and Immunities, but only after it had been agreed that it should undergo a revision process after two years.

By the time of the Convention's entry into force, the Member States had not yet agreed on the rules of procedure for the independent joint supervisory body whose primary task it is to ensure that the rights of the individual are not violated by the storage, processing and utilization of the data held by Europol. France continued to reject the idea of the body having judicial powers, and Germany opposed plans according to which it would have purely administrative functions. This, and the fact that France and Italy had not yet ratified the Protocol on Privileges and Immunities, meant that Europol was still not fully operational at the end of the year. However, in December, the Member States were able to reach agreement on the extension of Europol's mandate to combating terrorism and child pornography. They also started exploring the possibility of extending it further to the fight against falsification of money and other means of payment, a step which could be of considerable importance in view of increasing concerns about the vulnerability of the euro to falsification.

In spite of considerable delays and remaining difficulties, the entry into force of the Europol Convention must be regarded as a crucial element of progress for EU police co-operation. Although Europol has not been granted any operational powers, the Convention gives it comprehensive tasks in a wide range of areas. These include not only obtaining, collating and analysing information and intelligence and facilitating the exchange of information between Member States, but also the support of investigations in the Member States, the development of specialist knowledge of investigative procedures in the Member States, the provision of 'strategic intelligence' for operational activities at the national level and assistance to Member States in areas such as training of officers and research into crime prevention methods. The constant increase in information requests addressed to Europol's predecessor – the Europol Drugs Unit (EDU) – since 1994 is a clear indication that national police authorities appreciate more and more the central information agency role which forms the core of Europol's function as an essential instrument in their investigative work.

The Union also made progress with the implementation of the 1997 Action Plan to Combat Organized Crime. On 19 March, the Council adopted the Falcone programme (Joint Action 98/245/JHA) which provides for training programmes, joint projects to improve skills and operational methods in the fight against organized crime, the organization of traineeships, seminars and research activities and measures to improve information exchange. Although limited to 10m ECU for the period 1998–2002, the programme could make a valuable contribution to a better understanding by practitioners of the diversity of problems and methods in the fight against organized crime in the various Member States, and facilitate the development of common approaches and procedures.

In line with the Action Plan, Member States agreed on 21 December on a Joint Action (98/733/JHA) making it a criminal offence to participate in a criminal organization. This measure is of considerable significance because the mere participation in a criminal organization (without participation in the actual execution of crimes) had not in the past been punishable in all Member States by effective criminal penalties. According to the Joint Action, the Member States must now ensure that such penalties will be imposed on any person who takes part in the activities – criminal or not – of a 'criminal organization', as defined by the Joint Action, even if that person does not take part in the execution of that activity.

On 21 December, the Council also adopted a resolution on the prevention of organized crime. This, *inter alia,* emphasized the need for a greater involvement of civil society as a whole and, more particularly, of professions prone to infiltration by organized crime in the overall EU strategy, a better co-ordination of preventive action between local, regional and national bodies, and improved mutual information on experiences with different methods for the prevention of organized crime. This was followed on 22 December by a Joint Action on corruption in the private sector (98/742/JHA) which provides that Member States are to take the necessary measures to ensure that both passive and active corruption in the private sector are punishable by 'effective, proportionate and dissuasive criminal penalties' which in serious cases should involve prison sentences. Both measures reflect a new emphasis on the fight against the root factors of organized crime, but it still needs to be backed up by more concrete measures.

On 19 March, the Council adopted a statement in which it formally recognised the importance of the recommendations on the fight against transnational organized crime, terrorism and high-tech crime, which the G8 had adopted during 1996 and 1997. The Council announced that it would ensure coherence between the G8 recommendations – which place a greater emphasis on the challenges of high-tech crime – and its own 1997 Action Plan. Together with the signing of the Pre-Accession Pact on Organized Crime on 28 May (see below), this can be regarded as a clear sign that the Union is moving towards an integrated approach combining internal and external action in the fight against organized crime.

Judicial Co-operation

In the area of judicial co-operation in civil matters, the Council reached agreement – after several years of negotiations – on two new conventions of considerable importance:

On 28 May, the Council adopted the Convention on Jurisdiction and the Recognition and Enforcement of Judgments in Matrimonial Matters which represents a first major step towards mutual recognition and harmonization in matters of family law. Matrimonial matters had been excluded from the 1968 Brussels Convention because of their complexity and because they were not directly linked to economic integration. The fact that they have now become the object of a major EU legal instrument can be regarded as a decisive move in EU judicial co-operation on civil matters beyond the limits of economic integration, and that the Member States are willing and capable of dealing with the problems generated by the extraordinary disparity on civil law matters between the various systems of law.

The Convention introduces uniform basic standards for jurisdiction on divorce, legal separation or marriage annulment which are aimed at facilitating the automatic and rapid recognition of judgments in matrimonial matters given in any of the Member States. It establishes clear rules on the identification of the court of origin and provides that judgments given in a Member State shall be recognized in any other Member State without any special procedure being required. This constitutes a major increase of legal certainty for EU citizens and should drastically reduce protracted legal proceedings resulting from conflicts of jurisdiction. The Convention also lays down basic rules of jurisdiction concerning parental responsibility over the children of both spouses on the occasion of civil proceedings, and opens the possibility of giving jurisdiction to the ECJ to interpret the provisions of the Convention. Once ratified, it will become applicable *ex officio,* which means that the application of all of its rules will be compulsory and that those rules will at once become part of each Member State's national legislation.

During the negotiations, the Member States disagreed over the question of whether or not the possibility of requesting preliminary rulings by the ECJ on questions of interpretation should be limited to the highest national courts. In the protocol to the Convention establishing the principle of jurisdiction of the ECJ Member States were left with the possibility of indicating on an individual basis – at the time of the entry into force of the Convention – their choice of courts competent to make a referral to the ECJ. This constitutes another regrettable case of 'flexibility' in the EU legal order which is rather similar to that of new Art. 35(2) TEU as introduced by the Treaty of Amsterdam.

On 17 June, the Council adopted the Convention on Driving Disqualification which is aimed at giving a Union-wide effect to driving disqualifications. The Convention was motivated, in particular, by frequent cases of drivers disqualified from driving in a Member State other than that of their normal residence escaping the effects of their disqualification when residing in a Member State other than that of the offence. On the basis of a comprehensive definition of term 'driving disqualification', the Convention provides that the state of the offence shall immediately notify the state of residence of any driving disqualification and that the state of residence shall without delay give effect to the disqualification by executing the decision of the state of the offence, taking into account any period of disqualification which has already been served. The state of residence may refuse, however, to give effect to the disqualification if the conduct for which it has been imposed in the state of the offence does not constitute an offence under the law of the state of residence. The Convention can be regarded as a example of effective EU judicial co-operation on enforcement issues without any harmonization of national laws.

In the area of judicial co-operation in criminal matters, the Union made some progress on the practical implementation of mutual assistance between national judicial authorities. On 29 June, the Council adopted Joint Actions on good practice in mutual legal assistance in criminal matters (98/427/JHA) and on the creation of a European Judicial Network (98/428/JHA). The former provides that each Member State shall draw up a 'statement of good practice' in executing and sending requests for legal assistance. These statements must include undertak-ings in respect of a broad range of practical aspects of legal assistance, such as giving priority to requests marked 'urgent' by the requesting authority and providing explanatory reports in case of difficulties with the implementation of a request. It is also provided that each Member State should periodically review compliance with the 'statements'.

The establishment of the European Judicial Network was motivated by the aim of facilitating judicial co-operation by the creation of a network of contact points which could provide the legal and practical information to local judicial authorities in other countries to enable them to prepare an effective request for judicial co-operation. Since 1996, Member States had exchanged liaison mag-istrates in order to support requests for judicial assistance. This system had proved to be useful, but not sufficient. The European Judicial Network was designed to have a much broader remit, enabling local judicial authorities and other competent authorities in one Member State to establish the most appropri-ate direct contact with their counterparts in other Member States. The network is made up of the central judicial authorities of each Member State which are responsible for international judicial co-operation, both generally and for certain forms of serious crime, such as organized crime, corruption, drug-trafficking or terrorism. The Joint Action establishing the network not only provides for the contact points to serve as sources of information, but for the organization of periodic meetings between the contact points for the purpose of exchanging experiences and providing a forum for discussion of practical and legal problems encountered in the context of judicial co-operation. These can be passed on to the competent Council working parties to serve as a basis for the discussion of possible legislative changes.

The Joint Action of 3 December 1998 (98/699/JHA) on money laundering, the identification, tracing, freezing, seizing and confiscation of instrumentalities and the proceeds from crime was based partly on the judicial network, but also linked to the fight against organized crime. The main purpose of this Joint Action is to restrict the use by Member States of possible reservations with regard to confiscation of proceeds from certain offences defined in the 1990 Council of Europe Convention on Laundering, Search, Seizure and Confiscation of the Proceeds from Crime and also to restrict the use of optional grounds for refusal in respect to the enforcement of foreign confiscation orders. The European Judicial Network was entrusted with the task of providing, on the basis of 'guides' established by the Member States, information on the assistance which national authorities can mutually provide in identifying, tracing, freezing or seizing proceeds of crime.

Pre-accession Measures

The opening of accession negotiations with six of the applicant countries in March added a sense of urgency to the preparation of the potential new members in the areas of Justice and Home Affairs. Both Commissioner Anita Gradin and a number of ministers, the French Minister of Justice Elisabeth Guigou, prominent among them, repeatedly called for more comprehensive action by the Union on justice and home affairs in the pre-accession process. On 30 March, the Member States were finally able to reach agreement on the Union's *acquis* in the fields of Justice and Home Affairs which the new members will have to take over on accession (Council Document (DG H) 6473/3/98). The definition of the *acquis* was of vital importance to the development of a more concrete pre-accession policy in these fields. It comprises not only conventions, joint actions, joint positions, resolutions, recommendations, declarations and other decisions adopted by the Council under Title VI TEU, but also a range of relevant conventions and protocols of other international bodies, such as the Council of Europe and the United Nations, to which the EU Member States have become party. A number of important steps were then taken in May and June to increase pre-accession co-operation with the applicants.

These included a Pre-Accession Pact on organized crime, signed on 28 May by the Union and the ten central and eastern European countries (CEECs) and Cyprus. This pact is aimed at intensifying co-operation and assistance measures in the fight against organized crime during the pre-accession period. Under its terms, the EU-15 and the 11 applicants agreed to develop, with the assistance of Europol, a common annual strategy in order to identify the most significant common threats in relation to organized crime. It was further agreed to increase the exchange of law-enforcement intelligence and to give more mutual practical support in training and equipment assistance, joint investigative activities and special operations. The agreement is also intended to facilitate trans-border law enforcement and judicial co-operation and provided for the exchange of law enforcement officers and judicial authorities for traineeships. One of the primary aims the Union is pursuing with the pact is the gradual integration of the CEECs and Cyprus into the system of central law enforcement units responsible for the fight against organized crime which it has been establishing since the 1997 Action Plan. This consists of central national co-ordinating bodies, central national contact points for the exchange of information and the European Judicial Network.

Under the pact, the CEECs and Cyprus undertook to use the EU's 1997 Action Plan as a starting point for co-operation. They also agreed to 'consider' the establishment of similar national bodies, to make the necessary preparations enabling them to accede to the Europol Convention at the time of accession, to make the 'statements of good practice' provided for by the Joint Action on good practices in mutual legal assistance on criminal matters (see above) and to make progress towards enacting the legislation enabling them to accede to the 1995 and 1996 EU Extradition Conventions by the time of accession. The Union committed itself to promoting the funding of measures in favour of the applicants – particularly in the area of training – via appropriate Community programmes such as PHARE and MEDA and the relevant programmes in the fields of Justice and Home Affairs such as Oisin, Grotius, Stop, Odysseus and Falcone. In order to ensure adequate co-ordination and information exchange in the implementation of the pact, the signatories decided to set up a group of experts from all participating states, the 'Pre-Accession Pact Experts Group' (PAPEG).

In its 1997 *Agenda 2000* Report, the Commission had identified a range of weaknesses in several of the applicants as regards compliance with the principle of the rule of law in a democratic society. These could prove major obstacles to the capability of these applicants to take on the Union's *acquis* in Justice and Home Affairs. The Council, in its conclusions adopted on 28 May, felt it necessary to indicate to the applicants that full respect of the principle of the rule of law is an essential criterion of membership, pointing, in particular, to the need for an independent judiciary, effective access of citizens to justice, respect for judicial decisions, an objective system of public prosecutions and an adequate training of police forces, based on the principles of accountability of the police in the framework of the rule of law. The Council invited the Commission to continue to promote, both in the context of the PHARE horizontal Justice and Home Affairs programme and within the accession partnerships, projects aimed specifically at reinforcing the rule of law.

The persistence of legislative, structural and administrative deficits regarding the organization and operation of the judiciary and the police forces in the applicant countries led both the Member States and the Commission to take the view that the formal legal enactment of the Union *acquis* by the applicant countries would not necessarily guarantee effective implementation. The absence of such effectiveness could have serious adverse implications for the internal security situation of the 'old' Member States after accession. As a result, on 29 June the Council adopted a Joint Action (98/428/JHA) establishing a mechanism for collective evaluation of the enactment, application and effective implementation by the applicant countries of the EU *acquis* in Justice and Home Affairs. It led to the establishment of a group of experts, the 'Collective Evaluation Group' – under the supervision of Coreper and in close co-operation with the K-4 Committee – with the task of preparing and keeping up-to-date collective evaluations of the situation in the candidate countries. The Member States undertook to make available all relevant material on these issues compiled by national authorities, including information on their direct experience of working with the candidate countries, Schengen material, reports from embassies and Commission delegations in the applicant countries, reports from PHARE missions and reports from the Council of Europe on the implementation by the applicants of Council of Europe Conventions. The Member States also agreed to form, whenever it was considered necessary, ad hoc teams of representatives and experts of Member States and the Commission, which would carry out further missions on specific aspects. It was decided that the formation of such ad hoc teams should only require a decision by qualified majority. The Joint Action provides that the Collective Evaluation Group reports on its evaluations to the Council, and the Commission was invited to take its results into account in its proposals for significant adjustments of the priorities and objectives of the accession partnerships. It seems likely that this collective evaluation mechanism will also have a major impact on the accession negotiations in the fields of Justice and Home Affairs.

III. Preparations for the Implementation of the Treaty of Amsterdam

Throughout the year, the Council and a large number of its working parties, with active participation of the Commission, were engaged in intense and often difficult negotiations on the preparations for the entry into force of the Treaty of Amsterdam with its major and in some areas almost revolutionary changes to the bases of policy-making on EU Justice and Home Affairs. The main issues were the incorporation of the Schengen system into the EU framework, and the need to agree on a programme and priorities for EU Justice and Home Affairs after the entry into force of the new Treaty.

Problems with the Incorporation of Schengen

In order to proceed with the incorporation of the Schengen *acquis* into the Union, the Schengen members had to take two steps. First, they had to define the Schengen *acquis* and then allocate each part of this *acquis* to a legal basis either in Title IV of the EC Treaty or Title VI of the EU Treaty or in both of them. The definition of the *acquis* proved to be a much more difficult exercise than most of the Schengen members themselves had expected. Since 1985, thousands of pages of text had been adopted by the Schengen group, many of which – especially those adopted by subordinate bodies – lacked a clearly defined legal status and scope. The *acquis* also continued to evolve because of new decisions adopted by the Schengen group. As a result, a final and comprehensive list of the *acquis* was still not available at the end of the year. This attracted considerable criticism by, *inter alia,* the British House of Lords, which regarded it as an obstacle to effective scrutiny, and by some of the applicant countries which will have to take over the Schengen *acquis* upon accession.

The allocation of appropriate legal bases under the EC and/or EU Treaties is of considerable importance for the future development of EU Justice and Home Affairs because it can prejudice the scope of both Community competence under Title IV TEC and the areas remaining within the intergovernmental framework of Title VI TEU. Whereas some Schengen members preferred to allocate a TEC legal basis wherever possible, other members insisted on a 'third pillar' (Title VI TEU) legal basis for some parts of the *acquis*. Spain, for instance, wanted to retain an intergovernmental basis for most aspects of external border checks, surveillance and conditions which it considered to be essential for national security purposes. The majority of the Schengen members, however, felt that these areas should be based on the new TEC provisions dealing with external border controls, and that the Spanish proposals could undermine the communitarization of this field decided at Amsterdam. Serious difficulties also arose over the legal bases for certain provisions on the free movement of aliens, organized travel and the control of narcotic drugs, and provisions governing the Schengen Information System whose tasks of data exchange extend to both areas covered by Title VI TEU (such as police co-operation and extradition issues) and areas under Title IV (such as border controls and visa policy). By the end of the year, the Schengen members were still struggling to find a compromise on these issues and there remained a serious risk that they would fail to reach an agreement before the entry into force of the new Treaty. In that case all parts of the Schengen *acquis* on which no agreement had been reached would – by virtue of Art. 2 of the Schengen Protocol – automatically be deemed to be based on Title VI TEU.

Another problem resulting from the incorporation of Schengen is the fact that it has implications for the formal association of Norway and Iceland with the Schengen group. This is necessitated by the Nordic Passport Union which links three EU Member States (Denmark, Finland and Sweden) to the non-members Iceland and Norway. The Union had to engage in technically complex negotiations with the two countries in order to define the institutional and procedural aspects of their (limited) involvement in the adoption and implementation of Schengen decisions. A preliminary agreement on most of the issues was reached on 27 November.

The Action Plan of December 1998 and the Rationale of the 'Area of Freedom, Security and Justice'

While providing a more detailed set of objectives for EU Justice and Home Affairs, the Treaty of Amsterdam nevertheless sets only a broad framework for the development of EU policies in these areas. Both the Commission and the Member States felt that priorities and a precise agenda were needed in order to exploit fully the new possibilities of action provided by the new Treaty. On the basis of a Commission communication of 14 July (*COM*(1998) 459), the Member States agreed on an 'Action Plan on how best to implement the provisions of the Treaty of Amsterdam in an area of freedom, security and justice', which was formally adopted by the Justice and Home Affairs Council on 3 December. This plan is likely to be of considerable importance for the development of EU Justice and Home Affairs during the next five years.

First, it clarifies the rationale for the 'area of freedom, security and justice' which is only vaguely described in the Treaty of Amsterdam. As regards the concept of 'freedom', the Action Plan emphasizes that the new Treaty opens the way to giving freedom 'a meaning beyond free movement of persons across internal borders' and that includes the 'freedom to live in a law-abiding environment' protected by effective action of public authorities at the national and European level. This marks a clear step beyond the old Schengen rationale with its focus on free movement and mere 'compensatory measures'. On the meaning of 'security', however, the Action Plan takes a less progressive view, reflecting the concerns of several Member States about retaining control over internal security instruments. It states explicitly that the new Treaty, although aimed at developing common action in the fields of police and criminal justice co-operation and offering enhanced security to Union citizens, does not pursue the intention of creating a 'European security area' in the sense of uniform detection and investigation procedures, and that Member States' responsibilities for maintaining law and order will not be affected by the new provisions. On the concept of 'justice', the Action Plan is significantly more ambitious, declaring that Amsterdam is aimed at giving citizens 'a common sense of justice through-out the Union' with an impact on day-to-day life which includes both access to justice and full judicial co-operation among Member States. The wording may fall short of the idea of a 'European judicial area', but clearly goes beyond judicial co-operation as a mere accompanying process of economic integration.

The second important element of the Action Plan are the 'priorities and measures' listed in Part II. These comprise both a number of strategic objectives (such as the development of an 'overall migration strategy') and a broad range of more concrete measures in each of the main fields of Justice and Home Affairs, most of which have to be taken either within two or five years. Some of these measures are fairly technical, such as the examination of Europol access to investigation data of the Schengen Information System or the European Information System, but others are of considerable political significance, including the establishment of a coherent EU policy on readmission and return, and the examination of the possibility of approximating certain areas of civil law. Owing to the opposition of France and Spain, precise objectives on the issue of burden-sharing in the area of asylum policy had to be dropped from the plan. Yet, overall,

168   JÖRG MONAR

the plan appears to be a positive and constructive step: while not providing for
the establishment of any comprehensive common policy in the different areas of
Justice and Home Affairs, it nevertheless has the clear merit of combining a basic
conceptual approach with a list of limited, but concrete objectives which are
linked to clear deadlines. This should help the Union during the next few years
to realize at least some of the potential offered by the new Treaty.

References

Commission of the European Communities (1998) 'Amended proposal for a Joint
    Action concerning temporary protection of displaced persons'. *COM*(1998) 372.
Commission of the European Communities (1998) 'Proposal for a Community action
    programme to promote the integration of refugees'. *COM*(1998) 731.
Commission of the European Communities (1998) 'Proposal for a Council decision [...]
    establishing measures to provide practical support in relation to the reception and the
    voluntary repatriation of refugees, displaced persons and asylum applicants'.
    COM(1998) 733.
Council of the European Union (1998) 'Convention [...] on Jurisdiction and the
    Recognition and Enforcement of Judgements in Matrimonial Matters'. *OJ* C 221/1,
    16 July.
Council of the European Union (1998) 'Council Act of 17 June 1998 Drawing up the
    Convention on Driving Disqualifications'. *OJ* C 216/1, 10 July.
Council of the European Union (1998) 'Pre-accession Pact on Organised Crime between
    the Member States of the European Union and the Applicant Countries of Central and
    Eastern Europe and Cyprus'. *OJ* C 220/1.
Council of the European Union (1998) 'Joint Action [...] Establishing a Mechanism for
    Collective Evaluation of the Enactment, Application and Effective Implementation
    by the Applicant Countries of the *acquis* of the European Union in the Field of Justice
    and Home Affairs'. *OJ* L 191/8, 7 July.
Council of the European Union (1998) 'Joint Action [...] on Making it a Criminal
    Offence to Participate in a Criminal Organization in the Member States of the
    European Union'. *OJ* L 351/1, 29 December.
Council of the European Union (1998) 'Joint Action [....] on the Creation of a European
    Judicial Network '. *OJ* L 191/4, 7 July.
Council of the European Union/European Commission (1999) 'Action Plan of the
    Council and the Commission on how Best to Implement the Provisions of the Treaty
    of Amsterdam on an Area of Freedom, Security and Justice'. *OJ* C 19/1, 23 January.

Journal of Common Market Studies

Volume 37, Annual Review
September 1999

Developments in the Member States

BRIGID LAFFAN
University College Dublin

I. Introduction

This section of the *Annual Review* analyses the main political developments in the Member States that influence the ebb and flow of EU politics, and the European issues that have implications for domestic debate on the EU. 1998 was the year in which decisions were taken on membership of the single currency and it was also the year in which one of the central figures of European politics in the 1980s and 1990s, Chancellor Helmut Kohl, left office. In many ways, 1998 marked the end of one phase in the development of integration and the beginning of another with the decisions on EMU and the launching of the enlargement negotiations.

II. Elections and their Consequences

A number of elections in 1998, when added to the 1997 return of centre-left governments in the UK and France, marked a decisive shift in governmental power in western Europe to the left. By the end of 1998, 13 of the 15 governments in the EU were governed by parties of the left. Furthermore, the Union's three largest Member States, the UK, France and Germany, had social democratic governments. The impact of this realignment on European integration began to make itself felt in the latter part of 1998 and will continue to be felt in the years ahead.

Germany

The federal elections in Germany in September 1998 led to the defeat of the Christian Democrat–Free Democrat coalition that had governed Germany for 16 years. The election marked the end of Chancellor Kohl's dominance of German politics and was the first time in the history of the Federal Republic that political power changed hands as a result of an election. Throughout 1998, opinion polls suggested that Chancellor Kohl had a difficult political battle on his hands to retain power after such a long period in office. The re-election, in early March, of Gerhard Schröder as Prime Minister of Lower Saxony, with increased support (47.9 per cent) confirmed that he would be the Social Democratic Party (SPD) candidate for Chancellor in the autumn. The leader of the SPD, Oskar Lafontaine nominated his rival as candidate, once the results of the election in Lower Saxony were known. The choice of Schröder meant that the Social Democrats would be led by a pragmatic politician from the centre, rather than the left wing, of the party. During the election campaign, Schröder advocated what he called a 'new middle' *(Neue Mitte)* in German politics, and was somewhat reminiscent of Tony Blair in the tone and tenor of his political pronouncements. Like Blair, Schröder was determined to make his party electable and to ensure that the different factions in the SPD did not undermine the prospect of power.

From early March, Kohl, always a consummate politician, sought to overcome the adverse opinion polls by emphasizing his record in office and his commitment to European integration. His critics highlighted the worsening economic situation in Germany, particularly the rise in unemployment which breached the five million mark, and the worsening federal finances. Kohl could not reverse the swing away from the Christian Democrats and on 27 September the Social Democrats under Schröder polled 40.9 per cent of the vote, a rise of 5 per cent from the 1994 election, with the Christian Democrats polling only 35.1 per cent, a reduction of 5 per cent on the last election. Once it was clear that Schröder would be the next German Chancellor, attention turned to the coalition that would emerge in the aftermath of the election. The Green Party, with 6.7 per cent of the votes and 47 seats, had enough to form a government together with the SPD (see Table 1).

The election result marked the end of an era in German politics in a number of respects. First, it marked the end of Kohl as German Chancellor, a man who along with President Mitterrand had done more than any other to shape the direction of European integration in the 1980s and 1990s. Together they were the architects of the single market and the single currency. Their combined legacy left the EU a stronger and more ambitious project than when they took office in the early 1980s. Second, Kohl was the last Chancellor of the Federal Republic who had direct and personal experience of World War II and its aftermath. His political philosophy and foreign policy strategy were moulded by his desire to

Table 1: The German Election, 27 September 1998

Party	% Votes	% Seats
Social Democratic Party	40.9	298
Christian Democratic Union	28.4	198
Christian Social Union	6.7	47
Bündnis 90/The Greens	6.7	47
Free Democratic Party	6.2	43
Party of Democratic Socialism	5.1	36
Republicans	1.8	–
German People's Union	1.2	–

Source: «http://www.agora.it/elections/election/germany.htm»

embed Germany in the EU and the wider Europe. For him, German unification and European integration were two sides of the same coin. The election of Schröder marked an important shift in generation. Third, the new Chancellor would lead the relocation of the German government from provincial Bonn to Berlin, a potent symbol of the changes in Europe since the collapse of communism in 1989.

In the aftermath of the election, the focus was on the formation of the government and on the shape of Germany's first nationwide Red–Green coalition. The Social Democrats and the Greens agreed a 50 page programme of government in October. The Green element in the programme related to increases in ecological taxes, a withdrawal from nuclear energy and a wide-ranging reform of Germany's nationality laws. The leader of the Greens, Joschka Fischer, was given the Foreign Affairs portfolio in the new government. The SPD element was decisively shaped by the division in the party between the power of the Chancellor in office and the chairmanship of the party still held by Oskar Lafontaine. The latter was given the very powerful Finance Ministry portfolio, one that was strengthened by moving the European Affairs division and economic forecasting from the Economics Ministry to Finance. The key elements of the SPD's economic strategy included tackling unemployment with an alliance for jobs, reform of the taxation system to shift the burden from the employed to corporations, and measures to promote the stability of financial markets. Lafontaine, who was committed to boosting demand in a traditional Keynesian manner, was the driving force behind economic policy. In the early months, his chief adviser was Heiner Flassbeck, Germany's most committed Keynesian economist. After 15 years of supply-side economics, the emphasis was again on macroeconomic demand management.

The new government promised continuity in foreign policy, particularly in Germany's European policy. However, there was likely to be a change in emphasis. Chancellor Schröder's approach to the EU was likely to be less emotional than that of Kohl given their different experiences. Schröder suggested that, 'Germany standing up for its national interests will be just as natural as France or Britain standing up for theirs' (*Financial Times*, 10 November 1998). The exclusion of the Bavarian CSU from power meant an immediate change in the balance of forces on the reform of the Common Agricultural Policy (CAP). The emphasis in the programme on jobs heightened the salience of an EU Employment Pact. In addition, Lafontaine was determined to address what he felt to be unfair tax competition in the EU and sought to draw attention to unfair corporate taxation, arguing that the unanimity requirement in taxation should go. His emphasis on macroeconomic demand management led him fairly quickly into conflict with the German Bundesbank and the fledgling European Central Bank, as his requests for a reduction in interest rates were interpreted by the central bankers as interference in their domain and an attack on their independence.

The election seemed to presage a change in Germany's relations with the other two large states in the Union - France and the United Kingdom. During the election campaign, Schröder advocated closer ties with the Labour government in the UK and promoted the idea of a triangle involving Paris, London, Bonn/Berlin. Once elected, Chancellor Schröder made his first state visit to Paris, appearing to reaffirm the 'special relationship' with France, while at the same time insisting on the importance of a bigger role for the UK.

Denmark

In February, the Danish Prime Minister, Nyrup Rasmussen, called a snap election despite the fact that his coalition government had survived a crisis over the 1998 budget the previous October. The Prime Minister explained the election on the basis that he did not want political uncertainty to jeopardize the chances of a 'yes' vote in the referendum on the Treaty of Amsterdam. It suited his party, the Social Democrats, who were split on Europe, to keep the issue off the campaign agenda. Although the healthy state of the Danish economy augured well for the incumbent government, opinion polls during the campaign indicated that the opposition bloc, led by the former Danish Foreign Minister, Uffe Ellemann-Jensen, would win the election. Right up to election day, opinion polls were forecasting a win for the centre-right. In the event, the Social Democratic-led government was returned to power as a minority administration. They won 63 seats in contrast to 42 for the opposition (see Table 2). In the final week of the campaign, the Social Democrats and their allies, the Social Liberal Party, had managed to turn the tide in their favour.

Immigration emerged as the big issue of the campaign. The increase in immigration, especially of non-European origin, created a backlash from the

Table 2: The Danish Election, 11 March 1998

Party	% Votes	% Seats
Social Democratic Party	36.0	63
Liberals (Venstre)	24.0	42
Conservative People's Party	8.9	16
Socialist People's Party	7.5	13
Danish People's Party	7.4	13
Centre Democrats	4.3	8
Social Liberals	3.9	7
Red–Green Alliance	2.7	5
Christian People's Party	2.4	4
Progress Party	2.4	4
Faroes Liberals	–	1
Faroes Social Democrats	–	1
Greenland Liberals	–	1
Greenland Social Democrats	–	1

Source: «http://www.agora.it/elections/election/denmark.htm»

extreme right. The newly established Danish People's Party gained over 7 per cent of the popular vote and 13 seats. The impact of the election on Denmark's European policy is unlikely to be negative, although the success of the far right means that there are now more 'Eurosceptics' in the Folketing than in the past. During the campaign, Prime Minister Rasmussen said that he would not call a referendum on the Danish opt-outs from the Treaty on European Union without popular demand, and that this was unlikely for a number of years. Also during the campaign, the Danish Supreme Court began hearing a case brought by ten citizens on the constitutionality of the Treaty on European Union (TEU). In the event, the Court found that the Prime Minister had not been guilty of contravening the constitution when he signed the Treaty.

The Netherlands

The Netherlands faced a general election in May to determine whether the three-party coalition ruling since 1994, led by the Prime Minister Wim Kok of the Social Democratic Party (PvdA), would continue in power. During the campaign Frits Bolkestein, the leader of the free-market VVD party which formed part of the governing coalition, announced that he would challenge Wim Kok for the premiership if his party emerged as the largest party the election. Both the PvdA and the VVD did well in the elections, the Social Democratic Party winning an additional nine seats and the VVD an additional seven. The third coalition party,

Table 3: The Dutch Election, 6 May 1998

Party	% Votes	% Seats
Social Democratic Party (PvdA)	29.0	45
People's Party for Freedom and	24.7	38
Christian Democratic Appeal	18.4	29
Democrats 66	9.0	14
Green Left	7.3	11
Socialist Party	3.5	5
Reformatorian Political Federation	2.0	3
Political Reformed Party	1.8	3
Reformed Political League	1.3	2
Centre Democrats	0.6	–
General Elder People's League – Union 55+	0.5	–
Netherlands Mobile	0.5	–
Seniors 2000	0.4	–
Dutch Middle Class Party	0.3	–
The Greens	0.2	–
Platform of Independent Groups	–	–

Source: «http://www.agora.it/elections/election/netherln.htm»

D66, lost nine seats although they remained in government in the aftermath of the election. Their presence was viewed as necessary to broker agreement between the two larger coalition parties. The opposition Christian Democrats, who lost power in the 1994 election, did not manage to recover in this election, losing a further five seats (see Table 3). The return to power of Kok and the Finance Minister, Gerrit Zalm, augured well for continuity in EU policy.

Sweden

The September election in Sweden pitched the incumbent Social Democratic (SDP) government with Goran Persson as Prime Minister against Carl Bildt who was attempting to form a coalition between his party, the Moderate Party, the Liberals and the Christian Democrats. The SDP saw its vote fall from 45 per cent in the 1994 election to 36.4 per cent, although it remained the largest party with 131 seats in parliament. The Social Democrats were forced to seek the support of the former communists, the Left Party and the Greens, in order to form a government. The Green Party agreed to a parliamentary alliance which would see them support the government without entering into a formal coalition. Prime Minister Persson embarked in a major reshuffle of his cabinet in the aftermath of the election. On European issues, the Prime Minister pledged during the

Table 4: The Swedish Election, 21 September 1998

Party	% Votes	% Seats
Sweden Social Democratic Workers' Party	36.4	131
Moderate Rally Party	22.9	82
Left Party	12.0	43
Christian Democrats	11.8	42
Centre Party	5.1	18
People's Party Liberals	4.7	17
Environment Party, the Greens	4.5	16

Source:«http://www.agora.it/elections/election/sweden.htm»

campaign that a decision on Sweden's participation in the single currency would be put to the Swedish people either in a referendum or an election. Both the parties supporting him oppose Sweden's membership of the EU and EMU, demanding an early referendum as the opinion polls suggest that such a referendum would be defeated.

III. Other Political Developments

The United Kingdom

During 1998, Tony Blair continued to move the UK towards what could be termed 'constructive engagement' with the EU. He set a new tone in relations during the UK's six months in the Presidency (see Peter Anderson's summary, pp. 63–4 this issue) and announced a major initiative on defence in the autumn. The management of the single currency was, however, a major challenge for his government. Faced with non-membership in the first wave, the Blair government began to lay the groundwork for eventual membership after a referendum, which will not take place before 2002. But exclusion from this key development has made it more difficult for the Blair government to move to a position of equal influence in the system with Germany and France .

Internally, the constitutional changes resulting from devolution will have a significant impact on the UK's future management of EU business. The Scotland Bill received royal assent in November and was accompanied by intense preparations for elections to a Scottish Parliament in May 1999. The Scottish Parliament will have legislative powers over a wide range of policy issues and will be elected on the basis of a proportional representation electoral system. Preparations for a Welsh Assembly, which has significantly fewer powers than the Scottish Parliament, also took place in 1998. The devolution process in the United Kingdom is transforming the last centralized state in western Europe into

a multi-levelled system of governance. The impact of devolution on the traditional dominance of Whitehall and Westminster in the governance of the United
Kingdom will be unclear for some years to come.

The potential impact on the UK's management of EU business is likely to be
substantial, as the UK has a highly formalized and centralized system for
managing the interface between London and Brussels. The model is based on the
principle of 'singing from the same hymn sheet' and is designed to control and
contain flows between the UK and the Union. Although relations with the EU are
a reserved matter under the devolution legislation, constitutional reform challenges this model in a number of respects. First, Scotland and Wales will have
their own interests to pursue in relation to areas such as agriculture, structural
funds, transport and the environment. It will be more difficult to get a uniform
UK view, especially in relation to those areas where the devolved bodies have
power. Tensions between the different levels of government are likely. Second,
devolution raises issues of voice and representation in Brussels. The new
executives will take over responsibility for the representative offices in Brussels
and may seek to increase their presence in the UK Permanent Representation
(UKRep). Scottish ministers, though not their Welsh counterparts, may represent the UK at the Council level. Third, the new assemblies are in the process of
putting in place committee structures for the scrutiny of EU matters. Whitehall
and the devolved units have negotiated an administrative concordat, which will
establish the standard operating procedures for the co-ordination and management of EU matters across Whitehall and the devolved administrations. Regardless of how the concordats are designed, there is likely to be an unsettled period
as both new administrations battle for influence and presence on the Brussels
scene.

Britain and Ireland: The Good Friday Agreement

On Good Friday 1998, the political parties in Northern Ireland, and the British
and Irish governments agreed a peace settlement for Northern Ireland which was
designed to provide a system of government acceptable to both communities.
The Agreement was both a settlement and process involving three strands:
institutions of government for Northern Ireland (strand 1), a North–South
Ministerial Council on the island of Ireland (strand 2), and a British–Irish
Council and Intergovernmental Conference (strand 3). If the agreement becomes
operational, it will transform relations between the Republic of Ireland and
Northern Ireland and between Britain and Ireland.

There are considerable references to the EU in the text of the agreement and
traces of the EU model can be clearly seen in the institutional framework
established by the process. In strand 1, the proposed Northern Ireland Assembly
and the Executive Authority will have to organize themselves for the manage-

ment of EU business and will have to negotiate a concordat with Whitehall. The North–South Ministerial Council (strand 2) makes several references to the EU as an appropriate topic for North–South discussion and co-operation. The prospect of a North–South implementation body for EU programmes was signalled in the Agreement. Over the long term, it is possible that ministers or officials from Northern Ireland would participate in Irish delegations to EU meetings. The proposed British–Irish Council (strand 3) will comprise representatives of the British and Irish governments, devolved institutions in Northern Ireland, Scotland and Wales, the Isle of Man and the Channel Islands. EU matters are again cited as an appropriate topic of consultation and mutual co-operation.

Italy

Having succeeded in ensuring that Italy would qualify for membership of the single currency in the first wave, Prime Minister Prodi's 28-month old government went the way of so many Italian governments in the past. In October, it lost a vote of confidence in the Parliament, following disagreement about the 1999 budget, and Prodi was unable to put together an alternative coalition. This provided an opportunity for Massimo D'Alema, the leader of the Democrats of the Left (the former communists), to make a bid for political power. When it became clear that he could muster sufficient support to form an administration, D'Alema was appointed Prime Minister by the President, becoming the first ex-communist to hold political power in Italy. The new Prime Minister pledged continuity with the policies of the outgoing Prodi administration. This was underlined by the reappointment of Carlo Azeglio Ciampi as Finance Minister and Lamberto Dini as Foreign Minister. The programme for the new government involved a commitment to the policies of fiscal austerity which had been pursued by the previous government. Prime Minister D'Alema positioned his government towards the centre-left, a fact symbolized by the replacement of the hammer and sickle on the party banner with the red rose of social democracy.

Spain

While the Conservative government of José-Maria Aznar appeared secure in power, the opposition Socialist Party was confronted with a change at the top. In a primary designed to see who would lead the party into the next election, the party leader, Joaquín Almunia, was defeated by a surprise candidate, José Borrell. The former remains as leader of the party while the latter takes on the mantle of party candidate for the premiership in Parliament.

Economic and Monetary Union

After many years of preparation and speculation about membership of the single currency, 1998 was the year for decision about the first-wave entrants. The reports from the Commission and the European Monetary Institute (EMI) on the manner in which the Member States met the 'convergence criteria' laid down in the Treaty on European Union were published in March. The Commission report recommended that 11 states, having met the criteria, should join the single currency on 1 January 1999. The EMI's report agreed with the Commission that major strides towards budgetary consolidation had been made, but it was less than happy with deficit ratios of over 100 per cent in Belgium and Italy. Nevertheless, according to the EMI, the figures did not warrant their absence from the Euro-zone in the first wave. In March, Greece entered the ERM as a prelude to joining the euro when it met the convergence criteria. Ireland revalued the punt, so that it could bring its interest rates down to the EU average. Denmark, although not joining the currency in the first wave, pledged to adopt an economic policy designed to shadow EMU. In Germany, the Bundestag voted overwhelmingly in favour of the single currency by 575 votes to 35. The only parliamentary opposition came from the ex-communist party of Democratic Socialism (PDS), the former Socialist Unity Party (SED) of the old GDR. In the Bundesrat, 15 out of the 16 federal states supported the move. The SPD's candidate for Chancellor, Gerhard Schröder, dropped his previous hostility to the euro in the Bundestag debate. The Federal Constitutional Court (*Bundesverfassungsgericht*) in Karlsruhe rejected a challenge to EMU in April, thus removing a potential barrier to the May agreement on the launch of the euro. An effort by 155 economists in Germany to have an 'orderly postponement' of EMU was met with implacable political opposition from the Bonn government in February.

With positive reports from the Commission and the EMI on a broadly-based, 11-member Euro-zone from the outset, the stage was set for a smooth transition at the European Council meeting to decide on conversion rates in May. However, a very serious row broke out about the Presidency of the new European Central Bank (ECB) in the run-up to the Council, when the French government continued to support its candidate, Jean-Claude Trichet, against the incumbent President of the EMI, the Dutchman Wim Duisenberg, who had the full backing of all other Member States, including Germany. Both France and the Netherlands threatened to veto the candidate of the other country. This meant that the May Council was overshadowed by the need to find a compromise on the position of President. What emerged was a classic deal that saw Wim Duisenberg appointed as President of the European Central Bank with a 'gentleman's agreement', stipulating that he would retire early and hand over to Jean-Claude Trichet. This agreement has no basis in law and it remains to be seen if it will actually hold.

The row about the President soured relations between France and the Netherlands but also between France and Germany. The deal was widely condemned in the European Parliament (EP) and in a number of national parliaments, but it did not seem to trigger an adverse reaction in the financial markets. In the autumn, future tensions between the ECB and national governments were foreshadowed, when Wim Duisenberg reacted to what he felt was the danger of political interference from the new German government, particularly from Oskar Lafontaine, the then Finance Minister. The ECB was intent on protecting its independence and credibility with the financial markets in the run-up to the launch of the euro.

Agenda 2000

This July 1997 initiative was followed up, in March 1998, by detailed proposals on each chapter of the reforms. The Commission, in presenting its *Agenda 2000* blueprint, had clearly taken into account the mood of austerity among the net contributors, because it did not propose to increase the ceiling on 'own resources', which would have required ratification by national parliaments and would have increased the likelihood of acrimonious domestic debates on future financing. Because of their scope, managing the negotiations was an important part of the Austrian Presidency (in the latter half of 1998) – see Richard Luther's contribution, pp. 65–7, this issue. It was also top priority for the German Presidency in the first half of 1999. The *Agenda 2000* negotiations were viewed with great seriousness in national capitals, because they represented a critical juncture in the Union; relative benefits and costs alter and the rules of the game change. Moreover, the outcome of the budgetary debate could have implications for the overall dynamic of integration. The danger, as Quentin Peel pointed out in the *Financial Times*, was that it 'could unleash a bruising debate on burden-sharing, reminiscent of the debilitating battle fought by Baroness Thatcher, which brought most other decision-making to a standstill for several years' (*Financial Times*, 20 October 1998). The prospect of rich against poor, farm producers against the rest, possibly even Germany against France, and delay in the whole process of enlargement to central and eastern Europe demanded careful work on the key components of the various proposals and on the overall deal. As David Galloway shows in his article, the key cleavages among the Member States on the package became clear in 1998.

The growing 'net-contributors club' became extremely vocal in its demands for a fairer system of burden-sharing. There was agreement across the political spectrum in Germany that its contributions were too onerous. Both the outgoing government of Chancellor Kohl and the incoming government under Chancellor Schröder made it clear that it wanted a reduction in its net contribution of 10 billion ECU or 58 per cent of the annual total. The Dutch argued that, in 1996, they had become proportionately the Union's largest contributor and their Finance Minister Gerrit Zalm demanded 'an improvement of our net position, and we want a net limiter which should be general and not just a rebate for Britain' (*Financial Times*, 16 October, 1998). Sweden and Austria, two other net contributors, added to the chorus of states arguing for austerity and changes to the system of burden-sharing. The UK found itself in an increasingly difficult position, in that its rebate, negotiated by the Conservative government in 1984, appeared less justified then it once was. The UK, although part of the net contributors club, had the key goal of maintaining its rebate that placed it somewhat at odds with the austerity club.

The main beneficiaries of the EU budget, particularly the Mediterranean states, found their position under threat. They continued to argue the case of greater redistribution in the Union and were unwilling to see an eastern enlargement financed by reductions in budgetary flows to them. Spanish representatives were trenchant in their defence of cohesion policy and refused to countenance any significant reductions. The two smaller Mediterranean states, Greece and Portugal, were largely supportive of the Spanish position, although less strident in the expression of these views. Ireland found itself in the uneasy position of being a 'net contributor in waiting'. High growth rates in the 1990s had pushed Ireland well above the threshold for Objective 1 status and it was clear that Ireland would become a net contributor to the budget in the next financial period. For the Irish government, a key goal was to ensure that the reduction in receipts from the budget would be phased in so as to provide a soft landing for the Irish Exchequer. The other Member States, be they net beneficiaries or marginal net contributors, wanted to ensure that the outcome of the negotiations would not move them decisively into the net contributors club or if it did, that they could live with the budgetary costs.

The re-emergence of a burden-sharing debate led the Member States to request the Commission to undertake a study on the system of 'own resources', so that there would be an objective basis for the discussion. Although it had some reservations about calculating net balances (its traditional view has been that these were not an accurate analysis of the gains and losses from integration), it went ahead because most of the Member States based their attitude to the budget on such calculations. Not only were they therefore politically important, but the Commission concluded that it was better that the debate be based on Commission calculations rather than incorrect national figures. In addition, the Fontainebleau agreement in 1984 on the UK rebate had concluded that 'any Member State sustaining a budgetary burden which is excessive in relation to its relative prosperity may benefit from a correction at the appropriate time' (quoted in Institute of European Affairs, 1999, p. 34). Net contributors, other than the UK, began to claim an 'excessive burden' in the aftermath of the Delors II agreement. In October 1998, the Commission published its 'Report on Own Resources' that established, in a comprehensive and carefully argued text, who pays what and who benefits from the EU budget. The report confirmed that Germany, followed by Sweden, Austria, the Netherlands and the UK were the main contributors. The

Commission showed a strong preference for a strategy that would see the European Agricultural Guidance and Guarantee Fund (EAGGF) finance only 75 per cent of aid to farmers, instead of the existing 100 per cent. This would alleviate the costs of the CAP for the Union budget and would renationalize part of the subvention of farm incomes. This proposal found considerable support in Germany which concluded that it would cut its contributions significantly. The other members of the 'net-contributors' club' were also in favour of this strategy. France led the opposition to what it saw as a fundamental attack on the principles of the CAP; the French Agricultural Minister argued that co-financing would kill the Common Agricultural Policy (*European Report*, 30.11.98). Politically, the French did not want a taxpayer/farmer cleavage to emerge in domestic politics.

A veto on the renationalization of the CAP led to a demand for budgetary stabilization which would effectively freeze the size of the EU budget. The problem was to derive an agreement on what the Austrian Presidency called a 'model of reasonable stabilization' which did not compromise the Union's aims and commitments (*Agence Europe*, 7–8 December). Even Spain, characterized as the 'no, no, no state' by one (non-Spanish) diplomat, began to use the term stabilization but with preconditions. The 'net-contributors' club' wanted to address the revenue and not just the expenditure side of the budget in their search for budgetary discipline. The tone of the debate on the revenue side was set by the Commission's October 1998 report in which it was argued that reform of the existing system of financing was not indispensable to agreement on *Agenda 2000*, and that a better time to embark on a reform of the revenue side of the budget would be at the time of the first accession of the candidate countries. The Member States began to examine the own resources report at an official level in November and at the political level in December with a view to assessing if reform of the system was necessary. Several argued that any reform would have to await the outcome of the negotiations on budgetary stabilization, but a number also felt that in the long term, the system of own resources should be altered with a move to a generalized GNP resource replacing traditional own resources and VAT or just the VAT resource alone. This would link the system more closely to ability to pay and would avoid the regressive element in the VAT resource. Second, a debate developed on the question of a 'generalized corrective mechanism' or a 'net-limiter' which would establish a threshold for contributions above which Member States would get a rebate. The demand for a net-limiter was supported by Germany, the Netherlands, Austria and Sweden. The debate inevitably drew attention to the UK rebate mechanism which was regarded as unfair by the other large contributors, but on which the UK was adamant. The debate on the resource side of the budget was more about establishing the broad parameters of how the own resources system should develop in future rather than a serious attempt to renegotiate the system in this round of negotiations. Its importance was in establishing a range of options for future changes in the system of own resources.

Tax Harmonization

The EU debate on tax harmonization gathered pace in 1998. The Austrian Presidency highlighted it as an important issue for its term of office, particularly in the context of the launch of the single currency and the need for greater economic policy co-ordination. The debate concerned a EU-wide savings tax, corporation tax and ecological taxes. It was an extremely sensitive area for many Member States, but particularly the United Kingdom and Ireland. The UK is opposed to tax harmonization on policy grounds and in terms of sovereignty. Ireland is concerned that it will be asked to change its low levels of corporation tax which are seen as a key element of growth in the 1990s.

IV. Public Opinion

During 1998, the electorates in two Member States, Ireland and Denmark, voted on the Treaty of Amsterdam. The referendum in Ireland predated the Danish referendum by one week and took place on the same day as the referendum on the Good Friday Agreement, outlined above. The Irish electorate has tradition-ally been very supportive of Ireland's membership of the EU and has usually ratified new EU treaties by significant majorities. The Amsterdam Treaty was supported by all the political parties in the Parliament with the exception of the Greens and the nationalist party, Sinn Féin. The government and the main opposition parties strongly advocated a 'yes' vote and highlighted the benefits to Ireland of EU membership and the importance of the Treaty in European terms. Opposition to the Treaty came from a diverse range of groups such as the Immigration Control Platform, the Irish National Organization for the Unem-ployed, the Peace and Neutrality Alliance, in addition to the Greens, Sinn Féin and the Workers' Party. The 'yes' and 'no' camps disagreed on the impact of the Treaty on Irish neutrality, a sensitive issue for public opinion. There was also conflict about the employment chapter and the free movement provisions. Although the Irish electorate returned a 'yes' majority of 61.74 per cent, this was the lowest 'yes' vote in a EU referendum. The result suggests that the Irish electorate is experiencing 'referendum fatigue' on Europe and would like the system to stabilize for a number of years. The establishment of a Referendum Commission complicated the conduct of the referendum with responsibility for informing the Irish electorate of the benefits and disadvantages of the Treaty. Following the referendum, there was widespread agreement that the Commis-sion had failed in its information role.

Table 5: National Attitudes Towards EU Membership

	B	DK	D	GR	E	F	IRL	I
A good thing	47 +2	56 +3	48 +7	67 +8	63 +8	52 +2	79 –1	68 –1
A bad thing	9 –3	20 +1	11 –2	9 0	7 –1	12 –1	4 0	5 0
Neither good nor bad	36 +3	22 –2	30 –6	23 –2	25 –2	30 0	10 0	17 –1
Don't know	8 –2	3 –2	11 +1	1 –6	6 –5	6 –1	7 +1	10 +1
Total	100	101	100	100	101	100	100	101

Table 5: Cont.

	L	NL	A	P	FIN	S	UK	EU15
A good thing	77 +6	75 –2	38 +2	58 –3	45 +9	35 +3	37 –4	54 +3
A bad thing	6 0	6 +1	19 0	9 +2	21 –4	36 –2	22 +3	12 0
Neither good nor bad	15 –4	16 +2	36 +2	24 0	30 0	25 0	29 –1	26 –2
Don't know	2 –2	4 –1	9 –2	9 +1	3 –5	4 –1	13 +2	8 –1
Total	100	101	100	100	99	100	101	100

Source: Eurobarometer 50, 1999, «http://europa.eu.int/en/comm/dg10/infcomm/epo/eb/eb50/eb50en/eb50_en.pdf»
Notes: The printed version of *Eurobarometer 50* is not available until the second half of 1999.
Percentage of 'Don't knows' calculated on the basis of *Eurobarometer 49* totals.

Table 6: Perceived Benefits of EU Membership

	B	DK	D	GR	E	F	IRL	I
Benefited	44 0	70 +5	39 +3	76 +8	58 +13	53 +7	85 0	51 –6
Not benefited	32 0	20 +1	36 –7	17 –2	25 –3	53 +7	5 0	27 +10
Don't know	24 0	10 –6	25 +4	7 –6	17 –10	20 –3	10 0	22 –4
Total	100	100	100	100	100	100	100	100

Table 6: Cont.

	L	NL	A	P	FIN	S	UK	EU15
Benefited	69 +6	67 0	41 –2	67 –6	39 +6	27 +7	37 –3	49 +3
Not benefited	14 –9	22 +6	34 –3	19 +5	44 –8	53 –2	42 +3	31 –1
Don't know	17 +3	11 –6	25 +5	14 +1	18 +2	21 –5	22 0	20 –2
Total	100	100	100	100	101	101	101	100

Source: Eurobarometer 50, 1999, «http://europa.eu.int/en/comm/dg10/infcomm/epo/eb/eb50/eb50en/eb50_en.pdf»
Notes: The printed version of *Eurobarometer 50* is not available until the second half of 1999. Percentage of 'Don't knows' calculated on the basis of *Eurobarometer 49* totals.

There was considerable concern about the outcome of the Danish referendum following the majority 'no' vote in June 1992. In the lead-up to the referendum, opinion polls suggested that there was a majority in favour of the Treaty and that a second Danish 'no' was unlikely. The campaign was as lively and contentious as previous campaigns on the EU in Denmark which has a strong core of Eurosceptics in its electorate. The 'no' campaign was dominated by the Socialist People's Party, the far-right Danish People's Party, and the far-left Red–Green Alliance. The minority Social Democratic government strongly supported the Treaty but found that its rank-and-file were deeply divided. The free movement provisions were among the most contentious in the referendum, with fears of refugees and increased immigration if borders were to disappear. In the event, the 'yes' vote at 56 per cent ensured that this Treaty would be carried in Denmark without the need for further negotiations.

During 1998, two *Eurobarometer* surveys were conducted (Nos 49 and 50). The results indicate that support for the European Union is rising, having reached a low of 46 per cent in 1997. In reply to the standard questions about membership being a 'good thing' for the respondents' native country, 51 per cent replied in the affirmative in *Eurobarometer 49*, rising to 54 per cent in *Eurobarometer 50*. Support levels had increased in ten of the 15 Member States, especially in Spain, Greece, Germany and Luxembourg with increases of 6 per cent or over. Support for membership continued to be highest in Ireland (79 per cent), the Netherlands (75 per cent), Luxembourg (77 per cent) and Italy (68 per cent). Two new Member States, Sweden (35 per cent), Austria (38 per cent) together with the UK (37 per cent) record the lowest levels of support (see Table 5).

In a related question about perceived benefits from EU membership, 49 per cent felt that their country had benefited. This represents an increase of 5 per cent from autumn 1997. Irish respondents continued to be the most positive, with some 85 per cent saying that their country had benefited from EU membership. Sweden, with 27 per cent, the UK with 37 per cent and Finland with 39 per cent, are the lowest (see Table 6 for the variations across the Member States).

V. Implementation

The focus on implementation and enforcement in the 1997 Annual Report continued in 1998. The June 1997 *Action Plan for the Internal Market* bore fruit with the percentage of internal market directives not implemented falling to 14.9 per cent from 26.7 per cent in November 1997. This masks variation across the Member States, with Finland, Denmark, Sweden and the Netherlands the best performers. Austria, Germany and Belgium had improved their performance, whereas Luxembourg, Ireland and Portugal had fallen behind. Telecommunica-

Table 7: Notification of Transposition of European Community Law

Member State	Directives Applicable 31.12.97	Measures Notified	(%)
Belgium	1382	1269	91.8
Denmark	1378	1337	97.0
Germany	1384	1295	93.6
Greece	1380	1281	92.8
Spain	1380	1313	95.1
France	1382	1293	93.6
Ireland	1374	1293	94.1
Italy	1383	1278	92.5
Luxembourg	1380	1300	94.2
Netherlands	1382	1332	96.4
Austria	1379	1301	94.3
Portugal	1378	1289	93.5
Finland	1370	1319	96.3
Sweden	1376	1339	97.3
UK	1381	1308	94.7

Source: Commission (1998b), p. 9.

tions, public procurement, transport and intellectual property are the areas with the most serious implementation problems.

The Commission's *Fifteenth Annual Report on Monitoring the Application of Community Law* (Commission, 1998b), concluded that the level of implementation had improved, insofar as 94 per cent of national measures needed to implement the directives had been taken by 31 December 1997 (see Table 7). The most marked improvement took place in Sweden which ranked first on the scoreboard. Finnish implementation also improved, rising to 96.3 per cent, compared to 81 per cent in 1996).

References

Agence Europe, various issues.
Commission of the European Communities (1998a) *Eurobarometer 49,* Spring 1998.
Commission of the European Communities (1998b) 'Fifteenth annual report on monitoring the application of Community law 1997'. *COM* (98) 317 final, *Official Journal C 250/1,* 10 August.
European Report, various issues.
European Voice, various issues.
Financial Times, various issues.
Institute of European Affairs (1999) *European Agenda 2000. Implications for Ireland* (Dublin: IEA).

Journal of Common Market Studies

Volume 37, Annual Review
September 1999

A Guide to the Documentation of the European Union

IAN THOMSON
Cardiff University

and

JANET MATHER
Manchester Metropolitan University

Abbreviations

Bull.EU	*Bulletin of the European Union*
CEECs	Central and Eastern European countries
COM	Commission Document
CoR	Committee of the Regions
EC	European Community (when noted as the publisher, 'EC' means the office for Official Publications of the European Communities (EUROPE), L-2985, Luxembourg. EC publications may be obtained from the sales agents of EUR-OP in the Member States and elsewhere. In the UK the sales agent is HMSO.)
EEA	European Economic Area
EP	European Parliament
ESC	Economic and Social Committee
IGC	Intergovernmental Conference
OJ	*Official Journal of the European Communities* – Annex: Debates of the European Parliament – C: Information – L: Legislation
PE DOC	Committee Report of the European Parliament
SEC	Internal Commission General Secretariat Document
TEU	Treaty on European Union

Most publications and electronic sources cited in this guide are available for reference in European Documentation Centres (EDCs, mainly based in academic libraries) and EC Depository Libraries throughout the world.

Introduction

This guide lists a selection of the key EU documents and publications of 1998 that highlight the important institutional and policy activities and initiatives of the European Union with a selection of other significant new publications and series. Some titles issued in the closing weeks of 1997, or titles which only became available in 1998, are included. The guide is divided into five sections:

> General
> Governance and institutional developments
> Financing the Union
> Internal policy developments
> External policies and relations

Specific legislative proposals and legislation adopted during the year are not included (see *European Access* throughout 1998 in the 'Recent references' section for these).

The majority of references noted in the guide are to printed sources, but the growing significance of the Internet as a source of EU information is reflected throughout, and Internet addresses (URLs) are noted when appropriate.

Many of the documents noted within are available on the Internet. If a specific URL (site) is not indicated, try the EUROPA search engine to see if the text is available on the web «http://europa.eu.int/geninfo/query_en.htm», or «http://www2.echo.lu/search.htm». Sources noted as *Press Release, Document* and *Memo* are available on the RAPID database on the Internet «http://europa.eu.int/rapid/start/welcome.htm». For the text of European Parliament resolutions, the opinions of the ESC and the CoR, and the bulk of the sources cited from other EU institutions and agencies, try the home-pages of the institutions as listed below. Internet connections to all EU institutions, organizations and agencies can be found at 'Europe on the Internet' at: «http://www.europeanaccess.co.uk».

Note that 'EC' remains the standard term used in *European Access* for material published by the Office for Official Publications of the European Communities (EUR-OP).

General

For an overview of the activities of the EU in 1998 see the European Commission's *General Report on the Activities of the European Union 1998* (published by EUR-OP in February 1999) («http://europa.eu.int/abc/doc/off/rg/en/welcome.htm») and issues of the monthly *Bulletin of the European Union (Bull.EU)*: «http://europa.eu.int/abc/doc/off/bull/en/welcome.htm».

The major EU Internet development of 1998 was the launch of the EUR-Lex service («http://europa.eu.int/eur-lex»), which aims to offer free access to a mass of EU legislative and judicial information. Some of the information on EUR-Lex has been available on other websites for some time but two features launched in 1998 were genuinely new in terms of free access: the full text of all adopted EU secondary legislation currently in force and access to the full text of the last 20 days' issues of the 'L' and 'C' series of the *Official Journal* (from 1999 this will be extended to 45 days including the text of proposed legislation) (see Press Release (Commission), IP/98/951 (3.11.98)).

ECLAS, the electronic version of the catalogue of the European Commission Library, also became accessible on the Internet during 1998: «http://europa.eu.int/ eclas».

Agenda 2000

Each issue of the *Bull.EU* during 1998 contains a section called *Agenda 2000*, which draws together relevant developments within the EU. There is also an *Agenda 2000* website: «http://europa.eu.int/comm/agenda2000/index.htm».

Documents of interest include:

Commission: *Communication ... Agenda 2000: The legislative proposals. Overall view: COM* (98)182 final (18.3.98)

ESC: *Opinion: Commission Communication – Agenda 2000*: *OJ* C19, 21.1.98, pp. 111–15

Parliament: Resolution: *Enlargement – Agenda 2000; The 2000–2006 financial framework for the Union and the future financing system*: *OJ* C388, 22.12.97, pp. 17–30 (published 1998)
Related publications: PE DOC A4-331/97; *PE DOC* A4-368/97

Court of Auditors: *Opinion No.10/98 of the European Court of Auditors on certain proposals for regulations within the Agenda 2000 framework*: *OJ* C401, 22.12.98, pp. 1–47

Governance and Institutional Developments

Primary Legislation

It had been anticipated the Treaty of Amsterdam would be ratified before the end of 1998. However, this did not happen and the Treaty came into force in the summer of 1999:

Council: *Simplification of the Community Treaties. Explanatory report*: EC, 1998 ISBN: 92-824-1545-7 EC No. BX-10-97-251-EN-C

The Intergovernmental Conference

The Council continued to publish 'collected texts' issued during each EU Presidency in connection with the Intergovernmental Conference leading up to the signing of the Treaty of Amsterdam in October 1997. This included the 1997 Dutch Presidency:

> Council, General Secretariat: *Intergovernmental Conference on the revision of the Treaties. Dutch Presidency (January–June 1997). Collected texts:* EC, 1998; ISBN: 92-824-1523-6; EC No. BX-10-97-413-EN-C

The 1996 Intergovernmental Conference retrospective database, containing access to the key documents and many other sources, remains available on the Internet: «http://europa.eu.int/en/agenda/igc-home/».

The Amsterdam Treaty

The views of the EP and CoR were documented:

> Parliament: *Resolution on the Amsterdam Treaty*: OJ C371, 8.12.97, pp. 99–104 (published 1998)

> CoR: *Opinion: Outcome of the Intergovernmental Conference (IGC): OJ* C64, 27.2.98, pp. 98–100

The Council of the EU issued an introductory booklet on the Treaty of Amsterdam:

> Council, General Secretariat: *The Treaty of Amsterdam. Challenges and solutions:* EC, 1998; ISBN: 92-824-1517-1; EC No.BX-10-97-146-EN-C

The Commission issued a guide to the Amsterdam Treaty on its SCADPLUS website: «http://europa.eu.int/comm/sg/scadplus/leg/en/s50000.htm».

The Presidency and the European Council

There were two formal European Councils in 1998: Cardiff, 15–16.6.98, at the end of the UK Presidency, and Vienna, 11–12.12.98, at the end of the Austrian Presidency.

The programmes of the six-monthly Presidencies of the EU are formally presented to the European Parliament in January and July each year. The text of the verbal presentation by the current President of the Council, and the subsequent debate are published in the issues of the *OJ*: Annex covering the plenary sessions of January and July 1998. Summaries of the presentation and debate are published in the Parliament's *The Week* for the appropriate plenary sessions, which is available on the EUROPARL server listed under 'European Parliament' below. The full text of the statements and debates are also available on the EUROPARL server under the section 'Verbatim Report of Proceedings (Provisional Edition)' (not translated). See also the Presidency websites:

> UK Presidency, January–June 1998: «http://presid.fco.gov.uk/»

> Austrian Presidency, July–December 1998: «http://www.presidency.gv.at»

A review and debate of each Presidency take place in the European Parliament usually during the last month of each Presidency and following the European Council summit.

The Conclusions adopted at the end of European Council meetings are published in the *Bulletin of the European Union* for the appropriate month, as a *Document* on the RAPID database, on the EUROPA server, on the Council homepage, and on the Presidency homepages listed below. Following the European Council, Vienna, 11–12.12.98, the full text of all formal documents submitted to the European Council by the Council and Commission are available on the web at: «http://ue.eu.int/Newsroom» (click on 'Press Release Library/Miscellaneous').

No formal Conclusions were issued after the informal European Council, Pört-schach, 24–25.10.98 (see *Bull.EU*, No.10, 1998).

The Council of the European Union

Reports of all regular Council meetings in 1998 were issued as *Press Releases* accessible on both the RAPID database and the website of the Council «http://ue.eu.int/Newsroom» (click on 'Council'). Agendas for Council meetings are accessible in the 'Calendar' section of SCADPLUS «http://europa.eu.int/scadplus/».

There is a substantial delay in the publication of the Council annual review – the latest edition available covers 1995 and was published in 1997. No volume appeared in 1998.

Further information sources of interest include:

Council: *98/709/EC, ECSC, Euratom: Council decision of 7.12.98 amending the Council's Rules of Procedure: OJ* L337, 12.12.98, pp. 40–1

Council, General Secretariat: *Information handbook of the Council of the European Union.* May 1998: EC, 1998; ISBN: 92-824-1580-5; EC No.BX-01-96-608-EN-C

A Register of Council documents was launched on the Internet as from January 1999: «http://register.consilium.eu.int/isoregister/introEN.htm».

The European Commission

The Commission issued its annual review of 1997 in February 1998. For the first time, it appeared on the Internet as well as in printed format:

Commission: *General report on the activities of the European Union 1997:*EC, 1998; ISBN: 92-828-2445-4; EC No.CM-10-97-986-EN-C (also available on the Internet: «http://europa.eu.int/abc/doc/off/rg/en/welcome.htm»)

In October 1998 the Commission issued its Work Programme for 1999, divided into two sections: policy priorities and new legislative initiatives. The Programme is usually published as No.1 in the series *Bull.EU: Supplement* each year:

Commission: *The Commission's Work Programme for 1999: OJ* C366, 26.11.98, pp. 1–12

Related publications: COM (98)604 final (28.10.98); *COM* (98)609 final (28.10.98); Internet:«http://europa.eu.int/comm/off/work/1999/index_en.htm»

A report on the implementation of the Commission's work programme, and the Parliament's comments on it, was issued:

Commission: *Report on implementation of the Commission's work programme for 1998: COM* (98)610 final (28.10.98)

(This report is also available on the Internet: «http://europa.eu.int/comm/off/work/1999/index_en.htm»)

Parliament: *Resolution: Commission's work programme for 1998: OJ* C14, 19.1.98, pp. 185–90
Related publications: Bull.EU: Supplement, No.1, 1998

The European Parliament

Periodically the European Parliament issues a substantial volume providing information on the institutions and policies of the European Union, emphasizing the Parliament's role. The latest edition appeared in 1998 in printed form and on the Internet:

Parliament, DG IV: *Fact Sheets on the European Union:* EC, 1998; ISBN: 92-823-1074-4; EC No.AY-01-96-842-EN-C (Also available on the Internet at «http://www.europarl.eu.int/dg4/factsheets/en/default.htm»)

The latest edition of the EP's directory of Members published in 1998 is:

Parliament: *List of Members of the Bureau, Parliament, Political Groups, Committees and Interparliamentary Delegations, 28.10.98*: EC, 1998; ISSN: 0256-243X; EC No.AX-AE-98-003-1F-C

Further information sources of interest include:

Parliament, DG IV: *Rules of procedure.* 13th edn: EC, 1998; ISBN: 92-823-1096-5; EC No.AX-11-97-245-EN-C

Court of Auditors: *Special Report No.10/98 concerning the expenses and allowances of the members of the European Parliament together with the replies of the European Parliament: OJ* C243, 3.8.98, pp. 1–15

Parliament: *Resolution on a draft electoral procedure incorporating common principles for the election of MEPs: OJ* C292, 21.9.98, pp. 66–8
Related publications: PE DOC A4-212/98

Parliament, DG IV: *European Parliament: Bibliography 1990–1996*: EC, 1997
Internet: «http://www.europarl.eu.int/»

The European Court of Justice

The full text of judgments of the Court of Justice and Court of First Instance now appear on the day of the judgment on the ECJ's website at «http://www.curia.eu.int». As at the end of 1998 all judgments from June 1997 were still available on the ECJ webpage, contrary to expectations. The text of judgments is also accessible through the EUR-Lex service «http://europa.eu.int/eur-lex». As from 1998 the text of the opinion of the Advocate-General also appears on the ECJ website. For judgments and opinions before these dates use the printed sources and CELEX.

Further sources of information include:

> Court of Justice: *Annual report 1996. Synopsis of the work of the Court of Justice and of the Court of First Instance of the European Communities:* EC, 1998; ISBN: 92-829-354-0; EC No.DX-07-97-571-EN-C

> Court of Justice: *The Court of Justice of the European Communities:* EC, 1998; EC No. DY-05-97-357-EN-C (an introductory booklet)

> Court of Justice, Research. Documentation and Library Directorate: *Index A–Z. Numerical and alphabetical index of cases before the Court of Justice and the Court of First Instance of the European Communities since 1953. Situation oñ 31 August 1997:* EC, 1997; ISBN: 92-829-0361-3; EC No. DX-09-97-373-EN-C

The ECJ website also includes an up-to-date listing of all ECJ cases since 1953 in order of case number, with bibliographical references to the printed text of the judgment.

> Court of Justice, Research. Documentation and Library Directorate: *Legal bibliography of European integration. 1997.* 2 vols: EC, 1998; ISBN: 92-829-0405-9 (Vol.I)/ 92-829-0406-7 (Vol.II); EC No.DY-80-98-001/2-1F-C

The Economic and Social Committee

The ESC issued its annual report:

> ESC: *Annual report 1997:* EC, 1998; ISBN: 92-830-0285-7; EC No.EX-10-97-663-EN-C

New members were appointed during 1998:

> Council: 98/545/EC: *Council decision of 15.9.98 appointing the members of the ESC for period 21.9.98–20.9.2002: OJ* C291, 19.9.98, pp. 37–48

The ESC issued its 'half-term' report:

> ESC: *Bureau of the Economic and Social Committee of the European Communities: first two-year period of the 11th four-year term of office (1998–2000): OJ* C345, 13.11.98, pp. 4–5

Internet: «http://www.esc.eu.int/en/default.htm»

The Committee of the Regions (CoR)

The CoR began its second term of office and new members were appointed:

> Council: *98/110/EC: Council Decision of 26.1.98 appointing the members and alternate members of the Committee of the Regions for the period 26.1.98 to 25.1.2002: OJ* L28, 4.2.98, pp. 19–40

Internet: «http://www.cor.eu.int/»

The European Court of Auditors

The 21st annual report (for the financial year 1997) of the European Court of Auditors was issued in November 1998:

> Court of Auditors: *Annual report concerning the financial year 1997: OJ* C349, 17.11.98, pp. 1–177; i–xlix

The 1997 annual report now contains general observations on the findings of special reports and a summary of the audit conclusions adopted. Detailed work of the Court is published in a series of *Special Reports*. In 1998, 25 *Special Reports*, 10 opinions and 15 special annual reports were adopted. The full text of all of these can be found on the website of the Court of Auditors, along with *Information Notes* (summaries).

Internet: «http://www.eca.eu.int»

The European Investment Bank

The European Investment Bank published a new edition of its introductory booklet in 1998 to mark its 40th anniversary:

> European Investment Bank: *European Investment Bank. The European Union's financing institution. 40 years of lending in support of European integration:* EC, 1998; ISBN: 92-828-3208-2; EC No.IX-12-98-409-EN-C

In addition, two issues of *EIB Papers* were published in 1998 (Volume 3), the second being called the '40th anniversary issue' with a series of contributions on the theme 'International financial institutions in the 21st century'.

Internet: «http://www.eib.org»

Other EU Institutions and Organizations (Including Agencies)

Much information from these organizations is now available on the Internet. See the 'agencies' url below. Policy-related publications from these bodies are listed in the Internal Policy Developments section of this guide.

Internet: «http://www.emcdda.org»

The Foundation for the Improvement of Living and Working Conditions takes actions designed to increase and disseminate knowledge in fulfilment of its aims. It launched a monthly newsletter called *Communiqué* in October 1998 to replace its quarterly *Bulletin* and issued its annual report for 1997 and a programme of work for 1998 (which contained a summary of the activities planned by the Foundation in 1998 within the framework of its 1997–2000 programme 'Facing up to the Challenges of European Society'):

> European Foundation for the Improvement of Living and Working Conditions: *Programme of work for 1998:* EC, 1998 ISBN: 92-828-2808-5 EC No.SX-12-98-198-EN-C
> Internet: «http://www.eurofound.eu.int»

> European Foundation for the Improvement of Living and Working Conditions: *Annual report 1997:* EC, 1998; ISBN: 92-828-3804-8; EC No.SX-14-98-833-EN-C

The European Industrial Relations Observatory (EIRO) was established in 1997 with the aim of providing accurate and up-to-date information on and analysis of developments in industrial relations to social partners, national governments, the European Commission and other EU institutions. The EIROnline database service became available during 1998 on the Internet: «http://www.eiro.eurofound.ie/». EIRO also published its first annual review:

> European Foundation for the Improvement of Living and Working Conditions: *European Industrial Relations Observatory. Annual review 1997. A review of developments in European industrial relations:* EC, 1998 ISBN: 92-828-4375-0 EC No.SX-16-98-344-EN-C

CEDEFOP's work programme for 1998 follows the three major themes outlined in its medium-term priorities for the period 1997–2000: promoting competences and life-long learning, monitoring developments in the Member States and serving European mobility and exchanges:

> European Centre for the Development of Vocational training (CEDEFOP): *Work programme 1998:* EC, 1998; ISBN: 92-828-2390-3; EC No.HX-08-97-557-3A-C

In addition to CEDEFOP's main site on the Internet «http://www.cedefop.gr», a further site was launched in 1998 called the European Electronic Training Village: «http://www.trainingvillage.gr/».

A report on the fourth year of operations of the European Training Foundation featured National Observatories and the Tempus Programme:

Commission: *European Training Foundation. 1997 annual report: COM*
(98)481 final (28.7.98)
Internet: «http://www.etf.it/»

The EMI issued its annual report:

European Monetary Institute: *Annual report 1997:* EMI, 1998; ISSN: 1024-
560X

The ECB's rules of procedure restricted meeting attendance to accredited membership
including the President of the Council and one Commissioner. It also set out the
relationship between the Governing and the General Council and established confidentiality of proceedings as a general rule:

European Central Bank: *Rules of procedure: OJ* L338, 15.10.98, pp. 28–33
Internet: «http://www.ecb.int»

The Office for Harmonisation in the Internal Market issued its annual report:

Office for Harmonisation in the Internal Market: *Annual report 1997*: C, 1998
ISBN: 92-9156-015-4; No. AH-10-97-477-EN-C
Internet: «http://oami.eu.int»

The Monitoring Centre's General report listed its achievements in each area of its work
programme and documented activities undertaken with European and international
partners:

European Monitoring Centre for Drugs and Drug Addiction: *General report
of activities 1997:* EC, 1998; ISBN: 92-9168-047-8; EC No.AO-11-98-794-
EN-C
Internet: «http://www.emcdda.org»

1997 was the 3rd operational year for the EEA.

European Environment Agency: *Annual report 1997:* EC, 1998; ISBN:
92-9167-108-8; EC No.GH-15-98-277-EN-C
Internet: «http://www.eea.eu.int»

The European Agency for Safety and Health at work issued its annual report:

European Agency for Safety and Health at Work: *Annual report 1997*: EC,
1998; ISBN: 92-828-3811-0; EC No.AS-15-98-003-EN-C
Internet: «http://osha.eu.int/»

The Agency launched in 1998 a quarterly newsletter called *European Agency News*
(also available on the Internet site listed above).

Internet: Links to the homepages of the other agencies, foundations and centres set up by European Commission or European Council decisions are available at: «http://europa.eu.int/en/agencies.html».

Policy-making

The 15th report on the application of EC law related to the first year that the ECJ had been empowered to impose daily penalty payments on recalcitrant states:

> Commission: *Fifteenth annual report on monitoring the application of Community law (1997): OJ* C250, 10.8.98, pp. 1–204
> *Related publications: COM* (98)317 final (19.5.98); *OJ* C56, 23.2.98, p. 39 (EP Resolution on 1996 report); *PE DOC* A4-8/98

A report focused on the SLIM pilot project relating to the simplification of internal market legislation:

> Commission: *Communication ... Legislate less to act better: the facts: COM* (98)345 final (27.5.98)

The Commission's proposal would give the Commission the right to implement decisions, particularly upon CAP and programmes with budgetary implications unless the Council decided otherwise:

> Commission: *Proposal for a Council Decision laying down the procedures for the exercise of implementing powers conferred on the Commission: OJ* C279, 8.9.98, pp. 5–7
> *Related publications: COM* (98)380 final (16.7.98)

Improved efficiency was a feature of the Commission's aims:

> Commission: *Better lawmaking 1998. A shared responsibility. Commission report to the European Council: COM* (98)715 final (1.12.98)

The EP's transparency package encompassed policies on EMU, CCP, Euratom, agriculture, fisheries, development co-operation, competition and implementation of collective agreements:

> Parliament: *Resolution on improvements in the functioning of the Institutions without modifications of the Treaties – making EU policies more open and democratic: OJ* C167, 1.6.98, pp. 211–14
> *Related publications: PE DOC* A4-117/98

The prospect of the new simplified co-decision procedure prompted the EP to suggest informal trialogues at the first reading, with a direct presentation of the Council's common position at the second reading:

Parliament: *Resolution on the new co-decision procedure after Amsterdam: OJ* C292, 21.9.98, pp. 140–2
Related publications: PE DOC A4-271/98

The EP proposed that the principles underlying the Commission's delegated powers should guarantee full respect for the legislative procedure, ensure balance between institutions and include a precise definition of the Commission's degree of autonomy:

Parliament: *Resolution: Comitology: OJ* C313, 12.10.98, pp. 101–4

European Ombudsman

The Ombudsman's third report emphasized informing EU citizens of their rights. There had been an increase of 40 per cent of complaints on 1996 figures:

European Ombudsman: *Annual report for 1997:* EC, 1998; ISBN: 92-828-3507-3; EC No. ME-13-98-750-EN-C
Related publications: OJ C380, 7.12.98, pp. 1–162

The Ombudsman was particularly concerned with transparency issues in 1998:

European Ombudsman: *Special report from the European Ombudsman to the European Parliament following the own-initiative inquiry into public access to documents* (616/PUBAC/F/IJH): *OJ* C44, 10.2.98, pp. 9–13

Internet: «http://www.euro-ombudsman.eu.int»

European Access published a major two-part 'bibliographic snapshot' called 'EU governance and institutional developments' during 1998. It appeared in issues No.5, October 1998, pp. 32–9 and No.6, December 1998, pp. 40–9.

Financing the Union

Financing the Union – General

The Commission produced a comprehensive document presenting the history of the budget; an analysis of the period 1988–92; the new financial framework (1993–99); a detailed description of the budget adopted for 1998; the preliminary draft budget for 1999 and financial perspectives for the period 2000–06:

Commission: *The Community budget: the facts in figures. 1998 edn: SEC* (98)1100: EC, 1998; ISBN: 92-828-3743-2; EC No.C6-14-98-792-EN-C

The Commission demonstrated that accessions from CEECs and Cyprus could be financed without increasing the own resource ceiling of 1.27 per cent of Member State GDP:

Commission: *Communication ... on the establishment of a new financial perspective for the period 2000–2006: COM* (98)164 final (18.3.98)

The EP pointed out that the assumption that 1.27 per cent GDP would be adequate depended upon incalculable factors like growth, reform of EC policies and the outcome of the enlargement process:

Parliament: Resolution: *Agenda 2000. The 2000–2006 financial framework for the Union and the future financing system: OJ* C388, 22.12.97, p. 31; *PE DOC* A4-331/97

The Commission's report noted the advantages and disadvantages involved in introducing a new own resource and fixing permanently the rate of call of VAT:

Commission: *Financing the European Union. Commission report on the operation of the Own Resource System: COM* (98)560 final (7.10.98)
Related publications: *Bull.EU*: Supplement, No.2, 1998

See also section on *Agenda 2000* above.

1998 Budget

The full text of the 1998 budget was published in:

Parliament: *98/132/EC, ECSC, Euratom: Final adoption of the general budget of the European Union for the financial year 1998: OJ* L44, 16.2.98, pp. 1–1597
Related publications: OJ L323, 1.12.98, p. 1

A summary of the information on the current annual budget was issued for the first time:

Commission: *General budget of the European Union for the financial year 1998. The figures: SEC* (98)100; EC, 1998; ISBN: 92-828-2570-1; EC No.C6-09-97-462-EN-C

1999 Budget

The full texts of the draft budget as it passes through the various legislative stages are not published. Summaries are available from Part 1 Section 6 'Financing Community activities' in the *Bulletin of the European Union* for the appropriate months. For the European Parliament's role see issues of *The Week* covering the appropriate plenary sessions in October and December 1998 (available on the EUROPARL server: «http://www.europarl.eu.int»). For the Council's role see the *Press Releases* from the Budget Councils of 17 July and 24 November 1998 («http://ue.eu.int/Newsroom»; click on 'Council' and then 'Budget').

The Commission approved the preliminary draft budget for 1999 on 29 April 1998 (*Bull.EU*, No.4, 1998, pp. 73–7 and Press Release (Commission), IP/98/382 (29.4.98)). Further brief information about the draft budget at this stage is given in the 1998 edition of 'The Community budget: the facts in figures', pp. 101–7 (see Reference C1 above). The 1999 budget is the first to be expressed in euros.

The Council adopted a first reading draft on 17 July 1998 (*Bull.EU*, No.7–8, 1998, pp. 112–18 and *Press Release* (Council), PRES/98/253 (17.7.98). The European Parliament voted on the first reading on 22 October 1998. The Council approved a draft 1999 budget at a second reading on 24 November 1998 (*Press Release* (Council), PRES/98/406 (24.11.98)), although a continuing serious disagreement with the European Parliament meant that there was a further Budget Council and trialogue held on 8 December 1998 to resolve these disagreements (*Press Release* (Council), PRES/98/436 (8.12.98)). A compromise was reached and this enabled the European Parliament to adopt the 1999 budget on 17 December 1998.

The 1999 budget was published in *OJ* L39 12.2.99.

Financial Management

Two financial reports were issued in 1998:

> Commission: *Financial report 1996:* EC, 1998; ISBN: 92-828-0770-3; EC No.C6-06-97-351-EN-C
>
> Commission: *Financial report 1997:* EC, 1998; ISBN: 92-828-3777-7; EC No.C6-14-98-978-EN-C

A report noted lessons learned from the application of the 1993 Interinstitutional Agreement:

> Commission: *Report on the implementation of the Interinstitutional Agreement of 29.10.93 on budgetary discipline and improvement of the budgetary procedure. Proposals for renewal: COM* (98)165 final (18.3.98)

An interinstitutional agreement obviates the need to pass a basic act to enable EC action in relation to pilot schemes, preparation actions, actions of a specific nature or administrative actions:

> Parliament/Council/Commission: *Interinstitutional agreement of 13.10.98 on legal bases and implementation of the budget: OJ* C344, 12.11.98, pp. 1–4 *Related publications: Press Release*(Commission), IP/98/520 (10.6.98); IP/98/657 (15.7.98); IP/98/715 (29.7.98); Proceedings of the Court of Justice ..., No.13, 1998, p 5; *OJ* C313, 12.10.98, p. 5; *PE DOC* A4-296/98

1997 saw a 'substantial increase' in the EC's borrowing activities and an increase to 4.5 per cent (from 3 per cent in1996) in its investment:

Commission: *Annual report ... on the borrowing and lending activities of the Community in 1997: COM* (98)409 final (3.7.98)
Related publications: European Economy: Supplement A, No.6, June 1998, pp. 1–22

A report covered operations with macro- and microeconomic objectives related to former USSR states and an evaluation of risks re non-member countries:

Commission: *Report ... to the Budgetary Authority on guarantees covered by the General Budget – Situation at 31.12.98: COM* (98)252 final (27.4.98)
Related publications: COM (98)537 final (25.9.98)

The Commission responded to a Council Resolution of 9.3.98 promising a strengthening of the evaluation culture; the incorporation of measures taken into the *Agenda 2000* programme and a simplification of regulatory frameworks:

Commission: *Commission follow-up report on action taken in response to the Council recommendation on discharge in respect of the implementation of the general budget for 1996. Member States' replies to the Observations contained in the Court of Auditors' annual report for 1996: COM* (98)679 final (23.11.98)

A report issued triennially on the collection of VAT gave 'some clue as to the scale and importance of fraud and general principles for combating it':

Commission: *VAT collection and control procedures applied in the Member States. Third competition report: COM* (98)490 final (3.9.98)

A special report examined the EC budget's two main sources which account for 80 per cent of EC revenue:

Court of Auditors: *Special Report No.6/98 concerning the Court's assessment of the system of resources based on VAT and GNP together with the Commission's replies: OJ* C241, 31.7.98, pp. 58–80

Forty-five per cent of the EC's budget in 1997 was financed from VAT (in 1998 there was a maximum rate of 1.8 per cent). The auditors therefore concluded that it was important to avoid loss from VAT fraud:

Court of Auditors: *Special Report No.9/98 concerning the protection of the financial interests of the European Union in the field of VAT on intra-community trade together with the Commission's replies: OJ* C356, 20.11.98, pp. 1–17

Fraud

A series of reports traced the Commission's record in dealing with fraud and proposals for combating it in future:

Commission: *Protecting the Community's financial interests. The fight against fraud. Annual report 1997*: EC, 1998; ISBN: 92-828-3766-1; EC No.CM-13-98-306-EN-C
Related publications: COM (98)276 final (6.5.98)

Commission: *Protecting the Community's financial interests. The fight against fraud. Work Programme 1998–99*; EC, 1998; ISBN: 92-828-4104-9; EC No.CM-14-98-817-EN-C
Related publications: COM (98)278 final (6.5.98)

Commission: *Proposal for a Council Regulation (EC, Euratom) establishing a European Fraud Investigation Office*: OJ C21, 26.1.99, pp. 10–15
Related publications: COM (98)717 final (1.12.98)

Council: *Explanatory Report on the Convention on the fight against corruption involving officials of the European Communities or officials of Member States of the European Union*: OJ C391, 15.12.98, pp. 1–12

Court of Auditors: *Special Report No.8/98 on the Commission's services specifically involved in the fight against fraud, notably the 'unité de coordination de la lutte anti-fraude' (UCLAF) together with the Commission's replies*: OJ C230, 22.7.98, pp. 1–44

Parliament: *Resolution: Criminal proceedings in protection of the Union's financial interests*: OJ C138, 4.5.98, pp. 61–3
Related publications: OJ C339, 10.11.97, p. 68

See also 'Court of Auditors' above.

Internal Policy Developments

Agriculture

The Commission produced an introductory booklet on the CAP:

Commission, DG VI: *The common agricultural policy. Promoting Europe's agriculture and rural areas: continuity and change*: EC, 1998; ISBN: 92-828-3736-X; ISBN: CH-10-97-970-EN-C

(a series of *Fact Sheets* on specific aspects of the CAP also published during 1998, can be accessed on DG VI's website (see below).

Commission: *The agricultural situation in the European Union. 1997 report*: COM (98)611 final (8.12.98)

The Commission's report on EAGGF responded to Art. 10 of Council Regulation (EEC 727/70 on the financing of agricultural policy:

Commission: *Twenty-Seventh financial report concerning the European Agricultural Guidance and Guarantee Fund (EAGGF) – Guarantee section. 1997 financial year*: COM (98)552 final (5.10.98)

The Commission argued that the policy of stability and simplicity prevalent since 1992 on pricing of agricultural products was relevant to the *Agenda 2000* reform process. Its proposals related only to prices required for legal reasons:

Commission: *Commission proposal on the prices for agricultural products (1998/1999).* 3 vols: COM (98)51 final (4.2.98)/ *OJ* C87, 23.3.98, p. 1

The Commission set out proposals as a basis for the 1999 Council debates on CAP reform:

Commission: *Proposals for Council Regulations (EC) concerning the reform of the common agricultural policy*: COM (98)158 final (18.3.98)
(See also General Section, *Agenda 2000* above.)

Agricultural Products

The Commission issued a series of reports related to individual agricultural products: skimmed milk powder *(COM* (98)341 final (28.5.98)); milk consumption *(COM* (98)632 final (5.11.98)); pigmeat *(COM* (98)434 final (27.7.98)); laying hens *(COM* (98)135 final (11.3.98)); wine *(COM* (98)790 final (22.12.98) and *COM* (98)791 final (22.12.98)); and BSE *(COM* (98)282 final (6.5.98) and *COM* (98)598 final (18.11.98)).

The EFICS has operated for two full periods: 1989–93 and 1993–97. A report looked at the impact of the programmes:

Commission: *Report ... on the implementation of the European Forestry Information and Communication System (EFICS)... (+ related legislative proposal)*: COM (98)173 final (24.3.98)

Following this, the Commission proposed a 'coherent outline of the EU's forestry strategy':

Commission: *Communication ... on a forestry strategy for the European Union*: COM (98)649 final (18.11.98)

Internet: «http://europa.eu.int/comm/dg06/index_en.htm» (European Commission: DG VI)

See also General Section: Agenda 2000 above.

Citizens

European Commission President, Jacques Santer, and President of the Council, Tony Blair, launched a new service for citizens intended to give direct access to information and advice about the EU and citizens' rights in the single market by Internet («http://europa.eu.int/citizens») and by free phone numbers from all Member States (the UK's is 0800-581591):

> Commission, Spokesman's Service: *Europe Direct: Strengthening the dialogue with citizens and business*: *Press Release*, IP/98/544 (17.6.98)

The EP proposed a comprehensive resolution on citizenship:

> Parliament: *Resolution: Union citizenship*: *OJ* C226, 20.7.98, pp. 61–4
> *Related publications*: PE DOC A4-205/98

See Governance and Institutional Developments Section, 'European Parliament' above.

Competition

DG IV published its annual report in two parts; a brochure (also published in conjunction with the *General Report on the European Union – 1997*) and the *Report on the application of competition rules in the Union*:

> Commission, DG IV: *XXVIIth report on competition policy 1997*: EC, 1998; ISBN: 92-828-4057-3; EC No.CM-12-98-506-EN-C

DG IV published a report on merger control law:

> Commission, DG IV: *Merger control law in the European Union. Situation in March 1998*: EC, 1998; ISBN: 92-828-3997-4; EC No.CV-15-98-899-EN-C

The Commission sought to revise previous criteria on regional aid to make the process transparent, up-to-date and simple. All previous documentation was incorporated into one text:

> Commission: *Guidelines on national regional aid*: *OJ* C74, 10.3.98, pp. 9–31

The Commission identified a need for more systematic controls on regional aid to large investment projects:

> Commission: *Multisectoral framework on regional aid for large investment projects*: *OJ* C107, 7.4.98, pp. 7–18

There were 18 million people unemployed in the EU in 1998. The Commission argued that since firms were liable to locate in areas where there was an existing skilled workforce, training was of vital importance:

> Commission: *Framework on training aid*: *OJ* C343, 11.11.98, pp. 10–16

The Commission issued a code of conduct for business taxation:

Commission: *Commission notice on the application of the State aid rules to measures relating to direct business taxation*: OJ C384, 10.12.98, pp. 3–9

DG VI's sixth survey updated existing data including the new Member States for the first time and setting out an open policy on state aid:

Commission, DG IV: *Sixth survey on State aid in the European Union in the manufacturing and certain other sectors*: EC, 1998; ISBN: 92-828-5214-8; EC No.CV-18-98-704-EN-C
Related publications: COM (98)417 final (1.7.98)

A report examined state aid granted by France, Germany, Portugal, Spain and the UK. It declared that aid was compatible with the single market so long as it was granted in order to make progress on economic viability; solve social and regional problems or help an industry to adjust to environmental protection standards:

Commission: *Report ... on the application of the Community rules for state aid to the coal industry in 1995*: COM (98)186 final (24.3.98)

DG II's report discussed the relationship between competition and trade policies; outlined efforts made to establish an international framework for competition policy and examined proposals for further progress:

Commission, DG II: *Competition policy and trade*: European Economy: Reports and Studies, No. 3, 1997, pp. 171–97: EC, 1998; ISBN: 92-828-1329-0; ISSN: 0379-0991; EC No.CM-07-97-329-EN-C

The impact of competition law on Member States was analysed:

Commission: *The impact of Community law on the domestic legal systems of the Member States. Competition law*: EC, 1998; ISBN: 92-828-0997-8; EC No.C1-06-97-787-EN-C

DG II provided an overview of mergers and acquisitions from 1986–96, including details of the largest deals carried out in 1996, and the means by which the Commission controlled mergers:

Commission, DG II: *Mergers and acquisitions*: European Economy: Supplement A, No.11, November 1997, pp. 1–15 (published 1998)

Internet:«http://europa.eu.int/comm/dg04/index_en.htm» (European Commission: DG IV)

See also 'Energy' and 'North America' below.

Consumers

The Commission published its Consumer policy action plan:

Commission: *Communication ... Consumer policy action plan 1999–2001*: *COM* (98)696 final (1.12.98)

The Commission was concerned to enable consumers to be able to exercise their rights despite the cost and time-consuming nature of procedures:

> Commission: *Communication ... on 'the out-of-court settlement of consumer disputes' and Commission recommendation on the principles applicable to the bodies responsible for out-of-court settlement of consumer disputes*: *COM* (98)198 final (30.3.98)

A report on the European Home and Leisure Surveillance System programme noted that 83,000 deaths occurred annually in the home or in leisure activities (cf. 45,000 road and 6000 work fatalities):

> Commission: *Final report ... on the EHLASS programme*: *COM* (98)488 final (4.9.98)

DG XXIV of the European Commission launched a new journal called *Consumer Voice* in 1998, which replaces *INFO-C*.

Internet: «http:europa.eu.int/comm/dg24» (European Commission: DG XXIV)

Culture

A compendium of texts on culture was published:

> Council, General Secretariat: *Texts concerning culture at European Union level 1993–1997*: EC, 1998; ISBN: 92-824-1586-4; EC No.BX-14-98-809-EN-C

The Commission's Communication relates to a Council Decision of September 1997 requiring proposals for establishing a single instrument for the 'Culture 2000' programme:

> Commission: *Communication ... First European Community Framework Programme in Support of Culture (2000–2004)*: *COM* (98)266 final (6.5.98) *Related publications*: *OJ* C211, 7.7.98, p. 18

A summary of national reports from Member States and national reports from EFTA and EEA states discussed monitoring under the 'Television without Frontiers' directive in relation to digital television and an upsurge in the number of channels available:

> Commission: *Third Communication ... on the application of Articles 4 and 5 of Directive 89/552/EEC 'Television without Frontiers' for the period 1995–96 including an overall assessment of application over the period 1991–96*: *COM* (98)199 final (3.4.98)

Internet: «http://europa.eu.int/en/comm/dg10/culture/index-en.html»

Economic and Monetary Issues

DG II looked at recent developments especially in the light of turbulence in Asian markets. Forecasts were generally optimistic:

> Commission, DG II: *Economic forecasts for 1998–1999: European Economy: Supplement A*, No.3-4, March–April 1998, pp.1–30

This theme also applied to the longer term, with predicted increases in domestic demand. The Asian crisis had increased uncertainty in international finance, but the EU had been only mildly affected:

> Commission, DG II: *Economic forecasts for 1998–2000: European Economy: Supplement A*, No.10, October 1998, pp. 1–27

A Commission Communication focused on the current economic situation of the Member States during the final lead-up to the establishment of a single currency:

> Commission: *Communication ... Growth and employment in the stability-oriented framework of EMU. Economic policy reflections in view of the forthcoming 1998 Broad Guidelines*: COM (98)103 final (25.2.98) (This replaces the *Annual Economic Report* for 1998.)
> *Related publications: European Economy*, No.65, 1998; *OJ* C152, 18.5.98, p. 72; *OJ* C195, 22.6.98, p. 40

The Commission recommended high employment and a successful EMU as the main priorities for Member State and EU economic policies:

> Commission: *Commission's Recommendation for the Broad Guidelines of the Economic Policies of the Member States and the Community ...* : *COM* (98)279 final (13.5.98)

The Council provided a detailed response to the Commission's proposals:

> Council: *98/454/EC: Council Recommendation of 6.7.98 on the broad guidelines of the economic policies of the Member States and of the Community: OJ* L200, 16.7.98, pp. 34–8

The Commission followed up a debate relaunched by the European Council meeting at Pörtschach on infrastructure investment:

> Commission: *Communication ... Government investment in the framework of economic strategy*: *COM* (98)682 final (2.12.98)

The Council addressed the implementation of the third stage of EMU:

Council: *Resolution of the European Council of 13.12.97 on economic policy coordination in Stage 3 of EMU and on Treaty Articles 109 and 109b of the EC Treaty*: OJ C35, 2.2.98, pp. 1–4

The Commission's Communication aimed to heighten awareness of the importance of information and communication in introducing the euro:

Commission: *Communication ... on the information strategy for the euro*: COM (98)39 final (6.2.98)
(cf. also the related interactive publication: *Your Business and the EURO. A Strategic Guide,* EC 1999 (ISBN 92-828-6077-9, includes CD-ROM)).

An update on the Commission's *Communication* of October 1997 (*COM* (97)491 final (1.10.97)) was provided as a basis for the February 1998 round table discussions:

Commission: *Communication ... Update on the practical aspects of the introduction of the EURO*: COM (98)61 final (11.2.98)

The Commission issued a report on the first steps in the procedure set out in Art. 109j (TEC) which formed the basis of the European Council's decision in May 1998 as to which states could join the single currency:

Commission: *EURO 1999. 25 March 1998. Report on progress towards convergence and recommendation with a view to the transition to the third stage of economic and monetary union*: COM (98)1999 final (25.3.98). (This is also published in a two-volume publication format Vol.1: Recommendation (ISBN:92-828-2982-0; Vol 2: Report: 92-828-3271-6) Internet: «http://europa.eu.int/comm/off/rep/conver/index_en.htm».
Related publications: *European Economy*, No.65, 1998

The separate EMI (ECB) Convergence report is available at «http://www.ecb.int».

Recommendations on various aspects relating to conversion to the euro were issued covering standards of good practice, transparency measures and implementation methods:

Commission: *98/286/EC: Commission Recommendation of 23.4.98 concerning banking charges for conversion to the euro*: OJ L130, 1.5.98, pp. 22–5

Commission: *98/287/EC: Commission Recommendation of 23.4.98 concerning dual display of prices and other monetary amounts*: OJ L130, 1.5.98, pp. 26–8

Commission: *98/288/EC: Commission Recommendation of 23.4.98 on dialogue, monitoring and information to facilitate the transition to the euro*: OJ L130, 1.5.98, pp. 29–31
Related publications: OJ C160, 27.5.98, p. 1

The EP expressed its concern about the high level of independence granted to a future ECB, and listed its requirements for making it accountable to the Parliament:

Parliament: Resolution: *Democratic accountability in the third stage of EMU*: *OJ* C138, 4.5.98, pp. 177–9
Related publications: *PE DOC* A4-110/98

The EP asked that future membership of the single currency should be subject to consultation with the Parliament:

Parliament: *Resolution: Convergence and single currency*: *OJ* C152, 18.5.98, pp. 33–7
Related publications: *PE DOC* A4-130/98

The Council's Regulation confirmed the arrangements for the introduction of the euro as a medium of exchange and the subsequent introduction of banknotes and coins:

Council: *Council Regulation (EC) No.974/98 of 3.5.98 on the introduction of the euro*: *OJ* L139, 11.5.98, pp. 1–5

A highly specific Regulation listed the size, shape, thickness, weight, diameter, colour, composition and edge design of the future coinage, in denominations from one cent to two euros:

Council: *Council Regulation (EC) No.975/98 of 3.5.98 on denominations and technical specifications of euro coins intended for circulation*: *OJ* L139, 11.5.98, pp. 6–8

(See also: Council: *Resolution of 19.1.98 on denominations and technical specifications of euro coins intended for circulation*: *OJ* C35, 2.2.98, pp. 5–8)

Art. 109j(2) of the TEC requires the Council to assess each Member State's suitability to enter the single currency; Art. 109j(4) sets out the latest starting time for the third stage of EMU. All states assessed save Greece and Sweden met the criteria:

Council: *98/316/EC: Council Recommendation of 1.5.98 in accordance with Article 109j(2) of the Treaty*: *OJ* L139, 11.5.98, pp. 21–7

Council: *98/317/EC: Council Decision of 3.5.98 in accordance with Article 109j(4) of the Treaty*: *OJ* L139, 11.5.98, pp. 30–5

Ecofin expressed its intention to hold informal meetings with the intention of monitoring progress on EMU:

Council: *Declaration by the Council (Ecofin) and the Ministers meeting in that Council issued on 1.5.98*: *OJ* L139, 11.5.98, pp. 28–9

Wim Duisenberg was named as President of the ECB for an eight-year term, with Christian Noyer as Vice President for four years. An executive board of four members was recommended for varying terms of five to eight years:

> Council: *98/318/EC: Council Recommendation of 3.5.98 on the appointment of the President, the Vice-President and the other members of the Executive Board of the European Central Bank*: OJ L139, 11.5.98, p. 36
> *Related publications*: OJ L154, 28.5.98, p. 33

Council Regulations specified the minimum reserve basis for states participating in the single currency, and set upper limits for penalty payments on defaulters:

> Council: *Council Regulation (EC) No.2531/98 of 23.11.98 concerning the application of minimum reserves by the European Central Bank*: OJ L318, 27.11.98, pp. 1–3
> *Related publications*: OJ C246, 6.8.98, p. 6; OJ L356, 30.12.98, p. 1

> Council: *Council Regulation (EC) No.2532/98 of 23.11.98 concerning the powers of the European Central Bank to impose sanctions*: OJ L318, 27.11.98, pp. 4–7
> *Related publications*: OJ C246, 6.8.98, p. 9

Currency conversion rates were announced:

> Council: *Council Regulation (EC) No.2866/98 of 31.12.98 on the conversion rates between the euro and the currencies of the Member States adopting the euro*: OJ L359, 31.12.98, p. 1
> *Related publications*: *Press Release* (Commission), IP/98/1183 (31.12.98)

The euro will have an 'enormous circulation potential'; it will be unfamiliar to users; there will be numerous distribution points and one side of the coinage will vary depending upon the Member State issuing it. This created a high risk of counterfeiting:

> Commission: *Communication ... Protection of the Euro. Combating counterfeiting COM* (98)474 final (22.7.98)

The Commission traced its involvement with the establishment of economic and monetary union (EMU) and explained how it was intended to operate, indicating the roles of the EU's institutions in the project:

> Commission, Spokesman's Service: *The Commission and EMU*: *Memo*, No. 87, 1998 (14.12.98)
> *Related publications*: *Memo* (Commission), No.86, 1998 (14.12.98)

Many of the key Commission reports on the euro listed above are also issued in the *EURO Papers* series from DG II of the Commission available on the Internet (see below). See especially *EURO Papers*, No.7, October 1997 and No.25, July 1998 which reproduce the text of all legislation adopted in connection with the introduction of the euro.

Internet:
«http://europa.eu.int/comm/dg02/index_en.htm» (European Commission: DG II)
«http://www.ecb.int» (European Central Bank)
«http://europa.eu.int/euro» (EURO server)
«http://europa.eu.int/eurobirth/index.html» (EURO birth)
«http://europa.eu.int/comm/dg02/document/europap/eupidxen.htm» (*EURO Papers*)

Education, Training and R&D

A detailed report noted new developments and implementation of the framework programmes within RTD:

> Commission: *Research and technological development activities of the European Union. 1998 annual report*: COM (98)439 final (15.7.98)

The JRC acclaimed a 'year of significant achievements':

> Commission: *Joint Research Centre. 1997 annual report*: COM (98)483 final (29.7.98)

A Communication took stock of past and present initiatives and the developing cohesion at national and regional levels within RTD:

> Commission: *Communication ...Reinforcing cohesion and competitiveness through research, technological development and innovation*: COM (98)275 final (27.5.98)

An interim report examined the impact of TEMPUS II on countries eligible to participate: associated CEECs; non-associated CEECs and 12 countries of the former USSR and Mongolia:

> Commission: *TEMPUS II Programme. Interim report. March 1998* COM (98)379 final (24.7.98)

Internet:
«http://europa.eu.int/comm/dg12/» (European Commission: DG XII)
«http://europa.eu.int/en/comm/dg13/dg13.html» (European Commission: DG XIII)
«http://europa.eu.int/en/comm/dg22/dg22.html» (European Commission: DG XXII)
«http://www.cordis.lu (CORDIS R&D database)
«http://www.cordis.lu/fifth/home.html» (News of the Fifth Framework Programme)

Energy

The Commission noted existing barriers to trade in electricity and gas across and sometimes within national borders. EU prices were an average of 40 per cent higher than US prices. The Commission proposed a three-phase approach:

Commission: *Report ... on state of liberalisation of the energy markets*: COM (98)212 final (7.4.98)

The Council and Commission signified approval to the Energy Charter Treaty and Protocol:

Council/Commission: *98/181/EC, ECSC, Euratom Council and Commission Decision of 23.9.97 on the conclusion, by the European Communities, of the Energy Charter Treaty and the Energy Charter Protocol on energy efficiency and related environmental aspects: OJ L69, 9.3.98, pp. 1–116*

A Communication linked environmental and energy issues:

Commission: *Communication ... Strengthening environmental integration within Community energy policy*: COM (98)571 final (14.10.98)

A comprehensive survey on Member State aid to the coal industry was published:

Commission: *Mid-term report ... on the application of decision No.3632/93/ ECSC establishing Community rules for State aid of the Member States to the coal industry in 1994–97*: COM (98)288 final (8.5.98)

A second report on the disposal of radioactive waste and a fourth report on waste management were issued:

Commission: *Second report on the application in the Member States of Directive 92/3/EURATOM of 3.2.92 on the supervision and control of ship-ments of radioactive waste between Member States and into and out of the Community*: COM (98)778 final (22.12.98)

Commission: *Communication and fourth report ... on the present situation and prospects for radioactive waste management in the European Union*: COM (98)799 final (11.1.99)

A Communication presented the successes and failures of energy policy to date, refocused attention on promoting energy efficiency and prepared the ground for policies undertaken in the light of the Kyoto Agreement:

Commission: *Communication ... Energy efficiency in the European Commu-nity – towards a strategy for the rational use of energy*: COM (98)246 final (29.4.98)

The SAVE II programme, focusing on non-technological elements of energy efficiency, was approved for five years from 01.01.96. A report highlighted progress during the first 18 months:

Commission: *Communication ... Progress report on the multinational pro-gramme for the promotion of energy efficiency in the Community – SAVE II (Council Decision 96/737/EC Art.8.1)*: COM (98)458 final (17.7.98)

A study on nuclear energy was published:

> Commission: *Nuclear energy in Europe and world wide*: *Document* EC, 1998; ISBN: 92-828-3033-0; EC No.CS-12-98-564-EN-C

A comprehensive report provided an overview of world energy by region, with chapters on the EU, the rest of the OECD, CEECs, the former USSR and other world regions. It also reviewed the energy outlook for the EU, 1997–2000:

> Commission, DG XVII: *1997 Annual Energy review: Energy in Europe, Special Issue, September 1997 (published 1998)*: ISBN: 92-828-1194-8; EC No.CS-BR-97-003-EN-C (No 1998 issues of *Energy in Europe* had been published at the time of compilation of this guide.)

Internet:«http://europa.eu.int/en/comm/dg17/dg17home.htm» (European Commission: DG XVII)

See also 'Competition' above and the section on External Policies and Relations: 'Eastern and Central Europe' below.

Environment

The Commission issued a Communication responding to a obligation laid down by the Luxembourg European Council for the submission of a strategy for implementing the requirements of Art. 6 of the Treaty:

> Commission: *Communication ... Partnership for integration. A strategy for integrating environment into EU policies, Cardiff, June 1998*: *COM* (98)333 final (27.5.98)

The EEA produced a series of documents intended to update *Europe's Environment: The Dobris Assessment* (1995) presented in Sofia to Environment Ministers of all European countries. This conference asked the EEA to produce a second assessment for their meeting in Denmark in 1998:

> European Environment Agency: *Europe's environment: The second assessment. An overview*: EC, 1998; ISBN: 92-9167-087-1; EC No.GH-13-98-128-EN-C

The Commission's enquiry into the former East Germany's environment (in accordance with Council Directive 90/656/EEC) found that there were specific problems with the quality of drinking, bathing and fish farming waters:

> Commission: *Communication... State of the environment in the 6 Länder of the former East Germany*: *COM* (98)33 final (2.2.98)

The LIFE objective is 'to contribute to the development and, if appropriate, implementation of Community environmental policy and legislation'. A Commission report was prepared within the context of the LIFE Regulation and 'Sound and Efficient Management':

> Commission: *Report under Article 14 of Regulation (EC) No.1404/96. LIFE*: COM (98)721 final (4.12.98)

Proposals for action on sustainable urban development were issued:

> Commission: *Communication ... Sustainable urban development in the Europe an Union: a framework for action*: COM (98)605 final (28.10.98)

The Commission aimed to 'develop a robust, credible and cost-effective implementation strategy to reach the Union's Kyoto target', without which it was expected that CO_2 (carbon dioxide) emissions would increase by 40 per cent compared to 1990 levels:

> Commission: *Communication ... on transport and CO_2. Developing a Community approach*: COM (98)204 final (31.3.98)

The Commission also considered action to reduce CO_2 emissions from cars:

> Commission: *Communication ... Implementing the Community strategy to reduce CO_2 emissions from cars: an environmental agreement with the European automobile industry*: COM (98)495 final (29.7.98)

The Commission aimed to develop an effective climate change strategy to contrive reductions in CO_2, CH_2 (methane) and N_2O (nitrous oxide) by 15 per cent by 2010:

> Commission: *Communication ... Climate change – towards an EU post-Kyoto strategy*: OM (98)353 final (3.6.98)

A transition strategy to be submitted to the Montreal Protocol was developed:

> Commission: *Communication ... Strategy for the phaseout of CFCs in metered dose inhalers*: COM (98)603 final (23.10.98)

The case of the Brent Spar disposal in June 1995 had reactivated debate on waste management, given that there are over 600 redundant similar oil and gas installations in European waters. A Communication discussed the issues:

> Commission: *Communication ... on removal and disposal of disused offshore oil and gas installations*: COM (98)49 final (18.2.98)

Internet
«http://europa.eu.int/comm/dg11/index_en.htm» (European Commission: DG XI)
«http://www.eea.eu.int» (European Environment Agency)

See also section on External Policies and Relations, 'Eastern and Central Europe' below.

Fisheries

The Commission issued an introductory folder of information sheets on CFP:

Commission, DG XIV: *The common fisheries policy*: EC, 1998; ISBN: 92-828-3382-8; EC No.CU-12-98-441-EN-C

An EP resolution stressed the need to use CFP as a legal framework post-2002. It thought that fisheries should be treated like other sectors of economic activities, although it noted that the revision of CFP principles would have social and economic repercussions:

Parliament: *Resolution: Common fisheries policies after 2002*: OJ C358, 24.11.97, pp. 43–9
Related publications: PE DOC A4-298/97

A Communication provided an overview of achievements in fisheries monitoring since 1993. It analysed major omissions remaining and ways of remedying them:

Commission: *Communication ... Fisheries monitoring under the Common Fisheries Policy*: COM (98)92 final (19.2.98)

The Commission published its proposals for fixing total allowable catches (TACs). (The decisions on the 1999 TACs may be seen on the DG XIV website (see below). The formal text of the Regulation will be published in the *OJ* L series):

Commission: *Proposal for a Council Regulation (EC) fixing, for certain fish stocks and groups of fish stocks, the total allowable catches for 1999 and certain conditions under which they may be fished COM* (98)680 final (4.12.98)

Internet: «http://europa.eu.int/comm/dg14/dg14.html» (European Commission: DG-XIV).

Health

The third report provided an overview of EC policies affecting health and listed ways of developing health impact assessments in future:

Commission: *Third report ... on the integration of health protection require-ments in Community policies (1996)*: COM (98)34 final (27.1.98)

A Communication concluded that EC public health policy required a fundamental review, and proposed measures for a future policy:

Commission: *Communication ... on the development of public health policy in the European Community*: COM (98)230 final (15.4.98)

An annual monitoring report on safety at work was published:

Commission: *22nd annual activity report of the Advisory Committee on Safety, Hygiene and Health Protection at Work*: COM (98)522 final (1.12.98)

Internet:
«http://europa.eu.int/comm/dg05/phealth/main.htm» (European Commission: DG V: Public health)
«http://osha.eu.int» (European Agency for Safety and Health at Work)

Industry

A Communication relating to small and medium-sized enterprises followed a series of initiatives from the 1995 report to the Madrid European Council to the G 8 Employability Conference held in London February 1998:

Commission: *Communication ... Fostering entrepreneurship in Europe: priorities for the future*: COM (98)222 final (7.4.98)

A DG II paper described developments in competitiveness in the EU, US and Japan since 1988, with particular emphasis on the period from 1992:

Commission, DG II: *European competitiveness*: *European Economy: Supplement A*, No.7, July 1998, pp. 1–26

The Commission identified a need for better data and information so as to remove market barriers to enable business services to contribute to employment creation:

Commission *Communication ... The contribution of business services to industrial performance. A common policy framework*: COM (98)534 final (21.9.98)

A Communication proposed setting up a Commercial Communication Expert group:

Commission: *Communication ... The follow-up to the Green Paper on commercial communications in the Internal Market*: COM (98)121 final (4.3.98)

A third report built on two previous Communications (*COM* (97)236 final 29.05.97 and *COM* (97)504 final 8.10.97) on the telecommunications regulatory package:

Commission: *Communication ... Third report on the implementation of the telecommunications regulatory package*: COM (98)80 final (18.2.98)

A report confirmed that the EU should act to participate fully in the process of organization and management of the Internet, launched by a US White Paper:

Commission: *Communication... International policy issues related to Internet governance*: COM (98)111 final (20.2.98)
Related publications: COM (98)476 final (29.7.98)

The Commission summarized the present position related to the 'millennium bug', and set out its plans aimed at stimulating those responsible to act:

> Commission: *Communication ... The Year 2000 computer problem*: COM (98)102 final (25.2.98)

The Commission was optimistic about the potential of information technology. It logged its growth and commented that the EU was well placed to exploit its increasing opportunities:

> Commission: *Report ... Job opportunities in the Information Society: Exploiting the potential of the information revolution*: COM (98)590 final (25.11.98)

Internet:
«http://europa.eu.int/comm/dg03/index_en.htm» (European Commission: DG III)
«http://europa.eu.int/en/comm/dg23/index.htm» (European Commission: DG XXIII)

Justice and Home Affairs

An 'omnibus' resolution on JHA covered the means of dealing with its issues from January 1998 until the entry into force of the Treaty of Amsterdam:

> Council: *Council Resolution of 18.12.97 laying down the priorities for cooperation in the field of justice and home affairs for the period 1.1.98 to the date of entry into force of the Treaty of Amsterdam*: OJ C11, 15.1.98, pp. 1–4

The Commission listed the categories of third countries and the position of their nationals seeking entry into the EU:

> Commission: *Commission communication pursuant to Council Regulation (EC) No.2317/95 determining the third countries whose nationals must be in possession of visas when crossing the external borders of the Member States*: OJ C101, 3.4.98, pp. 4–11

Building on the initiatives of the European Year against Racism, the Commission proposed practical and procedural measures to prepare the ground for more radical action in the future:

> Commission: *Communication ... An Action Plan against racism*: COM (98)183 final (25.3.98)

The Commission attempted to define the concept of an area of freedom, security and justice and develop instruments of interinstitutional co-operation in the light of the Treaty of Amsterdam.

> Commission: *Communication ... Towards an area of freedom, security and justice*: COM (98)459 final (14.7.98)

A Communication on trafficking in women updated an earlier one (*COM* (96)567 final (20.11.96)):

Commission: *Communication ... for further actions in the fight against trafficking in women: COM* (98)726 final (9.12.98)

The Treaty of Amsterdam moves asylum, immigration, the free movement of persons and judicial co-operation in civil matters to the 'first pillar'. A report detailed an action plan:

Council/Commission: *Action plan of the Council and the Commission on how best to implement the provisions of the Treaty of Amsterdam on an area of freedom, security and justice – text adopted by the Justice and Home Affairs Council of 3.12.98: OJ* C19, 23.1.99, pp. 1–15

Internet:
«http://ue.eu.int/jai/default.asp?lang=en» (Council: JHA site)(new in 1998)
«http://europa.eu.int/pol/index-en.htm#justice» (European Commission)
«http://www.europol.eu.int/home2.htm» (Europol)(new in 1998)

Single Market

The Commission called upon the Council to emphasize the spirit and letter of the single market amongst the Member States:

Commission: *Communication ... Making Single Market rules more effective*: *COM* (98)296 final (13.5.98)

A report laid down measures for a suspensive procedure to prohibit release for free circulation, export, re-export or entry of counterfeit and pirated goods:

Commission: *Report ... on the implementation of Council Regulation (EC) No.3295/94 of 22.12.94 as regards border controls on trade in goods which may be counterfeit or pirated (+ legislative proposal): COM* (98)25 final (28.1.98)

A report responded to Art. 253 of Council Regulation No 2913/92/EEC which required a review of the customs code, in the light of the single market:

Commission: *Commission report on the Community Customs Code (+ legislative proposal): COM* (98)226 final (3.6.98)

The Commission issued an interim report in response to Art. 17 (3) of Decision No 210/97/EC covering the period 1.1.96–31.12.97. The aim was to ensure 'that customs administrations of the member states may operate as efficiently and effectively as would one single administration':

Commission: *Report ... on the implementation of the Customs 2000 Programme ...: COM* (98)471 final (24.7.98)

Following a request of the November 1997 Council meeting, a report described the relationship between the new approach (whose principles were laid down in 1985 – OJEC 136, 4.6.85) and standardization:

> Commission: *Report ... Efficiency and accountability in European standardisation under the New Approach*: COM (98)291 final (13.5.98)

A report described the state of play at 31.12.97 in relation to access to third country markets for community suppliers and service providers in water, energy, transport and telecommunications:

> Commission: *Third report ... concerning negotiations regarding access to third country public procurement markets in the fields covered by Directive 93/ 38 (the Utilities Directive)*: COM (98)203 final (23.4.98)

The Commission responded to the Action Plan agreed by the Amsterdam European Council which required Council and Commission to 'put in place common provisions to combat organized crime in the field of economic and commercial counterfeiting':

> Commission: *Green Paper. Combating counterfeiting and piracy in the Single Market*: COM (98)569 final (15.10.98)

The Commission aimed to reduce distortion in the single market, by preventing excessive losses of tax revenue and encouraging tax structures to develop in an employment friendly manner:

> Commission: *Communication ... First annual report on the implementation of the Code of Conduct for Business Taxation and Fiscal State Aid. Progress report on the work concerning the taxation of income from savings and a common system of taxation for interest and royalty payments between associated countries*: COM (98)595 final (25.11.98)

A Communication focused on two aspects of the free movement of persons: rights of entry and residence and improving citizens' awareness of their rights:

> Commission: *Communication ... on the follow-up to the recommendations of the High-Level Panel on the Free Movement of Persons*: COM (98)403 final (1.7.98)

Internet: «http://europa.eu.int/comm/dg15» (European Commission: DG XV)

See also 'Industry' above and 'Mediterranean and Middle East' below.

Social Policy and the Labour Market

The Commission followed its 1995–97 Social Action Programme, taking into account the increased significance of employment policy; additional key legislative proposals and the emergence of a set of ambitious work programmes:

Commission: *Communication ... Social Action Programme 1998–2000: COM* (98)259 final (29.4.98)

The Commission aimed to identify means whereby the social dialogue could be strengthened and made more adaptable, linking the social partners' work more closely to EU policies:

Commission: *Communication ... adapting and promoting the social dialogue at Community level (+ legislative proposal): COM* (98)322 final (20.5.98)

A paper aimed to launch a debate about undeclared work, considering sanctions and also adapting inappropriate legislation to reflect new labour market realities:

Commission: *Communication ... on undeclared work: COM* (98)219 final (7.4.98)

All Member States had produced National Action Plans from the Luxembourg Process by the end of April 1998. DG V provided an assessment:

Commission, DG V: *From guidelines to action: The National Action Plans for Employment: Employment and Social Affairs: Employment and European Social Fund;* EC, 1998; ISBN: 92-828-3916-8; EC No.CE-14-98-162-EN-C *Related publications: COM* (98)316 final (13.5.98); *Document* (Commission), DOC/98/5 and 6 (13.5.98)

The National Action Plans showed that public employment services took up 100,000 people. The Commission called for concerted action:

Commission: Communication ... *'Modernising public employment services to support the European employment strategy': COM* (98)641 final (13.11.98)

Employment has a new title under the Treaty of Amsterdam. A proposal from the Commission aimed to assist Member States towards meeting Treaty requirements:

Commission: *Communication ... Proposal for guidelines for Member State Employment policies 1999: COM* (98)574 final (14.10.98)

The EU's employment rate stands at 60.5 per cent, below that of the US and Japan:

Commission: *Employment rates report 1998. Employment performance in the Member States: COM* (98)572 final (14.10.98)

The EURES programme is intended to assist EU citizens interested in working in or recruiting from another EEA country. The Commission reported developments:

Commission: *Developing a European service in favour of mobility and employment. Report on EURES activities 1996–97 ... : COM* (98)413 final (3.7.98)

A report followed the establishment of a body of EC legislation adopted under Art. 118A TEC relating to health and safety of workers:

> Commission: *Mid-term report on the Community Programme concerning safety,hygiene and health at work (1996–2000)*: COM (98)511 final (3.9.98)

DG V's third report on social protection monitored progress on objectives set out in the Council's Recommendation 92/442/EC, and updated analysis of the 1993 and 1995 reports:

> Commission, DG V: *Social protection in Europe 1997: Employment and Social Affairs: Social Security and Social Integration*; EC, 1998; ISBN: 92-828-4248-7 EC No. CE-12-98-312-EN-C
> *Related publications*: COM (98)243 (23.4.98)

The first progress report on equal opportunities was based upon contributions from 18 DGs and horizontal services. Barriers which remained were owing to deficiencies in awareness of gender issues; of human and budgetary resources and of gender expertise:

> Commission: *Progress report ... on the follow-up of the Communication: 'Incorporating equal opportunities for women and men into all Community policies and activities'*: COM (98)122 final (4.3.98)

See also:

> Commission: *Equal opportunities for women and men in the European Union. Annual report 1997*: EC, 1998; ISBN: 92-828-3922-2; EC No. CE-13-98-815-EN-C
> *Related publications*: COM (98)302 final (13.5.98)

> Commission: *Interim report ... on the implementation of the medium-term Community action Programme on equal opportunities for men and women (1996–2000)*: COM (98)770 final (17.12.98)

The Daphne programme is to be opened up to applicant states. A Communication made provision for continuous assessment of a five-year programme (2000–04):

> *Commission: Communication ... on violence against children, young persons and women (+ legislative proposal to set up the Daphne programme): COM* (98)335 final (20.5.98)

The Youth For Europe programme targets 15–25 year-olds in the Member States, Iceland, Liechtenstein and Norway, with a budget of 24 m ECU from 1995–96. The CEECs and Cyprus were included from 1997:

> Commission: *Youth for Europe. Interim evaluation report*: COM (98)52 final (6.2.98)

The HELIOS programmes were set up by Council Decision 93/136/EEC 25.2.93. The Commission's 1998 report was based upon an independent evaluation of measures undertaken in the HELIOS II programme:

Commission: *Report ... on the evaluation of the Third Community Action Programme to Assist Disabled People (HELIOS II)*: *COM* (98)15 final (20.1.98)

Internet:
«http://europa.eu.int/comm/dg05/index_en.htm» (European Commission: DG V)
«http://www.eurofound.eu.int» (European Foundation for the Improvement of Living and Working Conditions)

Structural Policy

The reform of the structural funds involves reducing the number of objectives from seven to three and setting strict criteria for eligibility:

Commission: *Proposals to reform the Structural Funds*: *OJ* C176, 9.6.98, pp. 1–46 /*COM* (98)131 final (18.3.98)

The 9th annual report was issued in accordance with Art. 16 of Regulation 205/88/EEC and Art. 31 of Regulation 4253/88/EEC. It applied particularly to Objectives 1–6:

Commission: *9th annual report of the Structural Funds 1997*: *COM* (98)562 final (30.10.98)

See also:

Commission: *Report ... Mid-term review of structural interventions. Objectives 1 and 6 (1994–99). Developing a management culture through evaluation: towards best practice*: *COM* (98)782 final (7.1.98)

The first implementation report on TENs was issued, as required by TEN-T guidelines (Decision 1692/96/EC, 23.08.96). It was intended to act as a starting point for the first revision of TEN transport guidelines, and set out broad issues to consider:

Commission: *Trans-European Networks. 1997 annual report...*: *COM* (98)391 final (2.10.98)
Related publications: *COM* (98)614 final (28.10.98)

1997 was the fifth year of operation of the Cohesion Fund in the four beneficiary Member States. The report for 1997 stated that Ireland was no longer in deficit and noted that the Council had decided in May 1998 that Spain and Portugal were also not in deficit:

Commission: *Annual report of the Cohesion Fund 1997*: *COM* (98)543 final (7.10.98)

DG XVI looked at Member States' responses to economic and social cohesion:

Commission, DG XVI: *Economic and social cohesion in the European Union: the impact of Member States' own policies*: Regional Development Studies, No.29; EC, 1998; ISBN: 92-827-4039-0; EC No.CX-15-98-213-EN-C

Internet:
«http://europa.eu.int/comm/dg16» (European Commission: DG XVI)
«http://www.inforegio.org» (Inforegio database: details of the activities of the ERDF and Cohesion Funds)

See General Section: 'Agenda 2000' above and 'Transport' below.

Transport

The Common Transport Policy was assessed:

Commission: *Communication ... The Common Transport Policy. Sustainable mobility: Perspectives for the future*: COM (98)716 final/2 (21.12.98)

A report provided an overall assessment of the timetable and financial plans devised by Member States:

Commission: *Trans-European Transport Network: Report on progress and implementation of the fourteen Essen Projects, 1998*: COM (98)356 final (3.6.98)

A follow-up to a Green Paper on the Citizens' Network concluded that whilst good local/regional transport was essential, supplying it was a matter for national and sub-national authorities with the Commission providing tools to establish a policy framework:

Commission: *Communication... Developing the Citizens' Network. Why good local and regional passenger transport is important, and how the European Commission is helping to bring it about*: COM (98)431 final (10.7.98)

Variable charging systems on and for transport are charged throughout the EU. The Commission argued that there was a need for harmonization:

Commission: *Fair payment for infrastructure use: a phased approach to a common transport infrastructure charging framework in the EU. White Paper*: COM (98)466 final (22.7.98)

A Communication aimed to assess a directive calling for the creation of independent railways:

Commission: *Communication ... on the implementation and impact of Directive 91/440/EEC on the development of the Community's railways and an access rights for rail freight*: COM (98)202 final (31.3.98)

Internet: «http://europa.eu.int/en/comm/dg07/index.htm» (European Commission: DG VII)

See also 'Environment' and 'Structural Policy' above and External Policies and Relations Section: 'Mediterranean and Middle East' below.

External Policies and Relations

General

A report covered CEECs, the former Soviet Union and the Mediterranean area, emphasizing that the trend for moving macro-financial assistance to newly independent states had continued in 1996:

> Commission: *Report ... on the implementation of macro-financial assistance to Third Countries in 1996*: COM (98)3 final (13.1.98)

A report responded to a Finnish proposal at the Luxembourg European Council. December 1997:

> Commission: *Communication ... A Northern dimension for the policies of the Union*: COM (98)589 final (25.11.98)

Internet:
«http://europa.eu.int/comm/dg01/dg1.htm» (European Commission: DG I – Commercial policy, and relations with North America, the Far East, Australia and New Zealand)
«http://europa.eu.int/comm/dg1a/index.htm» (European Commission: DG Ia – Europe and the NIS, Common Foreign and Security Policy and External Missions)
«http://europa.eu.int/en/comm/dg1b/index.htm» (European Commission: DG Ib – Southern Mediterranean, Middle and Near East, Latin America, South and South East Asia and North–South co-operation)
«http://europa.eu.int/pol/ext/index_en.htm» (links to 'external relations' sites of EU institutions)

Common Foreign and Security Policy (CFSP)

Internet:
«http:europa.eu.int/comm/dg1a/cfsp/instruments_laws_proc.htm» (European Commission: DG Ia)
«http://ue.eu.int/pesc/default.asp?lang=en» (Council)

External Trade

DG II's report on world trade was divided into two parts: a factual analysis of EU trade in the aftermath of the Uruguay Round and a report on trade issues in relation to investment, environment and competition policy:

> Commission, DG II: *The European Union as a world trade partner: European Economy: Reports and Studies*, No.3, 1997: EC, 1998; ISBN: 92-828-1329-0; EC No.CM-07-97-329-EN-C

Internet: «http://europa.eu.int/comm/dg01/dg1.htm» (European Commission: DG I)

Asia

An EU policy on China was adopted in 1995. A report covered recent developments, all suggesting that there was a need to intensify and upgrade the initial policy:

> Commission: *Communication ... Building a comprehensive partnership with China: COM* (98)181 final (25.3.98)

The Commission outlined EU policy towards the Republic of Korea:

> Commission: *European Union policy towards the Republic of Korea: COM* (98)714 final (9.12.98)

The first report on Hong Kong concluded that basic rights, freedoms and autonomy had been broadly upheld, although the territory was suffering its worst recession for decades because of the Asian financial crisis.

> Commission: *First annual report by the European Commission on the Special Administrative Region of Hong Kong: COM* (98)796 final (8.1.98)

DG IB published a report reflecting the growing global prominence of both the EU and ASEAN and providing details of the different facets of their relationship in areas such as economic co-operation, business and development aid:

> Commission, DG IB: *EU–ASEAN relations. A growing partnership*: EU, 1998; ISBN: 92-828-5321-7; EC No.GV-15-98-140-EN-C

Internet:«http://europa.eu.int/comm/dg01/dg1.htm» (European Commission: DG I)

Eastern and Central Europe

1997 was a year of both consolidation and challenge for the PHARE programme, when it was mobilized to deliver aid to Bosnia-Herzegovina following the Dayton Agreement:

> Commission: *The PHARE Programme. Annual report 1996: COM* (98)178 final (24.3.98)

Restructuring the steel industries of CEECs is likely to have social and economic consequences. The Commission set out a framework for dealing with the situation:

> Commission: *Communication ... A global approach to promote regional and social conversion and to facilitate industrial restructuring in the Central and Eastern European countries: the case of steel: COM* (98)220 final (7.4.98)

A Communication provided a factual report monitoring compliance by Bosnia-Herzegovina, Croatia, the Federal Republic of Yugoslavia, Macedonia and Albania. Compliance was rated 'less than satisfactory' in respect of human rights, economic reform and regional co-operation:

> Commission: *Communication ... Operational conclusions: Regional approach to the countries of South-Eastern Europe: compliance with the conditions in the Council Conclusions of 29.4.97 ...* : *COM* (98)237 final (15.4.98)

CEEC candidate countries have both environmental liabilities and assets. The Commission considered means of reducing the former and maintaining the latter:

> Commission: *Communication ... on accession strategies for environment: Meeting the challenges of enlargement with the candidate countries in Central and Eastern Europe*: *COM* (98)294 final (20.5.98)

A document set out the framework for priority areas for CEEC candidate countries to enable them to meet the Copenhagen criteria (liberal democracy; market economy and ability to take on the EU's *acquis*):

> *Accession Partnerships* (Text of Accession Partnerships with Bulgaria, Czech Republic, Estonia, Hungary, Latvia, Lithuania, Poland, Romania, Slovakia and Slovenia) *OJ* C202, 29.6.98, pp. 1–102

The Commission reported that the *status quo* in relations covered by the regional approach should continue:

> Commission: *Regional approach to the countries of South-Eastern Europe: Compliance with the conditions in the Council Conclusions of 29.4.97.*
>
> *Commission Communication on operational conclusions (Bosnia and Herzegovina, Croatia, Federal Republic of Yugoslavia, Former Yugoslav Republic of Macedonia and Albania)*: *COM* (98)618 final (28.10.98)

Internet:
«http://europa.eu.int/comm/dg1a/index.htm» (European Commission: DG Ia)
«http://europa.eu.int/comm/dg1a/enlarge/checkpoint.htm» (European Commission: DG Ia – Enlargement)

See Governance and Institutional Developments Section 'Miscellaneous' above and 'Enlargement' below.

Latin America

Internet: «http://europa.eu.int/comm/dg1b/index.htm» (European Commission: DG Ib; click on 'Policies' and 'Publications')

Mediterranean and Middle East

The Commission concluded that the EU should continue in its political and economic efforts to enable the Middle East peace process to survive:

Commission: *The role of the European Union in the peace process and its future assistance to the Middle East*: COM (97)715 final (16.1.98)

The Euro–Mediterranean Partnership is based upon the establishment of a free trade area in goods and the liberalization of trade in services; the implementation of economic co-operation and an increase in EU aid to partners. MEDA is its main financial instrument, forming the major part of a five-year budget of 4,685m ECU:

Commission: *Communication... on the Euro–Mediterranean Partnership and the Single Market*: COM (98)538 final (23.9.98)

Commission: *Implementing MEDA. 1996–1997 report*: COM (98)524 final (14.9.98)

Internet:«http://europa.eu.int/en/comm/dg1b/euro-med_en.htm» (European Commission: DG Ib – Euro–Med Partnership)

North America

The EP welcomed the new transatlantic agenda and joint EU/US Action Plan, but wanted the partnership to be a 'genuine' one:

Parliament: *Resolution: Europe and the United States*: OJ C34, 2.2.98, pp.100–4

The US accounts for 19 per cent of the EU's total trade. The EU is also the biggest investor in the US, providing 59 per cent of its foreign investments. However, the Commission reported that there were still significant obstacles to trade and investment and proposed a plan to remove them:

Commission: *Communication ... The New Transatlantic Marketplace*: COM (98)125 final (11.3.98)

Whilst tariff barriers had been reduced in successive GATT rounds, the Commission's 14th report noted other impediments: extraterritoriality; other customs barriers and the use of trade defence instruments:

Commission, DG I: Report on United States barriers to trade and investment 1998 EC, 1998:
Internet: «http://europa.eu.int/comm/dg01/98usbtfo.htm»

A third report on the EC/US agreement on competition covered 1997:

Commission: *Report ... on the application of the Agreement between the European Communities and the Government of the United States of America regarding the application of their competition laws*: COM (98)510 final (3.9.98)

Internet:
«http://europa.eu.int/comm/dg01/euus.htm» (European Commission: DG I – USA)
«http://europa.eu.int/comm/dg01/eucana.htm» (European Commission: DG I – Canada)

Developing Countries

A decision approved the amended fourth Lomé Convention:

> Council: *98/344/EC: Council Decision of 27.4.98 concerning the conclusion of the Agreement amending the fourth ACP–EC Convention of Lomé, signed in Mauritius on 4.11.95*: *OJ* L156, 29.5.98, pp. 1–124

The Lomé Convention provides 71 ACP states with assistance under the European Development Fund. A report provided the financial details for 1997:

> Commission: *Communication … Balance sheets and accounts of the sixth and seventh European development Funds for the financial year 1997*: *COM* (98)442 final (14.7.98)

A document considered the partnership between the EU and the ACP states in the context of the fourth Lomé Convention:

> Commission: *Democratisation, the rule of law, respect for human rights and good governance, the challenges of the partnership between the EU and the ACP States*: *COM* (98)146 final (12.3.98)

Negotiations between the EU and the ACP States with a view to concluding a partnership agreement for development to succeed the Fourth Lomé Convention in 2000 were opened in Brussels on 30 September 1998:

> Council, General Secretariat: *Opening of EU–ACP negotiations*: *Press Release,* PRES/98/329 (30.9.98) («http://ue.eu.int/newsroom» and click on 'External relations')

The Commission provided a report at the end of a five-year period of operations with Asia and Latin America:

> Commission: *Report on financial and technical assistance to, and economic cooperation with the developing countries in Asia and Latin America, as covered by the Council Regulation (EEC 443/92) of 25.2.92 (OJ L52, 27.2.92, p. 1)*: *COM* (98)40 final (29.1.98)

A Communication summarized the existing situation and stressed the global responsibility in relation to AIDS:

> Commission: *Communication … For increased solidarity to confront AIDS in developing countries*: *COM* (98)407 final (3.7.98)

There was a reduction in funding within the ECHO programme from 656m ECU in 1996 to 441m ECU in 1997. The Former Yugoslavia and the Great Lakes regions had been the major recipients (33 per cent of the total):

> Commission: *Annual report on humanitarian aid 1997*: *COM* (98)448 final (15.7.98)

The EPRD programme completed its first full year. The budget for 1996 was 130m ECU; for 1997 it was 127.5m ECU:

> Commission: *European Programme for Reconstruction and Development (Council Regulation 2259/96) Annual Report (years 1996–1997)*: *COM* (98)502 final (3.9.98)

ECIP is an aid to the creation or development of joint ventures, and privatization or private infrastructure projects. It acts as a catalyst, unlocking other sources of finance, and thus supporting other financiers as well as the entrepreneurs themselves:

> Commission: *Report ... ECIP (European Community Investment Partners). Progress report 1995–1996–1997*: *COM* (98)752 final (18.12.98)

Internet:
«http://europa.eu.int/en/comm/dg1b/index.htm» (European Commission: DG Ib)
«http://europa.eu.int/comm/dg08/index_en.htm» (European Commission: DG VIII)

Turkey

A special action programme for Turkey of 135m ECU had been established. The Commission proposed a work programme for further development of relations:

> Commission: *Communication ... European strategy for Turkey. The Commission's initial operational proposals*: *COM* (98)124 final (4.3.98)

The Commission reported that the customs union with Turkey was still effective and that Turkey had continued in its harmonization programme with EC laws:

> Commission: *Report ... on developments in relations with Turkey since the entry into force of the Customs Union*: *COM* (98)147 final (4.3.98)
> *Related publications*: *OJ* C313, 12.10.98, p. 176; *PE DOC* A4-251/98

A report was issued by the Commission in response to the request of the Cardiff European Council, assessing Turkey's progress in relation to the Copenhagen criteria.

> Commission: *Regular report from the Commission on Turkey's progress towards accession*: *COM* (98)711 final (17.12.98)

Internet: «http:europa.eu.int/comm/dg1a/enlarge/report_11_98_en_turkey/ab.htm» (European Commission: DG Ia – Turkey)

Enlargement

The Commission produced informal draft proposals for Accession Partnerships in view of the limited time period available:

> Commission: *Proposals for Council Decisions on the principles, priorities, intermediate objectives and conditions contained in the Accession Partnerships*: COM (98)53 final (4.2.98)
> *Related publications*: OJ L121, 23.4.98, p. 1 (text of Council Decisions)

The Commission also put forward a framework for co-ordinating aid for application countries:

> Commission: *Proposal for a Council Regulation (EC) on coordinating aid to the applicant countries in the framework of the pre-accession strategy:* OJ C140, 5.5.98, pp. 26–8
> *Related publications:* COM (98)150 final (19.3.98); OJ C164, 29.5.98, pp. 4–13; COM (98)138 final (19.3.98); OJ C329, 27.10.98, p. 13; COM (98)551 final (30.9.98)

The European Commission completed the first round of 'screening' EU legislation with the five applicant countries which have not yet started accession negotiations (Bulgaria, Latvia, Lithuania, Romania and Slovakia):

> Commission, Spokesman's Service: *Update on enlargement: Commission completes first round of 'screening' with five 'pre-in' applicant countries*: Memo, No.60, 1998 (29.7.98)

The Commission prepared a 'composite paper' for the Council which contains a synthesis of the analysis in each of the regular reports on candidates for accession along with a series of recommendations. The document also set out the state of play on the negotiations and the reinforcement of the pre-accession strategy:

> Commission: *Composite Paper. Regular reports from the Commission on progress towards accession by each of the candidate countries*: COM (98)712 final (17.12.98)
> *Related publications*: COM (98)700-711 final (17.12.98)

Internet:«http://europa.eu.int/comm/dg1a/enlarge/checkpoint.htm» (European Commission: DG Ia – Enlargement)

Journal of Common Market Studies

Volume 37, Annual Review
September 1999

Chronology of Key Events in 1998

GEORG WIESSALA

University of Central Lancashire

January   Age limits for Commission competitions (*concours*) to be raised to 45 years, then to be phased out, on grounds of ageism.

1   UK takes over Presidency of the Council of Ministers, with the priority areas of EMU and economic reform, enlargement and policy reforms, crime, environment and foreign policy.

Telecommunications Market opened up to full competition for the first time.

Co-operation agreement with FYROM comes into force.

20   'Citizens First' initiative launched in the UK. Topics include living, working, studying, training and doing research in another Member State (initiative ends on 31 December).

February   For the first time, Member States give the Commission a mandate to negotiate maritime agreements with third countries (China and India).

1   Europe Agreements with Estonia, Latvia and Lithuania enter into force.
    They replace the 1993 Trade and Co-operation Agreements.

2   Priorities for countries planning to join the EU set out in ten draft Accession Partnership Agreements (AP).

18 Committee of the Regions begins its second four-year mandate.

19 Inaugural meeting of the European Group on Ethics in Science and New Technologies (EGE).

March   9   Commission extends GSP coverage to all least developed countries which are not party to the fourth Lomé Convention.

12 European Standing Conference on Enlargement launched in London. It brings together leaders of 26 countries.
    The priority areas are: fighting organized crime, environment, Foreign and Security Policy, competitive economies and regional co-operation. Turkey declined to attend the conference.

18 Commission sets out legal texts for *Agenda 2000* package.
    covering, *inter alia,* structural funds, the CAP, enlargement and the financial perspective for 2000–06.

25 Commission recommends 11 Member States take part in the Single Currency.
    The UK and Denmark have decided to stay out, Greece and Sweden fail to meet EMU criteria.

30 Formal accession process with the six 'first-wave' applicant countries formally opened
    (Cyprus, Czech Republic, Estonia, Hungary, Poland, Slovenia).

    Four genetically modified organism (GMO) crop products set to receive EU clearance, following a Regulatory Committee vote.

April   Council agrees to give consumers a minimum two-year guarantee on goods bought anywhere in the EU.

2   First ever EU–China summit in London.

3   Accession and screening process with the five other eastern applicants, who have not started accession negotiations, is officially opened
(Bulgaria, Latvia, Lithuania, Romania, Slovakia).

3–4   ASEM II summit in London brings together 15 EU and 10 Asian leaders.
The meeting helps Asia to come to terms with the financial crisis and builds on ASEM I in Bangkok in March 1996.

15   National Action Plans on Employment prepared and submitted to the Commission by the Member States.

16   European Energy Charter enters into force.

23   Commission approves 202 Jean Monnet Projects across the EU, amongst them 25 new Centres of Excellence. UK: 46 projects.

May   1–3   EMU Summit Brussels and Special Session of the European Parliament to decide on participation in EMU by the Euro-11
(Austria, Belgium, Finland, France, Germany, Ireland, Italy, Luxembourg, the Netherlands, Portugal and Spain).

6   Elections in the Netherlands.

14   EP approves directive on patents for biotechnological inventions.

15–17   G8 summit in Birmingham.

18   EU–US summit launches Transatlantic Economic Partnership.

21   First EU–Russia summit since the Partnership Agreement entered into force at the end of 1997.

28   Culture Council agreed to make Rotterdam and Porto cities of culture in 2001, Bruges and Salamanca in 2002, Graz in 2003 and Genoa and Lille in 2004. This will be followed by a 'rotating system' in 2005.

June   Figures show that more than 1,600 universities and 200,000 students
                will benefit from Erasmus exchange activities in 1998–99. With six
                new countries, the number of participating states is now 24.

        1   Hungary, the Czech Republic, Romania and Cyprus take part in the
                Leonardo da Vinci vocational training exchange programme for the
                first time, alongside 18 other countries.

                Establishment of ESCB and European Central Bank (ECB)
                brings EMI to a close.

                Agreement on Mid-term Review of the Fourth Lomé
                Convention enters into force.

        8   European Code of Conduct for Arms Exports adopted.

        14   Commission launches new information service ('Europe Direct').

        15   UK deposits instruments of ratification of the Treaty of
                Amsterdam.

     15–16   European Council in Cardiff ends UK Presidency.
                On the agenda are *Agenda 2000*, enlargement, employment, eco-
                nomic reform, the next financial perspective (2000–06) and external
                relations, amongst other topics.

        24   'Get-the Vote-Out' campaign launched, to encourage turnout for the
                June 1999 EP elections.

        30   European Central Bank (ECB) launched in Frankfurt
                a.M., with Wim Duisenberg as its first President.

July   1   Austria takes over Presidency of the EU for the first time
                since joining in 1995.
                Priorities include the euro, *Agenda 2000*, policy reforms and en-
                largement.

        6   Adoption of a directive prohibiting tobacco advertising.

     14–18   European Parliament plenary session: Jacques Santer
                presents the Commission's *Agenda 2000* package.

August	14	Commission adopts proposal regarding chemicals that reduce the ozone layer.

September 10 **Malta reactivates membership application**
following the General Election win of the Nationalist Party in Malta on 5 September. The Commission had adopted a previous *avis* on Malta in June 1993.

23 **Commission decides to cancel its pre-selection tests for new Commission posts (*concours*) of 14.9.99.**
Some candidates had been found using mobile phones during the tests and there were allegations that the exam papers had been leaked beforehand.

27 **German General Election**
brings Social Democrat–Green Coalition to power. Gerhard Schröder becomes Helmut Kohl's successor as German Chancellor.

General Election in Sweden.
The Social Democrats under Göran Persson remained the largest party, even though they lost 30 seats (largely to Christian Democrats).

30 Negotiations between the EU and the ACP states with a view to concluding a partnership agreement to succeed the Fourth Lomé Convention in 2000 open in Brussels.

October 202 new Jean Monnet projects across the EU begin operation. These include 25 new Jean Monnet European Centres of Excellence (*pôles Jean Monnet*).

1 **Europol Convention, signed in July 1995, enters into force.**

Elections in Slovakia.

5 **General Affairs Council agrees to start formal, substantive accession negotiations with the six leading applicants.**

6 **European Standing Conference on Enlargement**
(this second meeting was at foreign ministers' level)

7   EU budget reform options proposed by Commission.

14   Fines of 50.2 million ECU imposed on four UK sugar companies
         for operation of a sugar cartel.

24–25   (Informal) meeting of Heads of State or Government in
         Pörtschach
         The meeting discusses institutional reform, to improve decision-
         making and make the EU more relevant to the people and seeks
         to chart a new economic course for the Union, dealing with
         infrastructure, defence policy and the role of the WEU.

26   EU foreign ministers widen sanctions against Burma, but agree
         to allow Rangoon to be present at the next EU–ASEAN Joint
         Committee Meeting.

28   Commission adopts its Work Programme for 1999. The aim of
         implementing the EU's employment strategy is accorded high
         priority.

November 1   Commission President Santer meets Chinese leaders.
               (First visit on this level for 12 years, six months after the first EU–
               China summit in London in April and following the new China
               strategy from March 1999, which was adopted in June).

4   First regular Progress Reports on enlargement, updat-
         ing the Commission Opinions of 1997 (for CEE) and
         1993 (Cyprus).
         The process with the 12 applicant countries is broadly on track,
         opening of negotiations with further countries is not recommend-
         ed at this stage.

10   Ministerial-level negotiations with Cyprus, Czech
         Republic, Estonia, Hungary, Poland, Slovenia official-
         ly opened.

25   Commission lifts beef export ban for the UK and
         publishes political strategy on northern Europe.

December   JHA Council reaches agreement on setting up a computerized
               system for registering fingerprints of asylum seekers (the
               'EURODAC' Convention)

2   Commission President Santer announces to the EP plans for a structural review of the Commission.

10   Human Rights Declaration adopted by the EU.
It marks the 50th Anniversary of the Universal Declaration of Human Rights and envisages a new Human Rights Agenda.

Seven draft bilateral sectoral EU–Switzerland Agreements finalized.

Budgetary Control Committee of the EP adopts a Recommendation to grant the Commission the budgetary discharge for 1996.

11–12   European Council in Vienna ends Austrian Presidency.
'Vienna Strategy' identifies employment, economic growth and stability, security and quality of life and reforming policies and institutions as priority areas. The summit endorses a 'Declaration on Human Rights' and sets March 1999 as deadline for agreeing a package of changes to the EU budget.

17   MEPs vote 270 to 225 with 23 abstentions against approval of the budgetary discharge.

22   Council reaches agreement on the Fifth Framework Programme, covering research for 1998–2002.

31   The euro (€) is launched, after an Ecofin meeting fixes irrevocably the conversion rates for the currencies of the 11 participating Member States. The ECU is replaced by the € at 1:1.

Other Selected Events of Interest in 1998

European Monitoring Centre for Racism and Xenophobia starts work in January.

General Affairs Council does not support human rights resolution against China.

Commission establishes a 'Year 2000 Office'.

Agreement to revive the 'Silk Road' trading route between Europe and Central Asia is signed.

More than 3,000 schools in the EU log in for 'Netd@ys 98', investigating the Net and education.

Fraud becomes a more serious issue in 1998.

A Council Regulation lists size, shape, thickness, weight, diameter, colour, composition and edge design of the future coins from one cent to two euros.

The first report on Hong Kong after the 1997 handover is cautiously optimistic.

Sources:
European Access plus «http://www.europeanaccess.co.uk/»
European Voice «http://www.european-voice.com»
European Voice (1998) 'The European Union in 1998', pp. 62 ff.
Austrian Presidency website: «http://www.eu-presidency.gv.at/»
Commission 'Europa' website: «http://www.europa.eu.int»
Commission: «http://europa.eu.int/comm/dg15/en/index»
Commission: Financing the EU: «http://europa.eu.int/comm/dg19/en/agenda2000/» ownresources/index.htm
'Dialogue With Citizens and Business' service:«http://citizens.eu.int/originchoice.htm»
General Report on the Activities of the European Union 1998: «http://europa.eu.int/abc/doc/off/rg/en/welcome.htm»
EUR-Lex: «http://europa.eu.int/eur.lex»
The European
'The Week in Europe' website: «http://www.cec.org.uk»
Vienna Summit Conclusions: «http://europa.eu.int/council/off/conclu/dec98.htm»

Books on European Integration

BRIAN ARDY

and

JACKIE GOWER

Thames Valley University

The following list includes all books submitted to the *Journal of Common Market Studies* during 1998, whether these were reviewed or not. Each book is entered only once even though, inevitably, some titles are of relevance to more than one section.

General Studies

Bainbridge, T: *The Penguin Companion to European Union* (London, Penguin UK, 1998, 2nd edn, ISBN 0140268790) xvii+547pp., pb £10.99.

De Vree, J K and Jansen, M: *The Ordeal of Unity: Integration and Disintegration in Modern Europe* (Amsterdam, University of Amsterdam Press, 1998, ISBN 9076094020) ix+604pp., pb np.

Haynes, J: *Religion in Global Politics* (Harlow, Addison Wesley Longman, 1998, ISBN 058229312X) vii+243pp., pb £15.99.

Hrbek, R, Jopp, M, Lippert, B and Wessels, W (eds): *Die Europäische Union als Prozeß: Verfassungsentwicklungen im Spiegel von 20 Jahren der Zeitschrift* (Bonn, Europa Union Verlag, 1998, ISBN 3771305578) 677pp., pb np.

Le Galès, P and Lequesne, C (eds): *Regions in Europe* (London, Routledge, 1998, ISBN hb 0415164826, pb 0415164834) xvii+305pp., hb £55.00 $90.00, pb £15.99 $24.99.

Loth, W, Wallace, W and Wessels, W (eds): *Walter Hallstein: The Forgotten European?* (London, Macmillan, 1998, ISBN 0333717627) xvi+260pp., hb £45.00.

Maclay, M: *The European Union* (Stroud, Sutton Publishing, 1998, ISBN 0750919523) xiii+114pp., pb £5.99.

© Blackwell Publishers Ltd 1999, 108 Cowley Road, Oxford OX4 1JF, UK and 350 Main Street, Malden, MA 02148, USA

Pinder, D (ed): *The New Europe: Economy, Society and Environment* (Chichester, Wiley, 1998, ISBN 0471971235) ix+494 pp., pb £17.99.

Tilly, C: *Roads from Past to Future* (Oxford, Rowman & Littlefield, 1997, ISBN hb 0847684091, pb 0847684105) ix +433pp., hb £45.95, pb £17.00.

Tonra, B (ed): *Amsterdam: What the Treaty Means* (Dublin, Institute of European Affairs, 1997, ISBN 1874109354) viii+224pp., pb IR£15.00.

Westlake, M (ed): *The European Union Beyond Amsterdam: Concepts of European Integration* (London, Routledge, 1998, ISBN hb 0415168791, pb 0415168805) xvii+159pp., hb £45.00 $75.00, pb £14.99 $24.99.

Weidenfeld, W and Wessels, W: *Europa von A–Z: Taschenbuch der Europäischen Integration* (Bonn, Europa Union Verlag, 1997, 6th edn, ISBN 3771305519) 432pp., pb np.

Whiteside, N and Salais, R (eds): *Governance, Industry and Labour Markets in Britain and France: The Modernising State in the Mid-Twentieth Century* (London, Routledge, 1998, ISBN 0415157331) xi+294pp., hb £50.00.

Government and Institutions

Abromeit, H: *Democracy in Europe: Legitimising Politics in a Non-State Polity* (Oxford, Berghahn, 1998, ISBN 1571819851) ix+182pp., hb £25.00.

Blondel, J, Sinnott, R and Svensson, P: *People and Parliament in the European Union: Participation, Democracy and Legitimacy* (Oxford, Oxford University Press, 1998, ISBN 0198293089) xvi+287pp., hb £40.00.

Boix, C: *Political Parties, Growth and Equality: Conservative and Social Democratic Economic Strategies in the World Economy* (Cambridge, Cambridge University Press, 1998, ISBN hb 0521584469, pb 0521585953) xiv+280pp., hb £35.00, pb £12.95.

Broughton, D and Donovan, M (ed): *Changing Party Systems in Western Europe* (London, Cassell, 1999, ISBN hb 1855673274, pb 1855673282) xix+315pp., hb £55.00, pb £16.99.

Chryssochoou, D: *Democracy in the European Union* (London, Tauris Academic Studies, 1998, ISBN 1860643361) viii+280 pp., hb £39.50.

Corbett, R: *The European Parliament's Role in Closer EU Integration* (London, Macmillan, 1998, ISBN 0333722523) xx+424pp., hb £55.00.

Dumoulin, A and Remacle, E: *L'Union de l'Europe Occidentale: Phénix de la Défense Européenne* (Brussels, Établissements Émile Bruylant, 1998, ISBN 2802711105) xxii+605pp., pb FB 4.200.

Elgie, R and Thompson, H: *The Politics of Central Banks* (London, Routledge, 1998, ISBN 0415144221) ix+189pp., hb £50.00.

Gabel, M J: *Interests and Integration: Market Liberalization, Public Opinion, and European Union* (Ann Arbor, USA, University of Michigan Press, 1998, ISBN 0472108565) xiv+176pp., hb £35.00.

Greenwood, J and Aspinwall, M (eds): *Collective Action in the European Union: Interests and the New Politics of Associability* (London, Routledge, 1998, ISBN hb 0415159741, pb 041515975X) xvi+238pp., hb £55.00 $90.00, pb £16.99 $29.99.

McDonagh, B: *Original Sin in a Brave New World: An Account of the Negotiation of the Treaty of Amsterdam* (Dublin, Institute of European Affairs, 1998, ISBN 1874109400) xiv+249pp., pb IR£15.00.

Mény, Y and Knapp, A: *Government and Politics in Western Europe: Britain, France, Italy, Germany* (Oxford, Oxford University Press, 1998, 3rd edn, ISBN hb 0198782225, pb 0198782217) xvi+490 pp., hb £40.00, pb £15.99.

Moravcsik, A: *The Choice for Europe* (Ithaca and London, Cornell University Press, 1998, ISBN hb 0801435099, pb 0801485096) xxii+515pp., hb $49.95, pb $19.95.

Sandholtz, W and Stone Sweet A: *European Integration and Supranational Governance* (New York, Oxford University Press, 1998, ISBN hb 0198294573, pb 0198294646) 389pp., hb £45.00, pb £17.99.

Internal Policies and the Law

Betten, L and Grief, N: *EU Law and Human Rights* (Harlow, Addison Wesley Longman, 1998, ISBN 0582287162) xv+158pp., pb £15.99.

Cini, M and McGowan, L: *Competition Policy in the European Union* (London, Macmillan, 1998, ISBN pb 0333643011, hb 033364302X) xii+250pp., hb £45.00, pb £14.99.

Dehousse, R: *The European Court of Justice* (Basingstoke, Macmillan, 1998, ISBN hb 0333693167, pb 0333693175) xii+213pp., hb £40.00, pb £12.99.

Elliott, C and Quinn, F: *English Legal System* (Harlow, Addison Wesley Longman, 1998, 2nd edn, ISBN 0582327180) xxiv+500pp., pb £14.99.

European Academy of Bolzano: *Package For Europe: No. 10* (Bolzano, European Academy of Bolzano, 1998, ISBN 11253827) 262pp., pb np.

Golub, J (ed): *Global Competition and EU Environmental Policy* (London, Routledge, 1998, ISBN 041515698X) x+221pp., hb £47.50.

Golub, J (ed): *The Instruments for Environmental Policy in the EU* (London, Routledge, 1998, ISBN 0415156963) xiv+270pp., hb £50.00.

Hartley, T C: *The Foundations of European Community Law* (Oxford, Oxford University Press, 1998, 4th edn, ISBN hb 0198765320, pb 0198765312) lxiv+495pp., hb £50.00, pb £22.99.

Hine, D and Kassim, H (eds): *Beyond the Market: The EU and National Social Policy* (London, Routledge, 1998, ISBN hb 0415152380, pb 0415152399) x+231pp., hb £50.00 $85.00, pb £15.99 $24.99.

King, R and Black, R (eds): *Southern Europe and the New Immigrations* (Brighton, Sussex Academic Press, 1997, ISBN 1898723613) viii+210pp., hb £39.50.

Lowe, P and Ward, S (eds): *British Environmental Policy and Europe: Politics and Policy in Transition* (London, Routledge, 1998, ISBN hb 0415155002, pb 0415155010) xvii+326pp., hb £50.00 $85.00, pb £16.99 $27.99.

Mouton, J D and Soulard, C: *La Cour de Justice des Communautés Européennes* (Paris, Presses Universitaires de France, 1998, ISBN 2130490603) 127pp., pb np.

Neergaard, U B: *Competition and Competences: The Tensions between European Competition Law and Anti-Competitive Measures by the Member States* (Copenhagen, DJOF Publishing, 1998, ISBN 8757400679) xiv+385 pp., pb DKK 360.00.

Neven, D, Papandroupoulos, P and Seabright, P: *Trawling for Minnows: European Competition Policy Agreements Between Firms* (London, Centre for Economic Policy Research, 1998, ISBN 1898128340) xvii+227pp., pb £16.95.

Peterson, J and Sharp, M: *Technology Policy in the European Union* (Basingtoke, Macmillan, 1998, ISBN hb 0333656423, pb 0333656431) xviii+260pp., hb £47.50, pb £15.50.

Poiares Maduro, M: *We the Court: The European Court of Justice and the European Economic Constitution* (Oxford, Hart Publishing/Northwestern University Press (US), 1998, ISBN 1901362256) xii+194pp., hb £22.50.

Ross, J F L: *Linking Europe: Transport Politics in the European Union* (Westport, USA, Praeger, 1998, ISBN 0275952487) xvii+266 pp., hb £47.95.

Sauter, W: *Competition Law and Industrial Policy in the EU* (Oxford, Oxford University Press, 1997, ISBN 0198264933) xii+255 pp., hb £45.00.

Scott, J: *EC Environmental Law* (Harlow, Addison Wesley Longman, 1998, ISBN 0582291909) xiv+189pp., pb £15.99.

Slaughter, A M, Stone Sweet, A and Weiler, J H H (eds): *The European Courts and National Courts: Doctrine and Jurisprudence* (Oxford, Hart Publishing/Northwestern University Press (US), 1998, ISBN 1901362264) xii+400pp., hb £37.50.

Tracy, M (ed): *CAP Reform: The Southern Products* (Brussels, Agricultural Policy Studies, 1998, ISBN 2960004752) 174pp., pb £44.00.

Tracy, M: *Agricultural Policy in the European Union and Other Market Economies* (Brussels, Agricultural Policy Studies, 1997, 2nd edn, ISBN 2960004744) 104pp., pb £34.00.

Usher, J A: *General Principles of EC Law* (Harlow, Addison Wesley Longman, 1998, ISBN 0582277493) xxiii+167pp., pb £15.99.

Vanstone, B: *Understanding Law: Skills and Sources for Students* (Harlow, Addison Wesley Longman, 1998, ISBN 0582317207) xxii + 310 pp., pb £12.99.

Williams, D W: *EC Tax Law* (Harlow, Addison Wesley Longman, 1998, ISBN 0582305969) xxii+186pp., pb £15.99.

External Relations and Developments

Archer, C and Sogner, I: *Norway, European Integration and Atlantic Security* (London, Sage, 1998, ISBN 076195967X) x+191pp., hb £47.40.

Avery, G and Cameron, F: *The Enlargement of the European Union* (Sheffield, Sheffield Academic Press/UACES, 1998, ISBN 1850758530) 200pp., pb £9.95 $15.00.

Drysdale, P and Vines, D (ed): *Europe, East Asia and APEC: A Shared Global Agenda* (Cambridge, Cambridge University Press, 1998, ISBN 052163315X) xvii+304 pp., hb £35.00.

Eliassen, K A (ed): *Foreign and Security Policy in the European Union* (London, Sage, 1998, ISBN hb 0761956328, pb 0761956336) x+246pp., hb £49.00 np, pb £15.99.

European Commission: *The Future of North–South Relations: Towards Sustainable Economic and Social Development* (London, Kogan Page/OOPEC, 1998, ISBN hb 0749427086, pb 0749427833) x+159pp., hb £16.99, pb £9.99

European Commission: *The Mediterranean Society: A Challenge for Islam, Judaism and Christianity* (London, Kogan Page/OOPEC, 1998, ISBN hb 0749426985, pb 0749427094) viii+87pp., hb £16.99, pb £9.99.

European Commission: Vignon J: *Shaping Actors, Shaping Factors in Russia's Future* (London, Kogan Page/OOPEC, 1998, ISBN hb 0749427140, pb 0749427132) xi+141pp., hb £16.99, pb £9.99.

Gonzalez Alonso, L N: *Politica Commercial y Relaciones Exteriores de la Union Europea* (Madrid, Editorial Tecnos SA, 1998, ISBN 8430932100) 431pp., pb np.

Grabbe, H and Hughes, K: *Enlarging the EU Eastwards* (London, Cassell, 1998, ISBN hb 1855675250, pb 1855675269) x+130pp., hb £27.50, pb £11.99.

Henderson, K (ed): *Back to Europe: Central and Eastern Europe and the European Union* (London, UCL Press, 1999, ISBN hb 1857288866, pb 1857288874) xix+307pp., hb £45.00, pb £13.95.

Kyle, K: *Cyprus: In Search of Peace* (London, Minority Rights Group International, 1998, ISBN 1897693915) 40pp., pb £4.95.

Laurent, P-H and Maresceau, M (eds): *The State of the European Union Vol IV: Deepening and Widening* (Colorado, Lynne Rienner, 1998, ISBN 1555877206) ix + 374pp., hb £43.95.

Lister, M (ed): *European Union Development Policy* (London, Macmillan/ St Martin's Press, 1998, ISBN 0333716566) xviii+189pp., hb £40.00.

Lundestad, G: *'Empire' by Integration: The United States and European Integration, 1945–1997* (Oxford, Oxford University Press, 1998, ISBN hb 0198782128, pb 019878211X) viii+200pp., hb £40.00, pb £13.99.

Maitland, D and Hu, Y S: *Europe and Emerging Asia* (London, Federal Trust, 1998, ISBN 0901573698) 47pp., pb £9.95.

Mayhew, A: *Recreating Europe: The European Union's Policy Towards Central and Eastern Europe* (Cambridge, Cambridge University Press, 1998, ISBN hb 052163086X, pb 0521638976) xviii+403pp., hb £40.00, pb £15.95, $22.95.

Nicoll, W and Schoenberg, R (eds): *Europe Beyond 2000: The Enlargement of the European Union Towards the East* (London, Whurr, 1998, ISBN 1861560648) xii+355 pp., pb £24.50.

Peterson, J and Sjursen, H (eds): *A Common Foreign Policy for Europe? Competing Visions of the CFSP* (London, Routledge, 1998, ISBN hb 0415170710, pb 0415170729) xv+215pp., hb £50.00 $85.00, pb £17.99 $ 27.99.

Redmond, J and Rosenthal, G G (eds): *The Expanding European Union: Past Present and Future* (London, Lynne Rienner, 1998, ISBN 1555876234) viii+235pp., hb £35.95.

Rhodes, C (ed): *The European Union in the World Community* (London, Lynne Rienner, 1998, ISBN 155587780X) ix+259pp., hb £41.50.

Roberson, B A: *The Middle East and Europe: The Power of Deficit* (London, Routledge, 1998, ISBN hb 0415140447, pb 0415140455) x+228pp., hb £55.00, pb £16.99.

Sarma A, Faber G and Mehta P K: *Meeting the Challenges of the European Union: Prospects of Indian Exports* (London, Sage, 1997, ISBN 0803993900) 346pp., hb RS 425.

Smith, K E: *The Making of EU Foreign Policy: The Case of Eastern Europe* (London, Macmillan, 1998, ISBN 0333726057) xii+264pp., hb £45.00.

Stankovsky, J, Plasser, F and Ulram, P A: *On the Eve of EU Enlargement: Economic Developments and Democratic Attitudes in East Central Europe* (Vienna, Signum Verlag, 1998, ISBN 03854362625) 241pp., hb ATS 291/DM 39.80.

Whitman, R G: *From Civilian Power to Superpower? The International Identity of the European Union* (London, Macmillan, 1998, ISBN 0333694775) x+251 pp., hb £45.00.

Zielonka, J: *Explaining Euro-Paralysis: Why Europe is Unable to Act in International Politics* (London, Macmillan, 1998, ISBN 0333730402) x+266pp., hb £45.00.

Economic Developments in Europe and Beyond

Apel, E: *European Monetary Integration 1958–2002* (London, Routledge, 1998, ISBN 0415114330) xvi+222pp., pb £15.99.

Baldwin, R E, Lipsey, R E and Richardson, J D (eds): *Geography and Ownership as Bases for Economic Accounting* (Chicago, University of Chicago Press, 1998, ISBN 0226035727) x+346pp., hb £38.50.

Barry, N: *Business Ethics* (London, Macmillan, 1998, ISBN 0333551850) xi+191pp., hb £45.00.

Davidson, I: *Jobs and the Rhineland Model* (London, Federal Trust, 1997, ISBN 0901573647) 80pp., pb £12.95.

Duff, A (ed): *Understanding the Euro* (London, Federal Trust, 1998, ISBN 0901573728) 159pp., pb £12.95.

Dunning, J H and Narula, R (eds): *Foreign Direct Investment and Governments: Catalysts for Economic Restructuring* (London, Routledge, 1998, 2nd edn, ISBN hb 0415118204, pb 0415173558) xiii+455pp., hb £50.00 $85, pb £19.99 $32.99.

European Commission: *Towards a More Global Economic Order* (London, Kogan Page/OOPEC, 1998, ISBN hb 0749427116, pb 0749427124) xviii+105pp., hb £16.99, pb £9.99.

Ferner, A and Hyman, R (eds): *Changing Industrial Relations in Europe* (Oxford, Blackwell, 1998, 2nd edn, ISBN hb 0631205500, pb 0631205519) xxvi+550pp., hb £65.00 $74.95, pb £24.99 $41.95.

Forder, J and Menon, A (eds): *The European Union and National Macroeconomic Policy* (London, Routledge, 1998, ISBN hb 0415141966, pb 0415141974) xiii+210pp., hb £55.00 $85.00, pb £16.99 $27.99.

Giordano, F and Persaud, S: *The Political Economy of Monetary Union: Towards the Euro* (London, Routledge, 1998, ISBN hb 0415174422, pb 0415174430) xi+202pp., hb £50.00 $85, pb £15.99 $25.99.

Hale, M and Lachowicz, M (eds): *The Environment, Employment and Sustainable Development* (London, Routledge, 1998, ISBN hb 0415180295, pb 0415180309) xviii+199pp., hb £50.00 $85.00, £17.99 $27.99.

Jones, E and Freiden, J and Torres, F (eds): *Joining Europe's Monetary Club: The Challenges for Smaller Member States* (London, Macmillan, 1998, ISBN 0333746384) xi+258 pp., hb £40.00.

Jovanovic, M N: *International Economic Integration: Limits and Prospects* (London, Routledge, 1998, 2nd edn, ISBN hb 0415164508, pb 0415164516) xix+446pp., hb £60.00, pb £19.99.

Lannoo, K and Gros, D: *Capital Markets and EMU Report of a CEPS Working Party* (Brussels, CEPS, 1998, ISBN 9290792566) vii+99pp., pb 1,000 BF.

Lukauskas, A J: *Regulating Finance: The Political Economy of Spanish Financial Policy from Franco to Democracy* (Michigan, University of Michigan Press, 1998, ISBN 0472108360) xviii+326pp., hb £40.50.

McNamara, K R: *The Currency of Ideas: Monetary Politics in the European Union* (Ithaca, Cornell University Press, 1998, ISBN 0801434327) xi+185pp., hb £29.95.

Minkkinen, P and Patomäki, H (eds): *The Politics and Economics of Monetary Union* (Dordrecht, Netherlands, Kluwer, 1997, ISBN 079238041X) 250pp., hb £72.75.

Moss, B H and Michie, J (eds): *The Single European Currency in National Perspective: A Community in Crisis?* (London, Macmillan, 1998, ISBN 0333725484) ix+219pp., hb £45.00.

Nicoll, W, Norburn, D and Schoenberg (eds): *Perspectives on European Business* (London, Whurr, 1998, 2nd edn, ISBN 1861560605) vii+293pp., pb £19.50.

Parker, D (ed): *Privatisation in the European Union: Theory and Policy Perspectives* (London, Routledge, 1998, ISBN 0415154693) xvi+269pp., hb £50.00.

Perez, T: *Multinational Enterprises and Technological Spillovers* (Chur, Switzerland, Harwood, 1998, ISBN 9057022958) xv+186pp., hb £36.00.

Pesaran, M H and Schmidt, P (eds): *Handbook of Applied Econometrics Volume II: Microeconomics* (Oxford, Blackwell, 1997, ISBN 1557862095) viii+453pp., hb np.

Rittenberg, L (ed): *The Political Economy of Turkey in the Post-Soviet Era* (London, Praeger, 1998, ISBN 0275955966) xi+221pp., hb £47.50.

Rohner, K: *Marketing in the Cyber Age: The Why, the What and the How* (Chichester, Wiley, 1998, ISBN 0471970239) xviii+223pp., pb £19.99.

Schmidt, S K: *Liberalisierung in Europa: Die Rolle der Europäischen Kommission* (Frankfurt, Campus Verlag, 1998, ISBN 3593359715) 403pp., pb DM 78.

Sorensen, P B (ed): *Tax Policies in the Nordic Countries* (London, Macmillan, 1998, ISBN 0333642805) xiii+234pp., hb £47.50.

Towers, B and Terry, M (eds): *Industrial Relations Journal: European Annual Review 1997* (Oxford, Blackwell, 1998, ISBN 0631211489) 250pp., pb £19.99.

Underhill, G R D: *Industrial Crisis and the Open Economy: Politics, Global Trade and the Textile Industry in the Advanced Economies* (London, Macmillan / St Martin's Press, 1998, ISBN 033357849X) xviii+280pp., hb £45.00.

Ungerer, H: *A Concise History of European Monetary Integration: From EPU to EMU* (Westport, USA, Quorum Books, 1997, ISBN 089930981X) xii+338pp., hb £55.00.

United Nations Commission on Trade and Development: *World Investment Report 1998: Trends and Determinants* (Geneva, United Nations Publications, 1998, ISBN 9211124263) xxxi+428pp., pb £34.00.

Vaitilingam, R (ed): *Europe's Network Industries: Conflicting Priorities* (London, Centre for Economic Policy Research, 1998, ISBN 1898128375) xxiii+258pp., pb £15.00.

Virtanen, M: *Market Dominance-Related Competition Policy: An Eclectic Theory and Analyses of Policy Evolution* (Turku, Finland, Turku School of Economics and Business Admin, 1998, ISBN 09517389078) 419pp., pb np.

Member States

Baker, D and Seawright, D (eds): *Britain For and Against Europe: British Politics and the Question of European Integration* (Oxford, Clarendon Press, 1998, ISBN 0198280785) xiv+252pp., hb £35.00.

Cole, A: *French Politics and Society* (Hemel Hempstead, Prentice-Hall Europe, 1998, ISBN 0134339541) xvi+296pp., pb £14.95.

Deprez, K and Vos, L (eds): *Nationalism in Belgium: Shifting Identities, 1780–1995* (London, Macmillan/St Martin's Press, 1998, ISBN 0333657373) xvi+275pp., hb £45.00.

Hölscher, J and Hochberg, A (eds): *East Germany's Economic Development since Unification: Domestic and Global Aspects* (London, Macmillan, 1998, ISBN 0333724895) xvi+217pp., hb £45.00.

Holtermann, H (ed): *Denmark in International Affairs: Publications in Languages other than Danish 1967–1995* (Copenhagen, DJOF Publishing, 1997, ISBN 8757430241) 230pp., pb DKK 420.00.

Kaiser, W: *Using Europe, Abusing the Europeans: Britain and European Integration, 1945–63* (London, Macmillan/St Martin's Press, 1997, ISBN 0333649427) xviii+274pp., hb £45.00.

Lange, T and Shackleton, J R (eds): *The Political Economy of German Unification* (Oxford, Berghahn, 1998, ISBN 1571818804) viii+200pp., hb £30.00.

Larres, K (ed): *Germany Since Unification: The Domestic and External Consequences* (London, Macmillan, 1998, ISBN 031217747X) xvii+239pp., hb £45.00.

May, A: *Britain and Europe Since 1945* (Harlow, Addison Wesley Longman, 1998, ISBN 0582307783) ix+149pp., pb £6.99.

Pedersen, T: *Germany, France and the Integration of Europe: A Realist Interpretation* (London, Cassell, 1998, ISBN 1855675374) viii+229pp., hb £40.00.

Thomas, A H and Oakley, S P: *Historical Dictionary of Denmark* (Lanham, USA, Scarecrow Press, 1998, ISBN 0810835444) xxvi+533pp., hb $65.00.

Index

254   INDEX

Veil Group 70
Venezuela 114
Volkswagen 75

Waigel Declaration 72
Western European Union (WEU) 88
Westerndorp, Carlos 39
Williamson Report 50
Williamson, Sir David 50
Wolters Kluwer 75

Worker protection 126–7
Working Time Directive 64
World Bank 93
World Trade Organization (WTO) 2, 9, 34, 82,
    91, 92, 96, 102, 105, 106, 114

Yeltsin, Boris 96
Yugoslavia 99

Zalm, Gerrit 174, 179